THE CONSTITUTION OF THE WAR ON DRUGS

OTHER BOOKS IN THE SERIES:

INALIENABLE RIGHTS SERIES

. . .

SERIES EDITOR
Geoffrey R. Stone

Martha C. Nussbaum
ERNST FREUND DISTINGUISHED
SERVICE PROFESSOR, PHILOSOPHY,
LAW, DIVINITY, SOUTH ASIAN STUDIES
UNIVERSITY OF CHICAGO

Eric A. Posner
KIRKLAND & ELLIS DISTINGUISHED
SERVICE PROFESSOR OF LAW
UNIVERSITY OF CHICAGO
LAW SCHOOL

Richard A. Posner
JUDGE (RETIRED)
U.S. COURT OF APPEALS FOR THE
SEVENTH CIRCUIT

Jack N. Rakove
WILLIAM ROBERTSON COE
PROFESSOR OF HISTORY AND
AMERICAN STUDIES
STANFORD UNIVERSITY

Louis Michael Seidman
CARMACK WATERHOUSE PROFESSOR
OF CONSTITUTIONAL LAW
GEORGETOWN UNIVERSITY
LAW CENTER

Christopher H. Schroeder
CHARLES S. MURPHY PROFESSOR OF
LAW EMERITUS
DUKE LAW SCHOOL

Stephen J. Schulhofer
ROBERT B. MCKAY PROFESSOR OF
LAW EMERITUS
NEW YORK UNIVERSITY
SCHOOL OF LAW

Geoffrey R. Stone
EDWARD H. LEVI DISTINGUISHED
SERVICE PROFESSOR OF LAW
UNIVERSITY OF CHICAGO LAW SCHOOL

David A. Strauss
GERALD RATNER
DISTINGUISHED SERVICE
PROFESSOR OF LAW
UNIVERSITY OF CHICAGO
LAW SCHOOL

Kathleen M. Sullivan
DEAN EMERITUS
STANFORD LAW SCHOOL

Cass R. Sunstein
ROBERT WALMSLEY UNIVERSITY PROFESSOR
HARVARD LAW SCHOOL

Laurence H. Tribe
CARL M. LOEB UNIVERSITY
PROFESSOR OF LAW EMERITUS
HARVARD LAW SCHOOL

Mark V. Tushnet
WILLIAM NELSON CROMWELL
PROFESSOR OF LAW EMERITUS
HARVARD LAW SCHOOL

J. Harvie Wilkinson III
JUDGE
U.S. COURT OF APPEALS FOR THE
FOURTH CIRCUIT

Kenji Yoshino
CHIEF JUSTICE EARL WARREN
PROFESSOR OF CONSTITUTIONAL LAW
NEW YORK UNIVERSITY
SCHOOL OF LAW

GEOFFREY STONE AND OXFORD UNIVERSITY PRESS GRATEFULLY ACKNOWLEDGE
THE INTEREST AND SUPPORT OF THE FOLLOWING ORGANIZATIONS IN THE
INALIENABLE RIGHTS SERIES: THE ALA THE CHICAGO HUMANITIES FESTIVAL
THE AMERICAN BAR ASSOCIATION THE NATIONAL CONSTITUTION CENTER
THE NATIONAL ARCHIVES

The Constitution
of the War on Drugs

David Pozen

OXFORD
UNIVERSITY PRESS

OXFORD
UNIVERSITY PRESS

Oxford University Press is a department of the University of Oxford. It furthers
the University's objective of excellence in research, scholarship, and education
by publishing worldwide. Oxford is a registered trade mark of Oxford University
Press in the UK and certain other countries.

Published in the United States of America by Oxford University Press
198 Madison Avenue, New York, NY 10016, United States of America.

Library of Congress Control Number: 2023952606

ISBN 978–0–19–768545–7

DOI: 10.1093/oso/9780197685457.001.0001

Printed by Sheridan Books, Inc., United States of America

For Jessica,
my favorite drug

Contents

...

Introduction

IT IS HARD to think of a contemporary public policy regime more
discredited than the "war on drugs." For the past half-century, the
United States Congress and the legislatures of the fifty states have
made it a crime to own, use, grow, or sell a long list of psychoactive
substances. Police have stopped, searched, arrested, and jailed tens
of millions of Americans pursuant to these laws. Federal agencies
have exported and enforced them around the world. And yet it has
long been clear that many aspects of this regime, from the specific
substances that it targets to the overarching goal of a "drug-free"
society that it pursues, lack a coherent scientific or social-scientific
basis. The war undermines core tenets of liberalism, from the right
to self-rule to the protection of privacy to the freedom of religion. It
fuels mass incarceration and racial subordination. It costs billions of
dollars per year. It breeds distrust in government and disrespect for
law. On top of all that, the war doesn't even succeed on its own terms,
as rates of drug addiction, drug overdose, and drug-associated violence have only gone up since its inception.[1] Essentially every drug

The Constitution of the War on Drugs. David Pozen, Oxford University Press.
© Oxford University Press 2024. DOI: 10.1093/oso/9780197685457.003.0001

policy researcher agrees that the war has been an "abject failure," the cause of far greater harm than the problem it was meant to solve.[2] In the war on drugs, the curves of callousness and stupidity intersect at their respective maxima.[3] The regime is starting to unravel. Since the mid-1990s, dozens of U.S. states and foreign jurisdictions have legalized marijuana for medical use, recreational use, or both. The U.S. House of Representatives voted for the first time in 2020 to remove marijuana from the federal list of controlled substances.[4] Psychedelic drugs such as Ecstasy, LSD, and magic mushrooms, the *New York Times* reported the following year, "are on the cusp of entering mainstream psychiatry."[5] An ongoing crisis of prescription opioid abuse has called new attention to the ineffectiveness of our drug laws, as well as the degree of pharmaceutical industry capture. Across much of the globe, elected officials and civil society leaders have become increasingly bold in assailing the extant regime for its racism, colonialism, and perverse consequences. The war on drugs may at last be cooling off, or at least entering a next phase.

Drug reformers in this country have drawn inspiration and instruction from many sources, including racial justice movements, HIV/AIDS activists, and international human rights norms. But notably absent from their advocacy is one source that Americans are accustomed to seeing at the center of debates over civil liberties and civil rights: the Constitution. Other democracies that have liberalized their drug laws in recent years, in places as diverse as Argentina, Canada, Georgia, and South Africa, have done so as a direct or indirect result of their courts' constitutional rulings. American constitutional law, by contrast, has played almost no role in catalyzing efforts to dismantle the war on drugs.

As we will see, there are many different parts of our canonical legal document that might have been useful toward this end. Ever since the 1970s, however, U.S. courts have rebuffed constitutional challenges to drug prohibition. Legislative and executive branch actors have deferred to those judgments. Constitutional law not only failed to head off one of the most "obviously defective and destructive" policies in modern American history;[6] it also helped to validate and entrench that policy at critical junctures in its evolution.

This failure is all the more significant given the design of the international legal framework on drug control. Along with the vast majority of United Nations member states, the United States is party to a triad of U.N. drug treaties, beginning with the 1961 Single Convention on Narcotic Drugs. These treaties serve both an enabling and a constraining function. In addition to trying to stamp out the market for forbidden substances, they seek to ensure the global trade in chemicals essential to pharmaceutical production and modern medicine. By linking licit and illicit drug policy in this way, the U.N. treaties raise the stakes of noncompliance.[7] All three of them, however, contain constitutional escape clauses—clauses that condition the obligation to penalize illicit drug offenses on the "constitutional limitations" or "constitutional principles" of each party.[8] The upshot is that the United States could have eliminated its penalties for any number of drug offenses without violating international law and jeopardizing the interests of American drug companies if, and only if, such penalties were found to be inconsistent with the U.S. Constitution.[9]

Is it plausible to think that courts could have interpreted the Constitution to protect drug users? That notion may seem fanciful today, but the answer was not at all clear in the late 1960s and 1970s, when our drug policies began to take their current shape. Prior to 1915, American lawyers largely took it as given that the Constitution *does* protect drug users, in particular alcohol users, from laws that would forbid them from enjoying their preferred intoxicants; "judicial precedent abounded for the proposition that the right to possess alcohol for private consumption was an inalienable right."[10]

Although courts came to repudiate that proposition in the early to mid-twentieth century, and to endorse a more expansive understanding of the state's regulatory power, a variety of developments over the course of the 1960s and 1970s put the issue of drug rights back into play.

Across the country, surging use of illicit drugs by Vietnam veterans and by college-educated students and professionals created new, politically powerful constituencies for reform. A dozen states decriminalized marijuana between 1973 and 1978, from Maine to Mississippi, with President Jimmy Carter's blessing and law enforcement buy-in.[11] Carter's drug policy advisor expressed equal openness to legalizing cocaine, which he described in 1974 as "probably the most benign of illicit drugs currently in widespread use."[12] A spate of influential books highlighted the racial biases and flawed assumptions built into our drug policies.[13] In tune with these analyses, government commissions issued report after report urging relaxation of the drug laws—a stance that was echoed by comparable commissions abroad and that was embraced within the United States not only by civil libertarian outfits such as the American Civil Liberties Union (ACLU), the Playboy Foundation, and the National Organization for the Reform of Marijuana Laws (founded in 1970) but also by establishment groups ranging from the American Bar Association and the American Medical Association to the Consumers Union and the National Council of Churches. Counterforces were mobilizing, too, including an antimarijuana parents' movement that would go on to guide the Reagan administration's agenda. And the federal budget for enforcement was growing at the same exponential rate as the budget for treatment. But in both the general public and elite circles, the prohibitionist model of drug control was losing credibility. A more tolerant alternative, focused on education and rehabilitation rather than criminal punishment and supply-side interdiction, seemed to be ascendant.[14]

Inside the courts as well as outside, arguments for drug reform were making headway. Civil libertarian rulings proliferated after 1965 and started to unsettle assumptions about vice regulation. Drawing on these precedents, litigants brought "a tidal wave of . . . constitutional challenges" to state and federal drug prohibitions, especially prohibitions on marijuana.[15] Whereas judges in the 1950s and early 1960s had been wont to vilify drugs in their opinions, such rhetoric for the most part disappeared by the late 1960s—replaced by "skeptical references" to the drug laws' constitutive categories and pointed expressions of "disenchantment" with their effects.[16] After all, the defendant in a drug case, as two Michigan Supreme Court justices observed in a decision that drew national headlines, "could have been any mother's son or daughter."[17]

The U.S. Supreme Court mostly stayed above the fray in this period. But it issued a landmark ruling in 1962 that struck down a state law making it a crime to be a narcotics addict,[18] followed by a 1969 ruling that struck down the main provision of federal law used to prosecute marijuana offenses, in an appeal brought by countercultural icon Timothy Leary.[19] The *Leary* opinion was seen "to signal a Court sympathetic to liberalization of marijuana laws," if not of all drug laws.[20] Although many constitutional challenges to drug prohibition continued to fail, litigants won pathbreaking victories in state courts and lower federal courts under the Due Process Clause, the Equal Protection Clause, the Cruel and Unusual Punishment Clause, and the First Amendment. Experts predicted more constitutional victories to come if legislatures did not remove or relax penalties for drug possession.[21] Indeed, some predicted that the legal system would collapse in the absence of such a shift, given that the status quo had turned millions of otherwise law-abiding citizens into criminals.[22] The late 1960s and 1970s, in short, were a time of constitutional ferment and fluidity in the area of drug regulation. Constitutional law had shielded alcohol users from moralizing persecutors before; perhaps it would do something similar for users of marijuana, cocaine, and other substances widely understood to be more benign than booze.

In the end, however, the tidal wave was swept back to sea. The successful constitutional challenges of the late 1960s and early 1970s would go on to be overturned, minimized, or ignored by later courts. At this point, the U.S. jurisprudence is so moribund that most drug reformers don't even bother to enlist the Constitution in their cause. The possibility of constitutional drug rights moved from the mainstream to the margins in less than a generation, even as the drug laws themselves became more and more punitive.

How could a set of policies as draconian, destructive, and discriminatory as those that make up the war on drugs come to be deemed, by so many officials for so many years, to raise no serious constitutional problems? What does this constitutional complicity in the drug war tell us about the supreme law of the land? In view of this history and alternative approaches taken by courts abroad, where might we go from here? This book seeks to answer these questions and, in so doing, to throw new critical light on both drug prohibitionism and U.S. constitutionalism.

ANATOMY OF A CONSTITUTIONAL FAILURE

When trying to figure out why judicial doctrines evolved as they did, scholars divide into two main camps. *Internalists* (or legalists) focus on the role played by articulated principles, reasoned distinctions, institutional competencies—on the logic of the law and the ways it shapes and constrains paths of change. *Externalists* (or realists) focus on developments in the wider world that affect judges' preferences and perceptions—on the social, political, and cultural factors that make certain legal paths more or less likely to be taken.[23] Both perspectives can help us understand why constitutional attacks on the drug war flourished and then failed. The former has been almost entirely neglected in the literature and is, therefore, my primary subject.

Internal to constitutional law, this book will show how the adjudicative paradigm that took hold in the United States after the New Deal was peculiarly unequipped to handle the war on drugs. At first glance, drug claims may seem like good candidates for constitutionalization within this paradigm. Relative to its counterparts abroad, U.S. constitutional law is an outlier in the degree to which it fixates on "negative" rights to be spared state interference rather than "positive" rights to be given state support. But this feature posed no problem, as all of the legal challenges to the war on drugs were negative in character: they involved demands to be let alone, not pleas for government aid. American constitutional law is also comparatively stingy about letting people sue the state. This posed no problem either, as the volume of criminal drug prosecutions ensured a steady stream of defendants who would have standing to raise constitutional objections. On the merits, the Supreme Court's post-1950 rights jurisprudence has been accused by countless conservatives of coddling criminals, compelling integration, and elevating principles of personal autonomy over traditional values. The drug war threw hundreds of thousands of people into prison for behaviors that cause no direct harm to others, limiting adults' ability to control their own bodies, minds, and homes and turning large swaths of our urban landscape into racialized police states. Isn't this precisely the kind of government overreach that modern constitutional law was supposed to stop?

In area after area, however, the controlling legal tests developed in ways that blunted their capacity to reckon with the damage done by our drug regime. Under the Due Process Clause, for instance, courts came to require that liberty interests be "fundamental" to receive meaningful protection, when the problem with many drug prohibitions isn't necessarily that they offend an indispensable aspect of autonomy so much as that they cannot be justified on nonpaternalistic grounds. Under the Equal Protection Clause, courts came to focus on explicit racial classifications and conscious discriminatory intent as the key evils to overcome, when the racism perpetrated by the war on drugs tends to have a more implicit and structural character, and to be all the more tenacious for it. Across numerous lines of doctrine, the minimalist style of judicial review that liberals had championed at midcentury—demanding only a "rational basis" to justify most government measures—left courts with few resources for confronting a situation of profound policy failure. The long line of decisions in which judges declared that they had no choice but to uphold concededly dubious drug classifications amounted to a reductio ad absurdum of rational basis review and a perversion of this form of judicial deference's progressive origins. All of these doctrinal difficulties, moreover, were compounded by a constitutional culture that assigns an authoritative role to federal courts at the expense of other actors and that marginalizes modes of reasoning, such as cost-benefit analysis, that would have put the drug war's flaws front and center.

Hence, while there were many advantages that flowed from the so-called New Deal settlement, according to which courts jealously guarded certain civil rights and liberties while otherwise entrusting public policy to the legislative and executive branches, it had a massive blind spot through which the war on drugs slipped. A doctrinal framework designed to enable an active regulatory state was ill prepared to cope with a set of criminal justice and public health policies that were *themselves* criminogenic and a threat to public health. The analytical and institutional architecture of constitutional decisionmaking constrained possibilities for pushback. The logic of the law was confounded by the illogic of the war on drugs.

Yet that cannot be the whole story, because in various other areas this same doctrinal framework proved capable of generating bold deregulatory reform. Advocates of abortion rights, gay rights, and gun rights, to name just three examples, won major constitutional victories over the past half-century that few lawyers would have predicted in 1960. The fact that jurists and scholars identified substantive constitutional defects in drug policies throughout the 1960s and 1970s makes clear that something similar could have happened in this area as well, if the will had been there. Although the relevant legal tests may have been stifling, they were not straitjackets.

A web of external factors likely contributed to the demise of constitutional resistance to our drug regime. The policy literature points, for instance, toward the crack cocaine panic of the late 1980s, the bipartisan support for urban crime control, the neo-Victorian moralism of the Reagan administration and its successors, the financial and ideological benefits to law enforcement agencies from maintaining a "war" frame, and the racial prejudices braiding all of these.[24] As these reactionary forces became increasingly powerful, it became increasingly implausible that judges would tear down the regime's constitutional foundations. These forces had not yet come fully into place in the 1960s and 1970s, however—on multiple metrics the national trend toward greater toleration of drug use "would reach its peak in the years 1978–80"[25]—leaving judges with more room to maneuver. This was the key period in which the contemporary drug war could have been ameliorated or even averted in court, at least with respect to the personal use of popular substances like marijuana. Legal protections for nonviolent drug users could have been established and then entrenched to some degree against subsequent political change. We'll never know. By the time the war reached full maturity in the 1980s, the first-order fights over its constitutionality had already been resolved in the government's favor.

Meanwhile, no cohesive coalition stepped up to advance moral or identitarian claims about drug rights. What emerged instead after the tumultuous drug battles of the 1970s was, to adapt a phrase from Kenji Yoshino, an epistemic contract of responsible-drug-use erasure, whereby both law-and-order conservatives and professionally successful drug takers agreed, for very different reasons, to demonize illicit substances.[26] The emblematic legal figure here is Judge Ginsburg—not Ruth Bader Ginsburg, who ascended to the Supreme Court in 1993, but Douglas Ginsburg, whose high court nomination collapsed in 1987 after it was revealed that he had smoked pot while a professor. The Ginsburg debacle ensured that the New Deal settlement (which he vocally opposed) would survive, that elites who used illicit drugs would remain in the closet, and that mainstream civil society groups would retreat from the field. In what is still this country's most significant drug rights decision, a 1975 case called *Ravin v. State*, the Alaska Supreme Court went out of its way to "note that the Alaska Bar Association, American Bar Association, National Conference of Commissioners on Uniform State Laws, National Advisory Commission on Criminal Justice Standards and Goals, and the Governing Board of the American Medical Association" had all "recommended decriminalization of possession of marijuana."[27] Once these sorts of groups abandoned the cause of drug liberalization, judges were free to punish "druggies" and "pushers" with reputational impunity.

Moreover, internal and external variables were interacting dynamically. Many of the legal doctrines implicated by challenges to drug prohibition were themselves in flux in the 1970s. And across a range of doctrinal domains, judicial opinions rejecting such challenges served to steer the law in a rights-restrictive direction. That is to say, these opinions weren't merely the product of an unfavorable jurisprudence; they also played a part in making that jurisprudence unfavorable to abolitionist arguments of all kinds. This project proved so successful that the very notion of drug rights came to seem strange, even absurd, to many lawyers, to the detriment of both historical knowledge and contemporary advocacy.[28] Justice Samuel Alito's recent remark in *Dobbs v. Jackson Women's Health Organization* that the right to use illicit drugs lacks "any claim to being deeply rooted in history," made in support of overruling the Court's precedents on abortion, exemplifies this constitutional amnesia and the agendas it may serve.[29]

SETTING THE STAGE

In sum, this book recovers a lost history of constitutional challenges to draconian drug laws. Many critical works have examined how the war on drugs was designed as a political project.[30] By contrast, the story of how it was challenged, justified, and ultimately facilitated in court is unfamiliar even to most constitutional scholars, partly because few of these cases reached the U.S. Supreme Court and partly because they look hopeless from the vantage point of today. Recovering them can enrich our understanding not only of drug policy development but also of twentieth-century constitutional law, which promised a humane equilibrium—flexibility on social and economic regulation, stringency on civil libertarian rights—but which struggled to deal with policies straddling that divide and, more generally, with the eclipse of the welfare state by the penal state. In its moments of greatest legal peril, the war on drugs was rescued not by right-wing radicals but by progressive jurists desperate to defend the New Deal settlement.

Before delving deeper into this story, I need to offer a few notes of clarification. Any sympathetic study of drug rights claims is apt to provoke controversy. Some upfront explanation of this study's scope, limits, and premises will, I hope, help to orient the inquiry and dispel misreadings.

First, I should spell out what I mean by the "war on drugs." By that phrase, I refer broadly to the suite of federal and state policies that have imposed steep criminal as well as civil penalties for the possession, manufacture, and distribution of various psychoactive substances. The framework federal statute within this regime is the Controlled Substances Act, which was enacted in 1970 as part of the Comprehensive Drug Abuse Prevention and Control Act and has been amended many times over.[31] State controlled substances acts penalize a similar set of offenses. Among drug researchers, there is no consensus on what exactly the war on drugs comprises or when it began. As one historian notes, "scholars continue to debate fundamental questions of periodization, scope, and even capitalization."[32] Many attribute the war's launch to President Richard Nixon, who in 1971 declared drug abuse "America's public enemy number one."[33] Others associate the war with the Reagan administration, which escalated and militarized drug enforcement.[34] Still others identify the late 1940s through the 1960s as the formative period[35]—at the federal level, the Boggs Act of 1951 introduced mandatory minimum sentences for drug convictions, President Dwight Eisenhower announced a "new war on narcotics addiction" in 1954, and the Narcotics Control Act of 1956 increased penalties dramatically[36]— while the most expansive chronologies trace the war's origins to the initial wave of drug control laws in the early twentieth century.[37]

The details of these debates are not important for our purposes. On every account, the war on drugs has been marked by a *punitive* and *prohibitive* approach to drug control rather than an approach that regulates potentially dangerous substances primarily through education, taxation, licensing, zoning, medical supervision, age requirements, or the like. All of the constitutional challenges explored in this book question the legal foundations of punitive prohibitionism and thus of the drug war, however defined. They all ask, in one way or another, under what circumstances the state can categorically ban and severely sanction the choice to ingest certain substances. The many shifts in drug policy emphasis and enforcement over the years haven't altered the basic character of these constitutional disputes, which were ventilated most fully in the 1970s.

Second, I should explain the book's focus, on several fronts.

Geographically and temporally. — The war on drugs has been a global project from the start, no matter what start date one chooses, with especially devastating effects across Central and South America. In the chapters that follow, I will draw at points on other countries' constitutional rulings in an effort to place the U.S. jurisprudence in comparative context and to examine its strengths and weaknesses. The final chapter returns to this issue in greater depth. While I hope that these discussions can contribute reciprocally to foreign and international conversations on drug reform, the book's focus is on the United States from the 1960s onward.

Legally. — "One of the defining features of the war on drugs has been the use of especially intrusive investigative tactics":[38] no-knock raids, pretextual stops, electronic eavesdropping, aerial surveillance, undercover agents, paid informants, urine testing, and so forth. These tactics have given rise to a large number of constitutional challenges, brought mainly under the Fourth Amendment and its guarantee against "unreasonable searches and seizures." My focus is on substantive challenges to the drug laws themselves—challenges to the prohibitions and penalties that the laws impose, not to the procedures used to enforce them. Drug enforcement has been a highly visible source of social control in many Black and Brown communities. Reflecting this reality, it has been explored and excoriated in a vast literature, including Michelle Alexander's best-selling book *The New Jim Crow*.[39] The substantive constitutional issues raised by the drug laws have been overlooked in comparison. Yet in an important sense, they are "the heart of the matter"[40] because intrusive investigative techniques are a predictable, even inevitable, consequence of drug prohibition. As Alexander explains, "The ubiquity of illegal drug activity, combined with its consensual nature, requires a far more proactive approach by law enforcement than what is required to address ordinary street crime."[41] And the political and racial economy of law enforcement in the United States means that such "proactive" approaches will be concentrated in downscale drug markets and poor urban neighborhoods.[42] Logically and legally, prohibition precedes policing.

Chemically. — The Controlled Substances Act covers hundreds of substances with very different chemical properties and behavioral effects. Although other sorts of drugs will be addressed throughout, this book will concentrate on the physically nonaddictive "soft drugs," above all cannabis or, as I will most often call it, marijuana.[43] The criminalization of these drugs is hardest to justify as a matter of policy and has generated the lion's share of constitutional litigation. Marijuana is also the most widely used illicit drug and the drug that generates the most arrests: 8.2 million between 2001 and 2010, dwarfing the number of arrests made for all violent crimes combined (not including simple assault).[44] The war on drugs has been, in significant part, a war on marijuana.[45] "If you took marijuana out of the equation," the executive director of the ACLU remarked in 2000, "there would be very little left of the drug war."[46] This point arguably holds not just within the United States but globally as well.[47] The dramatic recent shifts in marijuana law therefore invite reconsideration of the war's constitutional underpinnings.

Third, I should acknowledge my motivating assumptions. The book proceeds from a pair of premises, namely, that the war on drugs has been a policy fiasco and that it is instructive to ask why constitutional law fell out of the reform picture. As far as I am aware, no serious scholar disputes that the war has been "a failure by any objective measure."[48] Nor is there any real dispute that illicit drugs "provide great pleasures to many, including many who are not in any sense addicted,"[49] or that our separation of substances into licit and illicit categories has been driven by politics, prejudice, and corporate interests as much as by pharmacology.[50] There is no comparable consensus on how to interpret the Constitution. But as long as one believes, or even suspects, that the drug war has been a ruinous affair, it becomes interesting to investigate how the war avoided constitutional curtailment during an era when, as Michael Sandel observed in 1989, constitutional law's motifs of "rights as trumps, the neutral state, and the unencumbered self . . . increasingly set the terms of political debate."[51]

Contemporary U.S. drug reformers invoke ideals of individual liberty, racial equality, and good government, yet they do not invoke our supreme law. In a country known for its extreme degree of Constitution worship—much of it oriented around those very ideals—I believe such disconnects are bound to be revealing.[52] An ever-growing array of social issues has been constitutionalized since the 1960s. Drugs have been *de*constitutionalized.

None of this is to deny that drug control presents vexing challenges for public policymakers as well as constitutional interpreters. Depending on how it is used, virtually any psychoactive substance can cause harm. The notion of a risk-free drug is as fantastical as the notion of a drug-free society. Addictions to alcohol and synthetic opioids are a particular scourge in the United States today, on top of less lethal but even more pervasive addictions and quasi-addictions to gambling, gaming, junk food, pornography, social media, and other commercial products.[53] And the regulation of even a relatively mild substance such as marijuana raises myriad complications,[54] as does the question of how to redress past drug policy injustices.[55] To recognize the war on drugs as a travesty is the beginning, not the end, of hard thinking in this area.

Fourth, I should clarify my approach. Expositionally, my aim is to be as efficient as possible in addressing nonlegal aspects of the war on drugs, keeping the focus on legal aspects that have received less attention. Analytically, my aim is to make sense of a failed constitutional reform movement without assuming that judges should have come to the rescue or that they would have done so absent a particular intervening cause. Because I believe the war on drugs to be a travesty, I am sympathetic to those who have opposed it on constitutional grounds. At the same time, I take seriously the constraints on judges who have heard these cases.

Although it offers some unflattering assessments, this book doesn't tell a tale of heroes and villains or prescribe any simple solutions. On the contrary, one of the points I wish to convey is how hard it is to engineer constitutional doctrine so that it will block the most objectionable parts of punitive prohibitionism, on the one hand, while avoiding judicial overreach and preserving worthy regulatory goals, on the other. Without purporting to resolve all of these trade-offs, I will suggest that the drug war's constitutional track record underscores the virtues of alternative models of rights enforcement, both inside and outside the courts.

PLAN OF THE BOOK

To put the inquiry yet another way: if the war on drugs has been so mean and misguided, why did the Constitution end up furnishing so little assistance to its victims, and what can this teach us?

The following chapters take up these questions from a variety of angles. Chapters 1 through 5 are organized around the clauses of the Constitution that have been the basis for challenges to the drug war. These chapters review the most active areas of substantive constitutional attack, both in lawsuits and in law journals. The resulting catalogue is not exhaustive—one of my senior colleagues tells me that his 1969 seminar on Drugs and the Law earnestly explored whether the freedom to "trip" on psychedelic drugs should be protected by the right to travel[56]—but it captures all of the constitutional claims that have gotten any traction in the mainstream legal community.

Chapter 6 expands the frame of analysis. It pans out from specific lines of doctrine to consider broader features of the U.S. constitutional order that have shielded the war on drugs from legal limitation. The overarching contention here as well is that while these features developed to serve valuable ends, their application to the drug war reveals alarming downsides. Finally, chapter 7 concludes with a discussion of how our constitutional practices might be improved in the coming years alongside our drug policies, either by altering the prevailing paradigm of judicial review or by relying less on judges in the first place.

* * *

As I write this introduction, drug reform experiments are cropping up across the nation and the world. Progress has been limited and fragile, however. Drug abuse is as rampant as ever. Punitive policies continue to be pervasive. Humane, holistic approaches remain in short supply.

Before we can move beyond the old regime, we need to understand how such a "monstrous, incoherent mess"[57] was made to seem nonmonstrous, coherent. Criminologists and historians have posited a host of reasons why the drug war persists despite overwhelming evidence of its failure, from anti-Black racism and the desire to protect "innocent" white youth[58] to religious hostility to chemically altered states of consciousness[59] to the bureaucratic imperatives of the military-industrial complex in the post-Vietnam and then post-Cold War moments[60] to the advent of neoliberalism and the recasting of economic and environmental problems as defects of individual character.[61] All of these reasons (and others) strike me as important. This book does not seek to supplant any of them but rather to add one more to the list: constitutional law and the many ways it has legitimated and obscured the drug war's costs to liberty, equality, and government rationality. Even if the ultimate legal outcomes have in some sense been determined, or overdetermined, by deeper social logics, forces within constitutional law have also contributed to the rise and fall of drug rights and to the deleterious consequences that followed.

This book's title thus carries a double meaning, for it aims to illuminate both how the war on drugs was legally constructed and how the Constitution became an asset to drug warriors, how our basic rights doctrines shaped prohibition and how prohibition shaped those same doctrines. Constitutional law helps explain the drug war's historical evolution and staying power. The drug war, in turn, helps explain constitutional law's strange brew of liberal and illiberal elements, of emancipatory possibility and carceral complacency.

CHAPTER I

. . .

Liberty, Privacy, and the Pursuit of Happiness

FROM THE BEGINNING of the American republic, individual liberty, personal privacy, and the pursuit of happiness have been singled out as special constitutional values. The Declaration of Independence pronounced it a "self-evident" truth "that all men . . . are endowed by their Creator with certain unalienable Rights, that among these are Life, Liberty and the pursuit of Happiness." Liberty figures explicitly in the U.S. Constitution's preamble, which invokes "the Blessings of Liberty," and in the Due Process Clauses of the Fifth and Fourteenth Amendments, which prevent the government from depriving "any person of life, liberty, or property, without due process of law." Although privacy does not appear by name in the constitutional text, numerous provisions of the Bill of Rights, as the Supreme Court has observed, "create zones of privacy" in a spatial, relational, or intellectual sense.[62] Happiness doesn't appear in the text either, and its legal significance has withered over time. Some version of the right to happiness made it into a supermajority of *state* constitutions, however.[63] And many commentators in prior periods understood this right, and the Declaration of Independence more

The Constitution of the War on Drugs. David Pozen, Oxford University Press.
© Oxford University Press 2024. DOI: 10.1093/oso/9780197685457.003.0002

generally, to reflect timeless principles of natural law that ought to inform interpretation of the federal Constitution—an approach that has been dubbed Declarationism.[64]

The three values also overlap and reinforce one another. Justice Louis Brandeis's famous dissent in *Olmstead v. United States*, a wiretapping case arising out of Prohibition, characterized the pursuit of happiness as the wellspring of constitutional privacy and liberty. It was because the "makers of our Constitution undertook to secure conditions favorable to the pursuit of happiness," Brandeis wrote, that they "conferred, as against the Government, the right to be let alone—the most comprehensive of rights, and the right most valued by civilized men."[65]

Punitive drug policies are hard to reconcile with liberty, privacy, and the pursuit of happiness on almost any account of those concepts. People use psychoactive substances for a wide range of reasons, including social lubrication, creative stimulation, spiritual and psychological exploration, mental and physical relaxation, pain relief, escapism, energy, sleep, sex—for "ends of great moral seriousness,"[66] frivolous fun, and everything in between. The decision to use such substances implicates a correspondingly wide range of civil libertarian interests, including the ability to govern one's body and brain, the freedom to make self-defining ethical and aesthetic choices, and Justice Brandeis's right to be let alone. Laws that criminalize drug taking are thus "inherently suspect from a liberal perspective."[67] They prevent people from controlling their own consciousness. They demand conformity with a certain image of the respectable citizen. And their enforcement requires invasive police tactics. Some drug restrictions may be justifiable in terms of liberty, privacy, or pursuit of happiness: for instance, if the restrictions paternalize children who lack relevant decisionmaking skills or if they target chemicals so debilitating or so addictive that their consumption is apt to "permanently or indefinitely impair our capacities for rational and moral agency."[68] But at least when it comes to most drugs in most contexts involving adults, the "autonomy costs" of prohibition are steep.[69]

The U.S. Constitution contains various provisions that can be read to protect liberty, privacy, and the pursuit of happiness, a set of values that helped motivate the entire constitutional project. Punitive drug laws imperil those same values both directly, through the personal choices and acts they forbid, and indirectly, through the enforcement techniques and biopolitics they generate.[70] How, then, would the Constitution be brought to bear on drug prohibition? The answer has varied dramatically over the past 150 years.

PROHIBITION AND THE POLICE POWER

If you asked a typical lawyer at the turn of the twentieth century whether the government could ban the possession or consumption of an intoxicant like alcohol, the answer would have been no. The federal government couldn't do so, it was understood at the time, because the "police power" to regulate in the interest of public health, safety, and welfare had been reserved by the Constitution to the states. State governments had broad discretion to legislate under their police powers, which grew tremendously in the period between the Civil War and the New Deal.[71] But many courts continued to enforce a crucial constraint: the legislation must not interfere with purely private behavior. As "vague and wide and undefined as it is," the Kentucky Court of Appeals opined in 1909 in dismissing a conviction for bringing booze into a dry town, the police power "has limits." "It is not within the competency of government," the court explained, "to invade the privacy of the citizen's life and to regulate his conduct in matters in which he alone is concerned, or to prohibit him any liberty the exercise of which will not directly injure society." And the "use of liquor for one's own comfort" causes "direct" injury only to the drinker, if anyone.[72]

On this view, the constitutional flaw in an alcohol ban wasn't that it prevented people from imbibing what they wished, but rather that it exceeded the state's regulatory remit; the problem was one of insufficient legislative authority, not of insufficiently respected individual liberty. These two logics were often difficult to distinguish, however, because the "unalienable Rights" named in the Declaration of Independence underwrote the belief that the police power shouldn't extend as far as the liquor cabinet. As the Kentucky Court of Appeals put the point, "the inalienable rights possessed by the citizens . . . of seeking and pursuing their safety and happiness . . . would be but an empty sound if the Legislature could prohibit . . . owning or drinking liquor."[73] Further complicating matters, some judges invoked the values of the Declaration not merely to justify structural limits on the police power but as a stand-alone basis for invalidating alcohol restrictions. The Indiana Supreme Court, for example, struck down a prohibitory law in 1855 under the state constitutional guarantee of "life, liberty, and the pursuit of happiness."[74] This bundle of rights, one justice observed in a companion case, "embraces the right, in each *compos mentis* individual, of selecting what he will eat and drink."[75]

The case law wasn't entirely uniform in other respects, too. Although in ostensible agreement with their Kentucky counterparts that the police power may be employed to criminalize only acts that "involve direct and immediate injury to another," judges in several western states upheld opium bans on the ground that excessive use of opium made people "liable to become a burden upon society."[76] Anti-Chinese prejudice and concerns about illicit sex often lay just beneath the surface of these opinions. According to a California court of appeals, "there is no such thing as moderation in the use of opium. Once the habit is formed the desire for it is insatiable, and its use is invariably disastrous"—with "a very deleterious and debasing effect upon our race."[77] The Tennessee Supreme Court upheld a local ban on cigarette smoking, describing cigarettes as "inherently bad, and bad only,"[78] whereas the Illinois and Kentucky high courts struck down similar measures.[79] And a clear majority of courts upheld restrictions on the manufacture and sale of intoxicating liquors after the 1850s, as this conduct was seen as nonprivate and therefore within the scope of the police power.[80] But again, the mainstream view was that personal drug possession and consumption could not themselves be banned unless, perhaps, the drug was so dangerous that its use would almost certainly lead to "disastrous" social consequences.

This legal framework fell apart in the 1910s. Between 1900 and 1920, nearly two dozen states enacted some sort of prohibition on alcohol; nearly a dozen states enacted some sort of prohibition on unprescribed marijuana; and every state enacted some sort of prohibition on unprescribed narcotics, including opium, morphine, and heroin.[81] Congress joined in the effort by enacting the first federal antidrug statutes, the Opium Exclusion Act of 1909[82] and the more sweeping Harrison Anti-Narcotics Act of 1914,[83] which effectively outlawed the nonmedical use of opium and coca products. In the coup de grâce, alcohol prohibition became the law of the land following the 1919 ratification of the Eighteenth Amendment (which would be repealed by the Twenty-First Amendment in 1933).[84]

As this unprecedented wave of legislation swept the country, courts came under increasing pressure to uphold prohibitory drug laws. Richard Bonnie and Charles Whitebread identify 1915 as "the watershed year for prohibitionists in the courts."[85] Across state after state, judges began to abandon the principle that the police power may not reach purely private conduct, along with the notion that inalienable rights may be implicated by the regulation of alcohol and other intoxicants. The result, critics complained, was "a kind of extra-legal Frankenstein—a monster Policeman who may defy and mock his creators."[86] In 1917, the U.S. Supreme Court unanimously blessed this new understanding of the police power in *Crane v. Campbell*, asserting with little elaboration that the power to prohibit the sale of alcohol carries with it a subsidiary power to prohibit possession and that "the right to hold intoxicating liquors for personal use is not one of those fundamental privileges of a citizen of the United States which no state may abridge."[87] During this same period, the Supreme Court struck down many progressive laws under the Due Process Clause for violating people's economic liberty. But *Crane* reflected the emerging consensus that drug laws would be spared, paving the legal path for the long century of what David Richards calls "American prohibitionist perfectionism."[88]

Nowadays, the notion that the police power is inherently limited to matters of public concern, lest it trench on the liberal ideals of the Declaration of Independence, would strike most lawyers as strange. The police power tends to be depicted, instead, as "plenary" or unlimited in nature.[89] Even less familiar is the connection between prohibitionism and plenaryism, or how the courts' accommodation of the first iteration of the war on drugs consummated this doctrinal shift. Constitutional law became much more hospitable in the early 1900s to state regulation in the name of public health and public morals, and much more disconnected from Declarationism, in part to enable prohibitory drug policies. In the process, antidrug sentiment helped erase the pursuit of happiness from our constitutional tradition.

THE *GRISWOLD* OPENING

From the late 1910s to the early 1960s, state legislatures effectively had constitutional carte blanche to penalize drug possession and consumption as well as production and distribution. After the Supreme Court endorsed an expansive understanding of the Commerce Clause at the turn of the 1940s, as the next chapter will discuss, Congress enjoyed similarly unfettered authority. The police power was no longer walled off from purely private conduct, and the pursuit of happiness no longer counted as a significant constitutional value. More generally, the Court retreated from the protection of unenumerated rights after the New Deal and came to insist that claims of individual liberty be grounded in a specific textual guarantee.[90] With rare exceptions, this meant that they had to be grounded in one of the guarantees set forth in the Fourteenth Amendment or the Bill of Rights, most of which the Court had applied to the states over the course of the mid-twentieth century.[91] And none of the provisions of the Fourteenth Amendment or the Bill of Rights seemed likely to be of much help. If drug-crime defendants or drug-reform advocates felt that the government had gone too far in limiting their freedom, they had no apparent constitutional hook on which to hang their arguments.

That changed in 1965. In June of that year, the Supreme Court issued a landmark decision in *Griswold v. Connecticut*, which recognized a new constitutional right of privacy and resurrected the protection of substantive liberty interests without a clear basis in the constitutional text. Seven justices in *Griswold* voted to strike down a Connecticut statute that banned the use of contraceptives by married couples, although they split on the rationale. Justice William Douglas, writing for the Court, found that the statute breached a "zone of privacy" created by the "penumbras" of the First, Third, Fourth, Fifth, and Ninth Amendments.[92] Justice Arthur Goldberg, joined by Chief Justice Earl Warren and Justice William Brennan, added that the Ninth Amendment compels the Court to protect fundamental rights, such as the right of privacy in marriage, not listed in "the specific terms of the Bill of Rights."[93] Justices John Harlan

II and Byron White argued in separate concurrences that the contraceptive ban was inconsistent with the Fourteenth Amendment's Due Process Clause, in Harlan's view because the ban "violate[d] basic values 'implicit in the concept of ordered liberty' "[94] and in White's view because it undermined "the freedoms of married persons" without significantly advancing the state's goal of deterring illicit sexual relationships.[95] Justices Potter Stewart and Hugo Black dissented. Although conceding that the Connecticut statute was "an uncommonly silly law," they protested that the "general right of privacy" announced by the majority could not be found in the Bill of Rights, in the Fourteenth Amendment, "or in any case ever before decided by this Court."[96]

Griswold was plainly a momentous ruling, but it left open many questions. Going forward, would the Court rely on penumbral inferences, the Ninth Amendment, or the Fourteenth Amendment to evaluate claims of government overreach that didn't correspond to the specific terms of the Bill of Rights? Would the Court's new right of privacy be "general" and expansive, as the dissent suggested, or would it be limited to married couples and their procreative choices? Or to conduct that takes place in the home? And how would the Court develop a jurisprudence of privacy without itself overreaching and repeating the sins of the recent past? In the late 1800s and early 1900s, as Justice Douglas acknowledged in *Griswold*, the Court had used the doctrine of substantive due process to strike down labor and price regulations that conflicted with the justices' laissez-faire ideology—leading to charges that the Court was "sit[ting] as a super-legislature to determine the wisdom, need, and propriety of laws that touch economic problems, business affairs, or social conditions."[97] The 1905 case *Lochner v. New York*, in which the Court invalidated a maximum-hours law for bakers, had come to stand for this discredited style of judicial review.[98] Douglas's dismissive reference to *Lochner* was, in effect, a concession that any new program of protecting substantive liberty interests would need to be distinguished, in terms of both interpretive methods and case outcomes, from the alleged activism of the *Lochner* era.

A series of decisions issued in the wake of *Griswold* confirmed that a new jurisprudence of personal autonomy was indeed emerging and that it would not be confined to the marital bedroom. In *Stanley v. Georgia*, the Court in 1969 recognized a right to possess and consume obscene material in one's home, even though obscenity does not qualify as speech within the meaning of the First Amendment and there is no right to buy, sell, or make such material. "Th[e] right to receive information and ideas, regardless of their social worth, is fundamental to our free society," the Court declaimed, as "is the right to be free, except in very limited circumstances, from unwanted governmental intrusions into one's privacy."[99] In *Eisenstadt v. Baird*, the Court in 1972 struck down a Massachusetts law that made it a crime to give contraceptives to unmarried persons. Although technically decided on equal protection grounds, *Eisenstadt* reaffirmed the *Griswold* right to privacy and, citing *Stanley*, redescribed it as a "right of the individual, married or single, to be free from unwarranted governmental intrusion into matters . . . fundamentally affecting a person."[100] The next year, the Court held in *Roe v. Wade* that the right of privacy, "founded in the Fourteenth Amendment's concept of personal liberty and restrictions upon state action . . . is broad enough to encompass a woman's decision whether or not to terminate her pregnancy."[101]

Just how broadly this new right would sweep, and how exactly these rulings meshed with one another, remained somewhat mysterious. Henry Friendly, the revered chief judge of the U.S. Court of Appeals for the Second Circuit, observed several months after *Roe* that "[i]f there is anything 'obvious' about the constitutional right to privacy at the present time, it is that its limits remain to be worked out in future cases."[102] Yet for all the ambiguity, everyone understood that some sort of rights revolution was underway, one that placed a new premium on individual freedom and self-determination and that gave less weight to majoritarian moral disapproval. The legal community quickly grasped that these rulings might be enlisted to attack prohibitory drug laws, especially with drugs like marijuana for which moral disapproval seemed to be the dominant rationale for prohibition. The National Commission on Marihuana and Drug Abuse, created by Congress in 1970 and stocked with President Nixon's appointees, acknowledged in 1972 that while courts had not yet "extended a 'right of privacy' shield to those charged with simple possession of marihuana . . . the analytical tools for such a determination are now available in *Griswold* and *Stanley*, as they have been interpreted in the abortion cases."[103] In light of those decisions and "the high place traditionally occupied by the value of privacy in our constitutional scheme," the commissioners added, application of the criminal law to private possession is "constitutionally suspect."[104] Citing *Griswold* and *Stanley*, retired U.S. Supreme Court Justice Tom Clark opined that same year that the Court "might find it difficult to uphold a prosecution for possession" of marijuana.[105]

Leading constitutional and criminal law scholars agreed.[106] Numerous academic articles contended that bans on marijuana were incompatible with *Griswold*'s right of privacy.[107] The ACLU, which launched a campaign to legalize marijuana possession in 1968, began to argue that such bans violate substantive due process by "abridging the right to privacy" and "depriving the consumer of the liberty to conduct his life as he desires so long as he causes no harm or unreasonable interference to the rights of others."[108] The American Bar Association (ABA), which had been questioning punitive drug policies since the 1950s, did not take a position on these constitutional questions but emphasized that it was "especially concerned" about the "impairments of individual liberties" and "invasions of privacy" caused by marijuana prohibition.[109] A California legislative

LIBERTY, PRIVACY, & THE PURSUIT OF HAPPINESS

committee issued a report in 1974 that said *Roe* "seems to compel
the conclusion" that "the right of an adult to possess and use marijuana in private is an act falling within the ambit of the fundamental
right of privacy."[110]

The reemerging constitutional debate over privacy and prohibition coincided with dramatic changes in patterns of drug use over
the 1960s and 1970s. I cannot begin to do justice here to the full
story of this cultural phenomenon, which persists in public memory
through tie-dyed images of hippies, Yippies, antiwar protests, sit-
ins, love-ins, and a newly unapologetic, politically assertive middle-
class movement for drug liberalization and social change. Marijuana
was a particular favorite within this scene, as was LSD. Usage rates
skyrocketed. In 1969, 8 percent of Americans ages eighteen to
twenty-nine reported to Gallup that they had tried marijuana; in
1973, that figure was 35 percent; in 1977, 56 percent.[111] Arrest rates
followed, from annual nationwide totals for marijuana in the tens
of thousands in the late 1960s to 420,000 in 1973 alone.[112] Criminal
defense lawyers began to specialize in cannabis cases.[113] A "cor-
nucopia" of pro-legalization groups were launched, most significantly the National Organization for the Reform of Marijuana Laws
(NORML) in 1970, and became political players.[114] Pro-legalization
magazine *High Times* ran its first issue in 1974 and, by 1978, had
a monthly circulation of 500,000, in line with *Rolling Stone*'s.[115]
Medical researchers and blue-ribbon commissions published a tor-
rent of studies attacking "myths" about marijuana's harms, many of
which had been promoted by the Federal Bureau of Narcotics for
decades.[116] Under the weight of this onslaught, legal scholars thought
it "evident that the assumptions underlying the marihuana prohibition were near collapse."[117]

Policy change came slowly, and then accelerated in the mid-
1970s. In 1973, Oregon became the first state to decriminalize cannabis, kicking off a state-level trend that would cover over a third of

the country's population by 1978. The Ford administration put out a paper in 1975 urging that drug policy be refocused on substances such as heroin that have "the highest costs to both society and the user," with "low priority" given to less damaging—and more white-identified—substances such as cocaine, hallucinogens, and marijuana.[118] The Carter administration openly supported marijuana decriminalization at the state and federal levels on the premise, articulated by President Carter in a message to Congress, that "[p]enalties against possession of a drug should not be more damaging to an individual than the use of the drug itself."[119] Propelling all of these developments, as Bonnie and Whitebread observed in 1970, was a generational and ideological turn toward placing higher value on "personal fulfillment," "personal identity, and the individualized, deinstitutionalized pursuit of happiness." After two hundred pages of scrupulously cautious legal analysis, Bonnie and Whitebread concluded that "marijuana prohibition is as inconsistent with this new cultural climate as it was predictable under the old."[120] Or as young people across the country told researchers in 1972, drug use shouldn't be criminal "because everybody does it, and because things done to oneself are constitutionally protected."[121]

Griswold thus opened the constitutional door in 1965 to a new sort of attack on the regulation of vice, just as the issue of illicit drug use exploded into the national consciousness and the cause of drug reform started to attract powerful new supporters. Would bans on drugs like marijuana meet the same constitutional fate as bans on contraception, abortion, and private possession of obscene material?

LIMITED LIBERTARIAN BREAKTHROUGHS

Some of the privacy- and liberty-based constitutional attacks on marijuana prohibition succeeded—at least initially, and at least in a few state courts. But not quite under the logic of *Griswold*. Most of the judges who recognized any sort of constitutional right to own or consume drugs made analytic moves that refined or departed from U.S. Supreme Court case law.

Before the privacy and liberty litigation came to a head, drug reformers secured a series of constitutional victories in the late 1960s and early 1970s on related rationales. A handful of state courts, for instance, found that laws making it a crime to be in the presence of illicit drug use were unduly vague or overbroad, and either struck down these laws or narrowly construed them to require knowledge of the drug use and control of the premises.[122] The U.S. Supreme Court deployed the void-for-vagueness doctrine to more far-reaching effect in the 1972 case *Papachristou v. City of Jacksonville*. Noting that "'wandering or strolling' from place to place" has "been extolled" in the American poetic canon, Justice Douglas's opinion for the Court struck down an antivagrancy ordinance that had been used to prosecute, among others, a reputed "narcotics pusher" who had been found with heroin on him.[123] Three years earlier, the Court unanimously accepted the argument of the country's best-known psychedelic proselytizer, Timothy Leary, that the 1937 Marihuana Tax Act's registration rules violated the Fifth Amendment privilege against self-incrimination.[124] (In order to obtain the required federal tax forms, Leary would have had to admit that he possessed pot in violation of state law.) Almost immediately, *Leary* proved a pyrrhic victory for drug liberalizers, as Congress simply replaced the Marihuana Tax Act the next year with a more sweeping and explicit criminal ban, which did not raise the same self-incrimination issues, and as Leary's increasingly eccentric antics arguably undermined what had been a burgeoning field of psychedelic research.[125]

At both the federal and state levels, direct challenges to marijuana possession bans started to make headway in the late 1960s. Several courts, while not outright endorsing such challenges, either construed bans in a manner that reduced their impact on the home[126] or hinted that they may raise privacy problems worthy of consideration in a future case.[127] More significant breakthroughs came soon thereafter, in a trilogy of widely followed state supreme court cases: *State v. Kantner* in Hawaii, *People v. Sinclair* in Michigan, and *Ravin v. State* in Alaska.

The *Kantner* decision came out first, in January 1972, and proved the least consequential. Bizarrely, the Hawaii Supreme Court upheld the state's ban on marijuana possession even though three of the five justices made it clear that they believed the ban to be unconstitutional. Two justices tersely sided with the state.[128] Justice Kazuhisa Abe concurred in this judgment, but only because in his view (and his view alone) the appellants had failed to raise the winning constitutional claim. Reiterating a stance he had articulated two years earlier, Justice Abe argued that under the Due Process Clause of the U.S. Constitution and a clause of the Hawaii Constitution recognizing a right to life, liberty, and the pursuit of happiness, there is a "fundamental constitutional right to smoke marijuana" as part of a broader right "to make a fool of [one]self as long as [one's] act does not endanger others."[129] In dissent, Justice Bernard Levinson contended that under those same two clauses, "a person has a constitutionally protected right purposely to induce in himself, in private, a mild hallucinatory mental condition through the use of marihuana." The drug stimulates "thoughts, emotions, and sensations" that are "among the most personal and private experiences possible," Justice Levinson elaborated, and *Griswold*'s right of privacy "guarantees to the individual the full measure of control over his own personality consistent with the security of himself and others."[130] Finally, Justice Bert Kobayashi dissented on the ground that the classification of marijuana as a narcotic was so unreasonable as to violate the U.S. Constitution's Equal Protection Clause.[131] Drug reformers in Hawaii never had a chance to capitalize on this "landmark package of opinions" deeming the state law unconstitutional,[132] as a rash of retirements on the court left only two votes for invalidation by the time the issue was revisited in 1975.[133] Later that same winter, the Michigan Supreme Court issued a fractured ruling of its own in *People v. Sinclair*. John Sinclair was a poet and political activist who had helped found the White Panther Party, an antiracist collective that supported the Black Panther Party, and the Detroit chapter of LEMAR, a grassroots organization dedicated to legalizing marijuana. After giving a pair of joints to undercover police officers who had been pestering him to do so for weeks, Sinclair was convicted in 1969 of unlawful possession of two marijuana cigarettes and sentenced to nine and a half to ten years in prison. The case drew widespread media attention and became, in the words of the Committee for a Sane Drug Policy, "symbolic throughout the United States of the barbarity of the marijuana laws."[134] Outrage over Sinclair's sentence led, in December 1971, to a fifteen-thousand-person protest rally in Ann Arbor. Performers and speakers included John Lennon, Yoko Ono, Stevie Wonder, Bobby Seale, and Allen Ginsberg. Lennon closed out the event with a song titled "Free John Sinclair."[135] Three days later, the Michigan Supreme Court ordered that Sinclair be released from custody. Three months later, the court issued its ruling.

All six of the participating justices agreed that Sinclair's conviction was unconstitutional. Two justices concluded that Sinclair had been "entrapped" by the police.[136] Three justices concluded that the Michigan legislature's "erroneous classification" of marijuana as a narcotic violated the Equal Protection Clause.[137] Three justices concluded that Sinclair's sentence amounted to cruel and unusual punishment in violation of the Eighth Amendment.[138] The most striking opinion belonged to Justice Thomas G. Kavanagh, who concluded that Michigan's marijuana ban "is an impermissible intrusion on the fundamental rights to liberty and the pursuit of happiness" as well as "the right to possess and use private property." Justice Kavanagh cited no legal authorities for this proposition. Drawing on John Stuart Mill's harm principle—which holds, roughly, that government restrictions on liberty may be justified only to prevent harm to others—and George Orwell's depiction of a totalitarian dystopia in *1984*, Kavanagh inveighed that " 'Big Brother' cannot, in the name of *Public* health, dictate to anyone what he can eat or drink or smoke in the Privacy of his own home."[139]

Sinclair achieved "seminal" status in Michigan jurisprudence[140] and has been credited, alongside *Ravin*, with "contributing to changing public sentiment and a partial relaxation of marijuana laws" in the years that followed.[141] "With the advent of such cases as *People v. Sinclair*," two attorneys wrote in the *Notre Dame Lawyer* shortly after the decision, "it seems only a matter of time before marijuana statutes will begin to fall."[142] Yet only Justice Kavanagh's approach would have prevented the Michigan legislature from reclassifying marijuana as a nonnarcotic and imposing a new ban with lesser penalties, which is exactly what happened in the spring of 1972.[143] The failure of any single constitutional claim to garner a majority made it easy for policymakers to maneuver around the ruling and for unsympathetic judges to ignore it. The Missouri Supreme Court, for instance, brushed aside *Sinclair* in 1978 as providing "very little authority for any singular proposition."[144] In Sinclair's conviction, so many plausible constitutional defects converged that, paradoxically, his legal victory repudiated none of them.

The final and most decisive breakthrough occurred three years later in *Ravin v. State*, when the Alaska Supreme Court ruled unanimously that the state's marijuana ban violated the right to privacy. The *Ravin* court declined to find that there is a "fundamental right" to possess or ingest the drug, given that—the court asserted without citation or explanation—"[f]ew would believe they have been deprived of something of critical importance if deprived of marijuana."[145] Under both U.S. Supreme Court precedents like *Griswold* and *Stanley* and a privacy amendment that had been added to the Alaska constitution in 1972, however, the Court found that Alaskans have a fundamental right to "privacy in their homes," which would "encompass the possession and ingestion of substances such as marijuana in a purely personal, non-commercial context in the home" unless the state could show "a close and substantial relationship between the public welfare" and a ban on such behavior.[146] The court then turned to the evidence on marijuana's effects. After reviewing the expert testimony that had been presented at trial along with scores of articles and books, the court determined that while "[r]esearch is continuing" and "[s]cientific doubts persist," "there is no firm evidence that marijuana, as presently used in this country, is generally a danger to the user or to others," except in the context of driving under the influence.[147] The state, accordingly, could not carry its burden of showing that a total prohibition sufficiently serves the public good.

In addition to limiting its holding to the home, the *Ravin* court went out of its way to emphasize that when it comes to drugs, the right to privacy may be outweighed even by indirect evidence of third-party harm. For example, if a drug were to cause such serious "withdrawal or amotivational syndrome" that its widespread use risked "significantly debilitat[ing] the fabric of our society," the state could intervene more forcefully.[148] Three years later, the Alaska Supreme Court applied this logic in declining to extend *Ravin* to cocaine, stating that, compared to marijuana, "it seems clear that cocaine is substantially more of a threat to health and welfare."[149] *Ravin*, however, continues to be good law in Alaska[150] and to inspire interest from judges and reformers abroad. In 2018, the Constitutional Court of South Africa cited *Ravin* extensively in finding that a marijuana ban violates the South African Constitution's right to privacy.[151] This reasoning was cited extensively, in turn, by the Eastern Caribbean Supreme Court in striking down Saint Kitts and Nevis's marijuana ban in 2019.[152]

CONSTRUCTING THE IMPLAUSIBILITY
OF DRUG RIGHTS, IN FOUR STEPS

Within the United States, *Ravin* proved less generative. No other court followed its lead, and by the early 1980s, the struggle to bring drugs into the rights revolution was effectively over. Certain psychoactive substances such as alcohol, nicotine, and caffeine remained legally available in every state, but only as a matter of legislative grace, not constitutional entitlement.[153] In rejecting privacy- and liberty-based challenges to marijuana prohibition, federal and state courts generally followed a common script.

First, the leading substantive due process precedents were distinguished. *Griswold* and *Roe* were about "marriage" and "procreation."[154] Older substantive due process precedents still held in esteem, such as *Meyer v. Nebraska*[155] and *Pierce v. Society of Sisters*,[156] were about "child rearing" and "education."[157] Smoking pot has nothing to do with these things. *Stanley*, meanwhile, was inapposite because it involved a regulation of people's " 'private thoughts,' "[158] not health and safety, and because footnote 11 of the Court's opinion had clarified, "What we have said in no way infringes upon the power of the State or Federal Government to make possession of other items, such as narcotics, firearms, or stolen goods, a crime."[159]

Second, it was explained that any autonomy interest not tightly tied to the text of the Bill of Rights must be "fundamental" or "implicit in the concept of ordered liberty" to receive meaningful constitutional protection.[160] The Supreme Court appeared to endorse this approach in *Roe*.[161] Requiring rights to meet such a standard brought some analytic discipline and normative coherence to substantive due process review, the opinions intimated, and it ensured that the *Griswold* opening would not lead to constitutional chaos.

Third, the possibility that a person's interest in using or possessing a drug like marijuana could qualify as "fundamental" was rejected out of hand. Whether in the home or anywhere else, this activity "does not involve important values."[162] Moreover, marijuana's reputation "as a 'recreational drug' undercuts any argument that its use is as important as, e.g., use of contraceptives."[163]

Finally, the specter of *Lochner* was invoked to confirm the propriety of deferring to the legislature. The *Lochner* Court had lost legitimacy and compromised democracy by second-guessing elected officials' efforts to protect public health and welfare. In light of that history, "Any court asked to undertake review of the multifarious political, economic, and social considerations that usually underlie legislative prohibitory policy should do so with caution and restraint."[164]

Add all this up, and it might seem that "[n]othing would be more inappropriate" than for a court to classify "personal possession [of marijuana] as a constitutionally protected right."[165]

DECONSTRUCTING THE IMPLAUSIBILITY OF DRUG RIGHTS

Each step in this line of reasoning was plausible, but also far from obvious. Recall that the National Commission on Marihuana and Drug Abuse, nine of the thirteen members of which had been selected by President Nixon, concluded in 1972 that bans on marijuana possession were "constitutionally suspect" on privacy grounds.[166] Those commissioners weren't political naïfs, nor were most of them liberals. If their conclusion now seems far-fetched, it is in part because the courts' reasoning in the marijuana cases came to inform not only how the legal profession thinks about drugs and privacy but also how the judiciary approaches substantive liberty claims in general. Against the notion that precedents like *Griswold* and *Roe* are easily distinguished by their connection to marriage and procreation, it would have been just as easy to read those cases as vindicating interests that bear on drug use, such as the right to be let alone, to control one's body, or to reach one's own decisions on sensitive personal matters. Several dissenting judges made precisely this move.[167] Before he became a Trumpian U.S. senator, Josh Hawley argued cogently that *Griswold*, *Roe*, and other modern substantive due process cases stand for a shared commitment to liberty as "the right to choose" one's own values and way of life.[168] The fact that certain drugs are anathema to religious conservatives and moral traditionalists only strengthens the analogy. Even though the Court found contraception and abortion to be constitutionally protected, none of the justices in *Griswold* or *Roe* wished to be seen as commending either practice, which many Americans believed to be sinful. Likewise, *Stanley* could have been read as standing for a principle of personal sovereignty or privacy in the home.[169] *Stanley*'s footnote 11, which was unnecessary to the resolution of the case and therefore not legally binding, could have been ignored or limited to especially dangerous drugs.[170]

Judges always have discretion in choosing how to characterize precedents and at what level of generality to describe previously protected rights—so much so that for many contested issues, "it is primarily in the interpretation of prior cases that the battle for constitutional meaning is joined."[171] And even those judges most skeptical of the emerging privacy jurisprudence had to concede that the precedents "def[ied] categorical description."[172] It was in the drug cases of the 1970s, as much as anywhere, that the judiciary repudiated any reading of *Griswold* as establishing a "general right of privacy."[173]

[38]

Against the notion that unenumerated rights must be "fundamental" to receive meaningful protection, more flexible approaches
to substantive due process were not only available but also in active use at the time. Constitutional law students today learn that
substantive due process jurisprudence has two tiers: government
intrusions on fundamental rights are subject to a very demanding
inquiry, known as strict scrutiny, while government intrusions on
nonfundamental interests are subject to a very deferential inquiry,
known as rational basis review (discussed in the next chapter). But
the Supreme Court had not fully developed this framework by
the mid-1970s. That much was evident on the face of *Griswold*,
Eisenstadt, and *Roe*, each of which employed a different, and indeed
sui generis, analytic method.

As Richard Fallon has detailed, throughout the 1960s and 1970s
the Court "appeared to engage in an ad hoc balancing of 'the liberty interest of the individual' against 'the demands of an organized
society'" in substantive due process cases "involving claims to avoid
confinement in mental institutions, to be allowed to travel, to re-
sist unwanted administration of antipsychotic drugs, and to receive
care and treatment while subject to government custody other than
criminal incarceration," among other matters.[174] There is no reason
in principle why such balancing couldn't have been performed in the
illicit drug cases as well. The Alaska Supreme Court did a version of
this in *Ravin*—rejecting "the rigid two-tier formulation" in favor of a
test that asks "whether the means chosen bear a substantial relationship to the legislative purpose"[175]—and concluded that the state's
marijuana policy interferes excessively with the right of privacy.

Against the notion that drug use couldn't possibly rank as fundamental, everything depends on how one organizes the inquiry. The
Supreme Court had given little guidance on how to ascertain fundamentality apart from the "implicit in the concept of ordered liberty"
formulation, which was both obscure in its own right and especially

confusing because it was sometimes suggested to be a *definition* of fundamentality and at other times suggested to be an *alternative basis* for strict scrutiny.[176] In later years, some of the Court's opinions insisted that a right also be carefully described and "deeply rooted in our legal tradition" to merit protection,[177] although other opinions rejected those requirements.[178] As discussed above, the right to possess and ingest intoxicating substances does have a strong claim to being "deeply rooted" in U.S. legal history, depending on how that equally enigmatic test is specified.

Regardless, it beggars belief to say that no "important values" are at stake with drug prohibition.[179] In general terms, once again, the right to be let alone is very much at stake, as are all of the autonomy interests associated with that right.[180] At a lower level of generality, theorists from diverse disciplines have described drug use as a "basic life choice"[181] and a moral right,[182] while anthropologists and historians have described drug use as a core component of the pursuit of happiness and "the constitution of culture" across virtually all known human societies.[183] Nothing comparable could be said about many of the other personal liberties that were actively litigated in the 1970s, such as the right to ride a motorcycle without a helmet.[184] As Justice Levinson suggested in *Kantner*, in a passage later endorsed by a chamber of the Mexican Supreme Court, psychoactive substances help many people access "thoughts, emotions, and sensations" that they experience as distinctly pleasurable if not profound.[185]

Shortly after *Kantner* came out, the Nixon administration suppressed a study commissioned by the U.S. Health, Education, and Welfare Department which reportedly found, as one of its "primary conclusions," that young people's use of psychedelics "can be a highly moral, productive, and personally fulfilling" pursuit.[186] Marijuana proponents, meanwhile, have long maintained that it helps them to appreciate more keenly not only the pleasures of music, food, and sex[187] but also the drawbacks of the rigid, hierarchical style of "straight thinking" that the fundamental/nonfundamental binary reflects and reifies.[188] Some drug users may be misguided or deluded in their self-assessments. But it's not clear how this could be objectively established[189] or why it should bear on the strength of their liberty interest, as opposed to the strength of the case for government regulation.

Finally, against the notion that undertaking rigorous review of prohibitory drug laws would be *Lochner* redux, there was—and is—no consensus on what makes *Lochner* an anticanonical case. It couldn't just be that *Lochner* protected unenumerated rights under the Due Process Clause, since *Griswold* had rehabilitated that tactic. In his *Kantner* dissent, Justice Levinson offered one possible basis for distinguishing the two opinions: whereas the *Lochner* Court had targeted "economic" legislation, *Griswold* and its progeny focused on legislation that "intrudes into the purely private sphere of human life."[190] Personal drug use would seem to fall firmly on the *Griswold* side of that line. Whether or not Levinson's distinction is persuasive, it is hard to see why striking down a marijuana ban would have been any more Lochnerian than striking down a contraception ban.

BEYOND DRUG RIGHTS "FUNDAMENTAL"-ISM

The idea that principles of liberty, privacy, and the pursuit of happiness constrain the state's ability to prohibit drug use has traveled a tortuous constitutional path. As this chapter has shown, the idea was commonplace in the late 1800s and early 1900s, routed in the 1910s to accommodate alcohol prohibition, revived in the 1960s by *Griswold* and follow-on cases, and then largely routed again in the 1970s. This history suggests, at a minimum, that there is nothing legally inevitable about the current conventional wisdom that happiness isn't an operative constitutional value or that drug rights don't exist in the United States.

The courts that rebuffed the post-1965 wave of challenges to marijuana prohibition invoked a standard set of doctrinal rationales which, as we have seen, were plausible but by no means ironclad. The most important of these rationales was that liberty interests not tightly tied to the text of the Bill of Rights must be "fundamental" to receive meaningful protection. Legal scholars often characterize this two-tiered framework—fundamental rights get special solicitude, every other right gets shown the door—as a means "to enshrine penitence for the sins of the *Lochner* era."[191] Yet in addition to being a backward-looking attempt to avoid a discredited style of judging, the construction and consolidation of this framework over the course of the 1970s was a forward-looking effort to close the floodgates *Griswold* had opened to all manner of personal autonomy claims and thereby preserve a space for paternalistic regulation, including drug regulation.

The proposition that there is a fundamental right to use mind-altering substances sits uneasily with the orderly instincts of many lawyers, a group more Apollonian than Dionysian by self-selection as well as training. The proposition is at least credible doctrinally and philosophically. But it challenges both legal progressives' faith in scientific expertise and legal conservatives' skepticism of freedom as libertinism. The genius of the Alaska Supreme Court's *Ravin* ruling was to break out of the two-tiered framework altogether and thus avoid conditioning constitutional protection on a finding of fundamentality. In this, as chapter 7 will explain, *Ravin* prefigured the "proportionality" approach to rights review that courts in other countries have employed in reaching similar results.

CHAPTER 2

. . .

Federalism and Rational Regulation

THE MOST COMMON constitutional challenges to prohibitory drug
laws throughout U.S. history have been founded on principles of
liberty, privacy, and the pursuit of happiness. These challenges, explored in the previous chapter, are essentially Millian in character.
In line with and sometimes inspired by Mill's harm principle,[192] they
contend at bottom that the state shouldn't be able to ban personal
choices that cause no direct damage to others. These challenges are
also the most far-reaching. If they were accepted, the state would
still be allowed to impose time, place, and manner restrictions on
drug use, as well as minimum age requirements and taxes on drug
sales. But the state would no longer be allowed to prohibit adults'
private possession or consumption of most, if not all, psychoactive
substances—as Mill himself maintained with reference to alcohol.[193]

Since the 1960s, the next most prominent set of constitutional
challenges to drug prohibition have focused not on principles of individual liberty but rather on principles of government responsibility
and rationality, not on whether people's freedom to ingest drugs
may be curtailed but on who gets to make such calls and according

The Constitution of the War on Drugs. David Pozen, Oxford University Press.
© Oxford University Press 2024. DOI: 10.1093/oso/9780197685457.003.0003

to what standards of justification. These challenges have taken two basic forms. First, litigants have argued that under principles of federalism, Congress lacks power to set drug policy. Second, litigants have argued that under the Equal Protection Clause, both state and federal officials must regulate drugs in a nonarbitrary manner, which entails a duty to ground policies in public reason and to treat like substances alike.

As with their Millian counterparts, these arguments enjoyed some success before ultimately being vanquished. Although their core contentions had undeniable historical and conceptual force, their odds in court were slim under the interpretive paradigm that emerged after the New Deal. Had they prevailed, these constitutional challenges wouldn't necessarily have stopped punitive prohibitionism in its tracks, but they would have required U.S. drug policy to be significantly more decentralized, evidence-based, and attentive to the different pharmacological properties of different substances.

FEDERAL POWER FROM THE HARRISON ACT TO
THE CONTROLLED SUBSTANCES ACT

As chapter 1 recounted, drugs have been at the center of historic debates over the scope of the states' police power to regulate in the interest of public health and welfare. The federal government, unlike the states, is said to have no police power, no "general authority to perform all the conceivable functions of government."[194] If Congress wishes to enact a law on a certain subject, it must identify a clause in the Constitution that authorizes it to regulate in that area. Sometimes, this exercise is straightforward. Article I, Section 8, Clause 7 grants Congress the power to "establish Post Offices and Roads," so no one disputes that Congress may set up a postal service.

In many instances, however, the fit between a legislative scheme and the language of Article I is more contestable. "[T]he question respecting the extent of the powers actually granted" to the federal government "is perpetually arising," Chief Justice John Marshall observed over two hundred years ago, "and will probably continue to arise, so long as our system shall exist."[195]

Drugs have been at the center of historic debates over this question as well. When Congress, in the 1910s, first determined to outlaw the nonmedical use of opium and cocaine, it was unclear what the constitutional basis for such legislation could be. The Commerce Clause, which grants Congress the power to "regulate Commerce . . . among the several States," might seem promising, since drugs are often sold for money. But most of the relevant drug transactions occurred within a single state rather than across state lines, and the Supreme Court's jurisprudence at the time did not permit the Commerce Clause to reach such local matters.

Congress therefore relied on a different power in passing the Harrison Anti-Narcotics Act of 1914, its power to "lay and collect Taxes." The statute imposed a nominal tax (increased five years later) on persons who produced, imported, or distributed opium or cocaine. Of greater consequence, the statute made it a crime to dispense those substances without having registered with the commissioner of internal revenue.[196] In addition to being one of the earliest federal forays into drug prohibition, the Harrison Act helped introduce strict liability into federal criminal law—relieving prosecutors of the burden of proving that defendants knew about the statute's rules or intended to violate them[197]—and was "certainly the most radical regulation of a consumer market yet attempted by the federal government."[198]

Many lawyers thought that Congress had pushed the tax power past its limit. Although the Harrison Act was framed as a revenue measure, everyone understood that the point was to root out the narcotics trade.[199] And it was blackletter constitutional law that "Congress, by merely calling an Act a taxing act," could not "make it a legitimate exercise of taxing power . . . if in fact the words of the Act show clearly its real purpose is otherwise."[200] The American Medical Association (AMA), moreover, came out in the 1920s against federal restrictions on the prescribing rights of physicians.[201] After upholding the Harrison Act in 1919 over the dissent of four justices,[202] the Supreme Court took the unusual step in 1926 of inviting another constitutional challenge.[203] Two years later, in *Nigro v. United States*, the Court upheld the statute once again. Chief Justice William Howard Taft, writing for the majority, conceded that "a mere act for the purpose of regulating and restraining the purchase of the opiate and other drugs . . . is beyond the power of Congress." Taft found, however, that the Harrison Act's drug control features were "genuinely calculated to sustain the revenue features."[204] The dissenters called bullshit. Justice James Clark McReynolds wrote that the act's "real and primary purpose is not difficult to discover, and it is strict limitation and regulation of the [narcotics] traffic."[205] "That conclusion is so plain," Justice Pierce Butler added, "that discussion cannot affect it."[206]

The *Nigro* Court's strained reading of the Harrison Act legitimated the tax power as a vehicle for prohibitory federal drug laws, a template that was repeated (in the form of a transfer tax) in the Marihuana Tax Act of 1937.[207] More than that, it gave the green light to all manner of federal regulatory taxes, aimed at encouraging or discouraging particular behaviors rather than filling the government's coffers. *Nigro* is today an obscure case. Yet whether or not it deserves the title of "most disingenuous Supreme Court opinion, ever," as one critic has charged, *Nigro* ranks as a milestone on the twentieth-century road to greater congressional authority.[208] Just as antidrug legislation helped defeat the idea of inherent limitations on the states' police power in the 1910s, so did it contribute, in the 1920s, to the demise of judicially enforceable limitations on the federal government's tax power.

A decade or so after *Nigro*, the Supreme Court unleashed congressional authority to a far greater extent. Following President Franklin Roosevelt's landslide reelection in 1936, the Court effectively abandoned judicial review of the enumerated powers doctrine. The Commerce Clause was reinterpreted to permit Congress to regulate any activity that, when aggregated nationwide, could have a substantial effect on interstate commerce—which is to say, almost every activity—and became the backbone of the modern regulatory state. From 1937 to 1995, not a single federal statute was struck down by the Court as exceeding the scope of the commerce power.[209] According to the New Deal settlement, as it came to be known, the political branches were presumptively free to set economic and social policy as they saw fit; allegations of government overreach stood a chance in court only if cast as violations of noneconomic civil libertarian rights protected by the Constitution's amendments. Hence, when Congress decided to enact new drug laws in the 1960s and 1970s, there was no need to engage in the old tax power "ruse."[210] Congress could simply outlaw disfavored drug behaviors under the Commerce Clause, which it did first in the Drug Abuse Control Amendments of 1965[211] and then more exhaustively in the Comprehensive Drug Abuse Prevention and Control Act of 1970.[212]

In 1995, however, the Supreme Court ruled that a provision of the Gun-Free School Zones Act exceeded the scope of the commerce power.[213] Five years later, the Court did it again with a provision of the Violence Against Women Act.[214] In these two cases, *United States v. Lopez* and *United States v. Morrison*, the Rehnquist Court indicated that federal laws might no longer be upheld under the Commerce Clause if they regulate local activities with an attenuated relationship to the interstate economy. Conservatives cheered the "federalism revolution" that seemed to be underway.[215] Liberals fretted that the Court's new jurisprudence would strangle congressional capacity to address urgent public problems. Momentum seemed to be on the conservatives' side, until drugs reentered the picture. In *Gonzales v. Raich*, two seriously ill California medical marijuana patients and their caregivers argued that the federal Controlled Substances Act (CSA) exceeds the scope of the commerce power to the extent that it prohibits local cultivation and use of marijuana in compliance with state law. The patients won in the court of appeals.[216] Surprising many, the Supreme Court in 2005 voted 6–3 to reverse. Justice John Paul Stevens, writing for the majority, explained that Congress could rationally conclude that the failure to criminalize such conduct would undercut its goal of destroying the interstate market in marijuana.[217] Justice Anthony Kennedy defected from his conservative colleagues to join Justice Stevens's opinion. Justice Antonin Scalia defected as well and concurred in the judgment.[218] In dissent, Justice Sandra Day O'Connor protested that the Court had reduced *Lopez* and *Morrison* to "nothing more than a drafting guide," easily circumvented by future Congresses, and "extinguishe[d]" any possibility of collective learning from California's "experiment with medical marijuana."[219]

It was easy to be cynical about Justice Kennedy's and Justice Scalia's embrace of federal power when it targeted a countercultural drug.[220] Rather than vote to uphold the CSA in its entirety, they could have adopted any number of intermediate positions that would have limited the statute's applicability in states that authorize medical marijuana under controlled conditions.[221] From the other side of the ideological spectrum, Justice Stevens dropped hints in *Raich* that he personally opposed marijuana prohibition,[222] which he later described as "futile."[223] The jurisprudential imperative, for Stevens and his liberal colleagues, was to put a stop to the Court's federalism revolution and shore up the New Deal settlement. In this they succeeded. The most significant constitutional challenge to the war on drugs in many years didn't just fail to deliver the knockout blow to that settlement; to the contrary, *Raich* united left- and right-leaning legal elites in reaffirming the de facto nationalization of the police power.

And yet Justice O'Connor's prediction about the death of state experimentation on marijuana policy proved quite wrong—in part because of another set of Rehnquist Court federalism rulings. In two cases from the 1990s, *New York v. United States* and *Printz v. United States*, the Court held that Congress may not compel states to adopt particular laws or to administer federal laws.[224] No one was thinking about drugs when this "anticommandeering" doctrine was developed. When states subsequently began to legalize marijuana for medicinal and then recreational purposes, however, this doctrine seemed to imply that Congress couldn't force them to recriminalize pot or to devote resources to enforcing the federal prohibition.[225] A Court that had never shown sympathy for drug users had, it turned out, created some breathing room for drug reformers. Although a separate principle of structural constitutional law dictates that federal legislation prevails over (or "preempts") state legislation whenever the two conflict,[226] the anticommandeering doctrine has also helped legalizing states to persuade judges that most of their actions are not preempted by the CSA.[227] The Obama administration reinforced this line of argument by urging the Supreme Court to stay out of the way[228] and by announcing that it would no longer enforce the CSA's marijuana provisions in states that had legalized the substance, except under limited circumstances.[229]

The current constitutional equilibrium is precarious. The more states do to support their marijuana companies and consumers, the more their policies will not just deviate from but will actively subvert the federal prohibition.[230] The same goes for psychedelics and any other substances that states might wish to legalize even though they remain illegal at the federal level. Unless Congress revises the

CSA, the Court revisits its federalism precedents, or the attorney general deschedules the drug, the anticommandeering principle will at some point run up against the preemption power as the cannabis industry matures.

CLASSIFYING DRUGS

In the meantime, the recent spate of marijuana legalizations at the state level, and the apparent absence of calamitous consequences from these reforms,[231] have spotlighted an old set of questions. Does it make any sense to penalize "soft drugs" like marijuana or magic mushrooms as harshly as "hard drugs" like heroin or fentanyl? For that matter, does it make sense to penalize marijuana at all when substances such as alcohol and nicotine are legal?

To millions of Americans who experimented with pot, psychedelics, and other mind-altering drugs in the late 1960s and 1970s, the answer seemed plain. Expert committee after expert committee confirmed through objective research what they felt they already knew from subjective experience: marijuana is basically benign in most settings, and certainly more benign than booze. Blue-ribbon bodies had reached similar conclusions in prior periods, most notably the Indian Hemp Drugs Commission in the 1890s, the Panama Canal Zone Governor's Committee in the 1920s and 1930s, and the La Guardia Committee in the 1940s.[232] In a 1966 essay titled "The Great Marijuana Hoax," the poet Allen Ginsberg lamented that these "medical-juridic reports . . . giving marijuana a clean bill of health" had fallen into obscurity.[233]

Reinforcement was about to arrive, however. The U.K. Advisory Committee on Drug Dependence announced in its 1968 Wootton Report that "[t]here is no evidence that [cannabis use] is causing violent crime or aggression, anti-social behaviour, or is producing in otherwise normal people conditions of dependence or psychosis," and "it is also clear that, in terms of physical harmfulness, cannabis is very much less dangerous than the opiates, amphetamines, and barbiturates, and also less dangerous than alcohol."[234] These findings were echoed in short order by the LeDain Commission in Canada,[235] the Baan and Hulsman Commissions in the Netherlands,[236] and the Baume Committee in Australia,[237] as well as a major study of Jamaican ganja users sponsored by the U.S. National Institute of Mental Health.[238] In the United States, the Kennedy administration acknowledged in 1962 that "the hazards of marihuana per se have been exaggerated."[239] Five years later, President Lyndon B. Johnson's crime commission advised that while marijuana "is equated in law with the opiates . . . the two have almost nothing in common."[240] Another five years later, President Nixon's National Commission on Marihuana and Drug Abuse, known as the Shafer Commission, concluded that intermittent use of marijuana "carries minimal risk to the public health" and that "neither the marihuana user nor the drug itself can be said to constitute a danger to public safety."[241]

These studies appeared just as the country was exiting the period from the 1930s through the 1960s when, as Lewis Grossman has recently shown, "Americans' confidence in government health regulators, the medical establishment, and pharmaceutical companies was at its peak."[242] Although the studies varied in many particulars and couldn't rule out the possibility of long-term risks or distinctive dangers for adolescents, they agreed that marijuana does not produce physical dependency, does not lead to lethal overdose, and poses little threat to most adults. From a public health perspective, as one influential scholar quipped in 1970 about the overall body of evidence, "It would seem clear . . . that we should treat marijuana considerably more respectfully than we do sugar candy."[243] Former U.S. Supreme Court Justice Tom Clark published an article two years later urging repeal of the marijuana laws because, "if we are to be honest with ourselves," the laws "have no basis in fact for their further existence. The findings are all to the contrary."²⁴⁴ These studies, moreover, debunked the rationales for marijuana prohibition that the government had touted for decades. In the 1930s, the Federal Bureau of Narcotics (FBN) and state officials described marijuana as a "killer weed" that induces violent conduct directly.²⁴⁵ In the 1950s, the FBN described marijuana as a "stepping stone" to heroin and other hard drugs that induces criminal conduct indirectly, "a rationale that the Bureau had expressly rejected in 1937."²⁴⁶ In the late 1960s and early 1970s, the Nixon administration described marijuana as the source of stupefying lethargy and passivity, an "amotivational syndrome" that threatened capitalist production and inverted the image of frenzied bloodlust conjured a generation before.²⁴⁷

Each of these theories had lost credibility by the mid-1970s. By then, most proponents of prohibition limited themselves to claims about temporary psychomotor deficits, the possibility of psychological dependency, or special risks associated with heavy consumption over time. The feared short-term effects, however, largely boiled down to the truism that "[a]ny psychoactive drug is potentially harmful to the individual,"²⁴⁸ depending on context, while the feared long-term effects could neither be proved nor disproved. And the clear pattern of shifting rationales for criminalization, empirically unfounded propaganda, and, as one judge put it in 1974, "official disdain of objective marijuana research"²⁴⁹ had eroded public trust in the prohibitionist narrative.

Compared to the hierarchy of drug dangerousness implied by the leading research studies and internalized by the generation that came of age in the 1960s and 1970s, the drug classifications written into federal and state law were hard to fathom. Nearly every state adopted drug laws in the mid-twentieth century that, in line with the 1932 Uniform Narcotic Drug Act, classified marijuana as a narcotic and criminalized simple possession.[250] The federal government had a chance to rethink this approach in 1970, when it developed a comprehensive regime for scheduling drugs in the CSA. As a political compromise, Congress placed marijuana in the CSA's most restrictive schedule—reserved for substances with "a high potential for abuse," "no currently accepted medical use," and "a lack of accepted safety for use . . . under medical supervision"[251]—on what was understood to be a provisional basis, until the Shafer Commission had a chance to complete its work. But when the Shafer Commission recommended decriminalization two years later, President Nixon dismissed its report and Congress took no further action. Marijuana remained stuck in Schedule I along with heroin, LSD, mescaline, magic mushrooms, and various other hallucinogens, amphetamines, and opiates.

Disappointed reformers saw this scheme as a reflection of, and roadmap to, the ideological biases and special interests that dominated U.S. drug policy. The Consumers Union, for instance, assailed the official classifications in 1972 as "illogical and capricious," "shocking" in their equation of marijuana with heroin, and susceptible to the suspicion that "corrupt legislators" had created them "to protect the tobacco and alcohol industries."[252] In fact, the CSA was a boon not only to those industries but even more so to domestic pharmaceutical manufacturers—amounting, in the view of historian Kathleen Frydl, to "one of the most remarkable feats of trade protectionism in modern U.S. history,"[253] as the act placed no limits on their production of licit painkillers while banning foreign imports of competing chemicals. Legacies of racism also shaped a number of the CSA's categories, as the next chapter will explain.

Whatever unholy mix of forces lay behind it, the CSA's classification matrix struck critics at the time as a kind of Bizarro World of drug regulation: not merely outdated or overbroad but, in important respects, the *opposite* of what rational risk assessment called for. And so it still seems to many. When a team of U.K. drug experts rated twenty psychoactive drugs in 2010 based on their aggregate harm to users and to others, the highest-scoring drug by far was alcohol (in part because it is so widely used). Heroin came in a distant second. Cannabis was determined to be less than a third as harmful as alcohol, and magic mushrooms the least harmful drug of all.[254] Although the construction of any such index is bound to be vexed, the basic conclusion that marijuana and mushrooms are safer for most users and third parties than alcohol, cigarettes, and heroin is difficult to dispute.

The drug classifications embedded in the CSA and its state analogues are so bizarre, a growing chorus of commentators began to argue in the late 1960s and 1970s, as to violate the Constitution. Specifically, these commentators argued that misclassification on such a scale violates the Fourteenth Amendment's Equal Protection Clause by laying "an unequal hand on those who have committed intrinsically the same quality of offense."[255] Marijuana was once again the focus of critique. Compared to the cluster of substantive due process claims reviewed in chapter 1, these equal protection claims were simple and unvarying. The U.S. Supreme Court unanimously instructed in 1964 that judges reviewing equal protection challenges "must reach and determine the question whether the classifications drawn in a statute are reasonable in light of its purpose."[256] And what could be more unreasonable than lumping a mild euphoriant with heavy narcotics in a health-oriented statute, while giving alcohol and nicotine a free pass?

RECLASSIFYING CANNABIS (AND COCAINE AND ECSTASY)
IN COURT

In a series of cases from the late 1960s and 1970s, a dozen-odd courts accepted this argument and either held or implied that states' classification of marijuana as a narcotic, or together with narcotics, violates the Equal Protection Clause. These courts employed the weakest form of Fourteenth Amendment scrutiny, known as rational basis review, because no fundamental rights or specially protected groups were deemed to be at issue. And they found that the laws couldn't meet even this low bar. Drawing on the latest medical research, these rulings detailed the relative harmlessness of marijuana, acknowledged the widespread disillusionment and disobedience caused by its legal status, and were emphatic in concluding that its categorization as one of the most dangerous drugs flouted basic norms of rationality.

The first such rulings came out of Colorado. In the mid-1960s, a Colorado trial judge suggested that the classification of marijuana as a narcotic violated equal protection, before opting to invalidate the state Narcotic Drugs Act on an alternative ground (that it failed to specify all the drugs to which it could apply). Several years later, another Colorado trial judge held that this same classification was unconstitutionally arbitrary based on the uncontradicted testimony of the defendant's expert witness. The state supreme court reversed both of these rulings without addressing their empirical premises.[257] The second supreme court opinion ended with the anti-Lochnerian disclaimer, "Although we, as individual judges, may disagree with the legislative classifications and the penalties prescribed for the several violations, we, as courts, cannot . . . invalidate the law in order to bend the legislature to our views."[258]

The Washington Supreme Court took the next step in 1970, finding that marijuana fell outside the state Narcotic Drug Act in light of the medical "consensus" that "cannabis is not a narcotic" and the equal protection problems that would be raised by a criminal classification "contrary to all the evidence."[259] The following year, the Illinois Supreme Court became the first to strike down a statute on this basis in *People v. McCabe*. After reviewing the "voluminous materials" presented by the parties on the effects of marijuana compared with those of other drugs, the *McCabe* majority concluded that its classification under the state Narcotic Drug Act lacked "any rational basis."[260]

Judicial pushback accelerated after *McCabe*. Over the course of 1972, three of the six Michigan justices participating in *People v. Sinclair* endorsed *McCabe*'s equal protection rationale;[261] Justice Kobayashi defended this view at length in his *Kantner* opinion and added that "a more reasonable and rational approach in this area would be to regulate marijuana in a manner similar to that of alcohol or tobacco";[262] the New Jersey Superior Court ruled that marijuana does not count as a narcotic under the state Motor Vehicle Act;[263] the Oklahoma Court of Criminal Appeals ruled that a trial judge committed "clear" legal error in instructing the jury that marijuana was a narcotic;[264] and the federal district court for the Eastern District of Virginia ruled that the classification of marijuana as a narcotic under Virginia law is "violative of the equal protection clause" given, among other things, "the vast weight of medical authority" and "common knowledge" that marijuana is not physically addictive.[265] In the nation's capital, a trial judge launched an indirect attack on the rationality of the cannabis laws by construing the District of Columbia's prohibition to cover only one strain, and dismissing all charges in which possession or distribution of that particular strain hadn't been proved—as it never was.[266] "By the end of 1972," reformers enthused, "there appeared to be growing judicial recognition . . . that marijuana is not a narcotic and, in fact, is a relatively harmless substance."[267]

In hindsight, however, we can see that 1972 was not the start of a wave so much as its crest, for reasons I will turn to shortly. Some jurists continued to build on *McCabe*. A Massachusetts trial judge ruled in 1976 that the state's "erroneous classification" of cocaine as a narcotic violates equal protection. All the "myths" that lay behind this classification, the judge wrote, "are now destroyed by reliable scientific data," which show alcohol and nicotine to be more dangerous.[268] Or as one of the defense attorneys put the point more colorfully in a press interview, the legislators who classified cocaine didn't "know their ass from second base when they pass[ed] these laws."[269] An Illinois appellate court reached the same conclusion in 1981 and was quickly overruled.[270] As far as I can tell, the Massachusetts case remains the only one in which a cocaine charge was thrown out on such grounds. Harvard law professor Alan Dershowitz hailed the opinion at the time as "a very important and heroic first step toward eliminating victimless crimes."[271]

In the more familiar context of cannabis, the high court of the Trust Territory of the Pacific Islands, which the United States administered at the time, "agree[d]" with *McCabe* in 1974 in striking down a Micronesian law that penalized marijuana offenses more severely than opium and heroin offenses.[272] A Florida trial judge urged the state supreme court in 1976 to reconsider its precedents on pot, as "the evidence clearly indicates that marijuana does not represent any serious threat to the well-being of American society" and that its criminalization "does greater harm to the youth of our nation than marijuana could ever do."[273] Two years later, the same judge went ahead and held that the state's marijuana ban is "without a rational basis," only to be summarily reversed.[274] Also in 1976, a Connecticut trial judge issued the most comprehensive ruling to date on the irrationality of classifying marijuana with harder drugs and was likewise reversed by the state supreme court. After documenting the many ways in which the effects of marijuana are different from and milder than the effects of drugs such as amphetamines and barbiturates, the judge warned that "the dangers of an irrational classification undermine a fundamental respect for the law" while imposing "staggering" costs on individuals and society.[275] In addition, the D.C. Superior Court became the first to accept a medical necessity defense against a marijuana possession charge, in a case involving a glaucoma sufferer whose ophthalmologist testified that he would go blind without regular use of the drug. Whereas the defendant had established a compelling need for the substance, the judge reasoned, "research has failed to establish any substantial physical or mental impairment caused by marijuana."[276]

The last gasp of this line of rulings came from an unexpected source. In 1988, the chief administrative law judge of the Drug Enforcement Administration (DEA), Francis Young, issued an opinion recommending that marijuana be moved from Schedule I of the CSA to Schedule II, reserved for drugs that have a high potential for abuse but also a currently accepted medical use. Four years earlier, Young had recommended that MDMA (also known as Ecstasy or Molly) be placed in Schedule III on account of its safety in psychiatric practice and modest abuse potential. Young's marijuana opinion came in response to a rescheduling petition that NORML had filed way back in 1972, on which the DEA and its predecessor, the Bureau of Narcotics and Dangerous Drugs, had dragged their feet for as long as the courts allowed. It "is clear beyond any question," Young observed, "that many people find marijuana to have, in the words of the [CSA], an 'accepted medical use'" for treating diseases such as cancer. Schedule I is therefore inapposite unless one refuses to credit these patients' lived experiences as a valid source of evidence. "In strict medical terms," Young further observed, "marijuana is far safer than many foods we commonly consume" and indeed "is one of the safest therapeutically active substances known to man."[277]

The administrator of the DEA overruled this opinion, just as he had overruled Young's previous opinion on MDMA.[278] In so doing, he chided Young for relying on the "pro-marijuana" testimony of patients and doctors who had used or prescribed the drug, rather than the testimony of government experts. And he described Young's analysis as not merely mistaken but "irresponsible" and "appalling"—so much so that Young had "failed to act as an impartial judge in this matter."[279] The administrator seemed oblivious to the irony of such an allegation coming from the head of an agency that simultaneously schedules drugs and enforces criminal drug laws, creating a structural bias in favor of criminalization, and that has never once granted a rescheduling petition not submitted by a pharmaceutical company.[280]

REINING IN RATIONAL BASIS REVIEW

By the time Judge Young questioned the validity of marijuana's scheduling, the regular (nonadministrative) judiciary had already abandoned this project. The New Deal settlement stood not only for the expansion of federal regulatory authority, as explained earlier, but also for the diminution of equal protection review. Over the middle part of the twentieth century, the Supreme Court developed an approach to equal protection analysis that reserved heightened scrutiny for a small set of fundamental rights and historically freighted forms of discrimination, above all racial discrimination. Every other claim of unequal treatment was to be tested for mere "rationality." In this way, it was hoped, the most pernicious forms of government discrimination would be checked by courts while policymakers would otherwise be free to fashion a modern administrative state. If the justices in *Raich* who rejected a federalism challenge to the CSA saw themselves as defending the broad scope of federal power won in the 1930s, the judges who rejected equal protection challenges to marijuana's classification saw themselves as defending the other half of the New Deal settlement: judicial deference to legislative and executive judgments about which social problems to tackle in which ways, without regard for the resulting distribution of policy burdens and benefits.

Many of the key opinions in this line of cases were strikingly candid about the *irrationality* of marijuana's classification, even as they maintained that role fidelity compelled them to uphold it. The Colorado Supreme Court, for instance, acknowledged in 1974 in evaluating a challenge to marijuana's classification as a narcotic that, "[w]ithout an authoritative exception, those medical authorities who have examined marijuana have concluded that it has no narcotic properties"; that the "legal and sociological commentators are in agreement as well"; and that the continued classification of marijuana as a narcotic undermines the "integrity" of the law, invites "overzealous police practices," and imposes a "heavy burden" on courts and prison officials. Notwithstanding these seemingly devastating critiques, the majority concluded that it was "require[d]" to "defer to the legislative body as the proper forum for the resolution of this controversy."[281] The Hawaii Supreme Court acknowledged in 1975 that the argument that alcohol is more dangerous than marijuana has "considerable persuasive power," before admonishing that the notion that courts may "hold laws unconstitutional when they believe the legislature has acted unwisely . . . has long since been discarded."[282] The Michigan Court of Appeals acknowledged in 1978 that "[m]any of the former 'truths' about marijuana have been shown to be myths," before capitulating and "urg[ing] the Legislature to reevaluate the entire marijuana 'problem.' "[283] The U.S. Court of Appeals for the Second Circuit's influential opinion in *United States v. Kiffer* acknowledged "[i]t is apparently true that there is little or no basis for concluding that marihuana is as dangerous a substance as some of the other drugs included in Schedule I," before upholding marijuana's placement within that schedule.[284] A number of forceful dissenting opinions echoed these same themes, differing only in the judges' ultimate vote to strike down rather than sustain the classification.[285]

The lawyers bringing these equal protection challenges relied heavily on two U.S. Supreme Court cases. In *Skinner v. Oklahoma*, the Court in 1942 invalidated a state law that provided for the forced sterilization of individuals with two or more convictions for grand larceny while sparing those with two or more convictions for embezzlement—"a clear, pointed, unmistakable discrimination" without logical foundation.[286] In *McLaughlin v. Florida*, the Court in 1964 invalidated a state law that prohibited unmarried interracial couples, but not other couples, from cohabitating—a distinction that was inconsistent with the statute's ostensible purpose of preventing adultery and fornication.[287] Even if particular features of these laws had led the Court to apply a heightened standard of review, both opinions contained language that could be read to require courts to scrutinize the reasonableness of *all* substantive criminal classifications.[288] Most judges in the 1970s, however, declined to extend *Skinner* or *McLaughlin* beyond the context of the eugenics movement and the Jim Crow South. *Skinner* became a Fourteenth Amendment oddity, converted over time from an equal protection ruling into a substantive due process precedent.[289] *McLaughlin* became an anti-apartheid case, with little bearing on laws that make no explicit reference to race.

Rather than build on *Skinner* or *McLaughlin*, the courts that rejected equal protection challenges to marijuana's classification pointed to ongoing controversy and uncertainty around the drug— and insisted that the existence of such controversy and uncertainty was itself sufficient to satisfy rational basis review. *Kiffer* is representative in this regard. The *Kiffer* court, once again, all but announced that marijuana's placement in Schedule I of the CSA makes no sense. Yet even if the argument that marijuana is relatively safe "may be persuasive," the court observed, "it is not undisputed." For all the studies suggesting that marijuana is significantly less dangerous than other Schedule I substances such as heroin and than unscheduled substances such as nicotine, "there is a body of scientific opinion that marihuana is subject to serious abuse in some cases, and relatively little is known about its long-term effects." The government did nothing irrational, accordingly, in electing to take a "cautious approach" by placing marijuana in the most restrictive schedule.[290] As another widely cited opinion put it, "The continuing questions about marijuana and its effects make the classification rational."[291] Similar logic was used to reject challenges to the rationality of classifying cocaine as a narcotic, even though cocaine is a stimulant and this classification therefore rests on "the slender threads of minimum rationality."[292]

The courts further noted that even if drugs like heroin and nicotine really are much more destructive than marijuana, equal protection doctrine doesn't require a legislature to " 'cover the waterfront.' It may attack different aspects of a problem in different ways, or go about the matter piecemeal."[293] Under these principles, the Connecticut Supreme Court explained, it's irrelevant that marijuana may be a "relatively slight . . . health hazard." The legislature can still "rationally conclude that traffic in such a drug should be prohibited by a seven-year penalty."[294]

To appreciate just how limited—and arational—was the model of review that allowed judges to concede that marijuana seems harmless while accepting its categorization as one of the most dangerous of drugs, consider this passage from a more recent opinion upholding marijuana's inclusion in Schedule I of the CSA:

> Under the deferential standard of rational basis review, then, as long as there is some conceivable reason for the challenged classification of marijuana, the CSA should be upheld. Such a classification comes before the court bearing a strong presumption of validity, and the challenger must negative every conceivable basis which might support it. The asserted rationale may

rest on rational speculation unsupported by evidence or empirical data. The law may be overinclusive, underinclusive, illogical, and unscientific and yet pass constitutional muster. In addition, under rational basis review, the government has no obligation to produce evidence to sustain the rationality of a statutory classification.[295]

It is hard to imagine how a challenger could ever satisfy this standard. There would need to be near-perfect agreement among all actors credible to courts as to a drug's blatant misclassification. Given the complexity of drug science and drug politics, as well as the benefits that the status quo affords to powerful interests ranging from law enforcement agencies to pharmaceutical companies to social conservatives, the prospect of such consensus is a pipe dream.

As acutely as any set of cases in the late twentieth century, the constitutional challenges to marijuana's scheduling tested whether rational basis review would do any work in the face of apparent arbitrariness. And the answer that won out in the 1970s was: no. Even as it became easier in this period to challenge federal agency rulemakings as arbitrary under the Administrative Procedure Act,[296] it became harder to challenge criminal prosecutions as arbitrary under the Constitution. If the courts' treatment of substantive due process challenges to drug prohibition helped narrow the path to strict scrutiny, the courts' treatment of equal protection challenges to drug classification helped ensure that rational basis review would remain a rubber stamp.

REASONS STATED AND UNSTATED

In fact, there was a coherent policy rationale behind the criminalization of cannabis. The main reason why marijuana remained in restrictive drug schedules throughout the 1960s and 1970s, the historical record suggests, had much more to do with fears of social dislocation and decay than with fears of medical harm. This point was widely appreciated at the time. The leading legal tomes on marijuana prohibition, familiar to all judges who issued rulings on the topic, bore it out in painstaking detail. Kaplan's book *Marijuana: The New Prohibition* explained how marijuana had "become the symbol of a host of major conflicts in our society" along cultural, ideological, and generational lines, which thwarted "any attempt at a rational solution to the problem."[297] Bonnie and Whitebread's article "The Forbidden Fruit and the Tree of Knowledge" documented how the marijuana laws were "irrational," in that they failed to advance their putative ends, but nonetheless responded to a set of widely held "moral" intuitions.[298] The Shafer Commission described how many Americans felt "threatened" by marijuana because of its association with countercultural challenges to "the dominant social order"—reflected in "the adoption of new life styles," "campus unrest," "communal living, protest politics, and even political radicalism"—rather than because of any well-founded concerns about its effects on health or safety.[299]

The problem for the government attorneys who defended marijuana's classification in court was that this threat-based account of its legal status, while persuasive as a descriptive diagnosis, was uncomfortably repressive in character, impervious to counterevidence, tinged with racism and religious dogmatism, and inconsistent with the statutory language, which demanded that drug scheduling be based on medical criteria, not moral sentiment. These features only became more problematic after the Supreme Court clarified in 1973 that "a bare [legislative] desire to harm a politically unpopular group," such as "hippies," "cannot constitute a legitimate governmental interest."[300] The government attorneys therefore shunned this line of argument, limiting their equal protection defense to a public health framework in which their claims looked transparently weak. The goal wasn't so much to persuade judges that marijuana causes significant damage to bodies or brains as to sow doubt about the emerging consensus to the contrary and, in so doing, to divert attention from the real drivers of prohibition.

On the other side of the litigation, the constitutional challengers also pulled their punches. Almost all of their arguments about marijuana's misclassification focused on its relative lack of dangerousness and, after the 1980s, on its potential utility for pain relief and other medical applications. The dominant trope in their brief for irrationality was *harm*: the (modest) amount of physical and psychological harm caused by marijuana; the (substantial) amount of physical and psychological harm caused by other drugs in the same statutory schedule; the economic and social harm caused by enforcement of the marijuana laws; the value of marijuana for relieving harm caused by medical ailments. Entirely ignored were the "recreational" reasons why most people consume cannabis and other psychoactive substances, reasons that have less to do with the avoidance of discomfort than with the pursuit of pleasure, adventure, alterity, insight, or the like.

In addition to downplaying these affirmative dimensions of marijuana use, the challengers also downplayed the difficulties of assessing drug dangers so as to avoid conceding any health risks that might be seen to satisfy rational basis review. The result was a constitutional stance that legitimated the always unstable medical/recreational divide, overstated the degree of scientific certitude, and undersold the case for reform. Banning a substance will invariably appear more reasonable if the benefits that most users believe they derive from it are simply put to the side.

In the absence of any honest account of the nonmedical motivations for illicit drug taking, the legal debate became increasingly stilted and surreal. One of the DEA's most recent denials of a petition to reschedule marijuana incorporates an analysis by the Department of Health and Human Services (HHS) of the drug's psychoactive effects. The analysis begins, disarmingly, by explaining that marijuana use is "pleasurable to many humans" and that among the most "common subjective responses" are "relaxation, increased sociability, and talkativeness"; "increased merriment and appetite, and even exhilaration at high doses"; "heightened imagination, which can lead to a subjective sense of increased creativity"; and "enhanced sensory perception, which can generate an increased appreciation of music, art, and touch." HHS then proceeds to characterize all these effects not as evidence of marijuana's positive attributes, to be weighed against its downside risks, but rather of its "abuse potential"—and hence its suitability for Schedule I and maximal punishment under the CSA.[301]

In this discourse, the pursuit of pleasure hasn't just been marginalized; it has been pathologized. Illicit drug users must be saved from experiences that may seem enjoyable and rewarding but that, through this very mechanism, are sources of seduction and corruption. And this holds even for drugs that produce no physical dependency. Euphoria is "the devil's work."[302] It is only through the *trivialization* of marijuana's hedonic benefits under the "recreational" rubric, together with the *transvaluation* of many of those benefits into costs, that a complete criminal ban could hope to come across as rational. For all their zeal and creativity, the drug laws' constitutional challengers never questioned this pillar of prohibitionist ideology. Just as the attorneys defending these laws obscured the main reasons why politicians enact them, the attorneys attacking these laws obscured the main reasons why people defy them.

CHAPTER 3

· · ·

Racial Equality

FOR MANY WHO invoke the label, the war on drugs is synonymous with racial injustice. Commentators have described this package of policies as "a war against minorities,"[303] "a system of apartheid justice,"[304] and "the new Jim Crow."[305] Historically, racial prejudice has influenced the government's decisions to criminalize certain psychoactive substances while sparing others. And to this day, the implementation of prohibitory drug laws generates profound racial disparities in rates of arrest and imprisonment, notwithstanding broadly similar rates of illicit drug behavior across racial groups. It is now conventional wisdom among academics that the war on drugs has been "a racial system of social control of urban minority populations,"[306] as well as a driver of mass incarceration at home and imperialist power projection abroad.

One might assume that the Fourteenth Amendment's Equal Protection Clause would have something to say about this. Ratified after the Civil War, the clause forbids government officials from

The Constitution of the War on Drugs. David Pozen, Oxford University Press.
© Oxford University Press 2024. DOI: 10.1093/oso/9780197685457.003.0004

denying to any person "the equal protection of the laws." Although the precise meaning and scope of this guarantee remain the subject of intense debate, judges agree that it is centrally concerned with the problem of invidious discrimination against African Americans and that laws that discriminate on the basis of race should be subject to the most rigorous scrutiny. Allegations of racist state action tend to be analyzed, in constitutional law, through an equal protection lens.

The preceding chapters explained how constitutional challenges to prohibitory drug laws based on principles of individual liberty and government rationality made significant inroads in the late 1960s and 1970s, including under the Equal Protection Clause, before losing out. The story of race-based challenges is a little different. The main litigation campaign emerged not in the late 1960s and 1970s but in the late 1980s and 1990s, and the focus was not marijuana but cocaine—in particular, the differential treatment of its crack versus powder forms. Nevertheless, there are important parallels across these areas. With the race-based challenges as with the others, litigants won a few high-profile victories in the state courts and lower federal courts, victories that pointed the way toward a more rights-protective jurisprudence. The campaign then collapsed in a manner that both reflected and reinforced an increasingly inhospitable doctrinal framework, to the point that it's almost impossible to see how a claim of racial discrimination in drug policy could succeed in court today. Unless the plaintiff is white.

BIAS IN, BIAS OUT: DISCRIMINATORY ORIGINS, DISPARATE OUTCOMES

Racism's first opportunity to shape drug prohibition arises at the threshold, in the choice of which drugs—among the countless chemicals that could prove dangerous to some users at some doses in some settings—will be criminalized and which will be allocated to legal markets. As a large body of scholarship details, racism has contributed to these choices at pivotal junctures throughout U.S. history.

Opium is the original case in point. Hostility toward Chinese immigrant labor was a driving force behind the first wave of prohibitory laws in the American West during the late 1800s and early 1900s. In press reports and legislative hearings, opium dens were assailed as sites of racial intermixing, moral contamination, and sexual vice.[307] "Johnny Comprador [a generic term for Chinese immigrants] has impoverished our country, degraded our free labor and hoodlumized our children," the San Francisco *Daily Evening Post* inveighed in 1879. "He is now destroying our young men with opium."[308] A federal judge acknowledged in 1886, in the course of denying habeas corpus to a Chinese immigrant who had been convicted of selling opium under a recently enacted Oregon law, "[I]t may be that this legislation proceeds more from a desire to vex and annoy the 'Heathen Chinee' . . . than to protect the people from the evil habit."[309]

Cocaine came next. "Just as the Chinese had been linked with opium use and singled out for tailor-made legislation and subsequent law enforcement," Coramae Richey Mann has written, "the second campaign against narcotics was directed at blacks and cocaine."[310] Advocates of cocaine prohibition in the early 1900s identified the drug with Black males and with violence against whites, including the rape of white women. The lead architect of the Harrison Anti-Narcotics Act of 1914, for instance, informed Congress, "[I]t has been authoritatively stated that cocaine is often the direct incentive to the crime of rape by the Negroes of the South and other sections of the country."[311] Drug historian David Musto has collected many more examples of similar statements in the media and in medical journals that painted "a lurid and fearful picture of 'the Negro cocaine fiends' who terrorized the South."[312]

Marijuana prohibition followed a similar script, with Mexican Americans as well as African Americans the target of racialized appeals throughout the 1910s, 1920s, and 1930s.[313] Following an influx of Mexican immigrants into the Southwest, prohibitionists began to refer to cannabis as "marihuana" or "marijuana"—and later as "loco weed" or "demon weed"—to highlight the ethnic link.[314] They also began to assert that even casual use of the drug induces insanity and aggression. Harry Anslinger, the founding commissioner of the Federal Bureau of Narcotics and a central figure in the development of the U.S. drug control bureaucracy, helped to popularize both of these rhetorical moves. Anslinger collected and disseminated stories of violent crimes and lewd acts allegedly fueled by marijuana, often with a racial charge. And he persisted in vilifying the drug with reckless disregard for the truth throughout his thirty-two years as head of the Bureau. Marijuana reformers looking to discredit the prohibitionist project could hardly have dreamed up a better historical villain. (Perhaps in the hope of making a good story even better, Anslinger's critics do seem to have dreamed up certain details of his villainy.)[315]

The early twentieth-century campaigns to outlaw a number of substances at the heart of the war on drugs thus traded on racial stereotypes and fears. To varying degrees, so did the contemporaneous movement to outlaw alcohol, the midcentury movement to increase heroin penalties, and the drug policy programs of the Nixon and Reagan administrations.[316] Conversely, the decriminalization campaigns that gained traction in the latter part of the twentieth century were aided by the "whitening" of certain drugs' popular image. Cannabis and cocaine reformers benefited from this dynamic in the 1970s. Medical marijuana reformers benefited from it even more in the 1990s. The president of the Washington chapter of the NAACP, Harry Toussaint Alexander, pointed out to Congress in 1977 that not until marijuana had "spread its tentacles into the majority section of society in their schools, neighborhoods, and universities did there become a hue and cry for decriminalization. This did not come, however, until countless Black, poor, and oppressed people had been sentenced to countless numbers of years in prison."[317]

Whatever led to their enactment, the enforcement of punitive drug laws has disproportionately swept Black and Brown individuals into the criminal system. Illicit drugs are so pervasive in the United States, changing hands hundreds of millions of times each year, that enforcement of these laws is bound to be partial and selective. Since the 1950s, commentators have decried the "racial logic" behind the government's use of this discretion to harass communists and disrupt Black political mobilization, both domestically and overseas.[318] Since the 1970s, surveys and field studies have indicated that Black and white Americans consume and sell illicit drugs at comparable rates. Yet drug-related arrest rates have been three to six times higher for Blacks than for whites over this period.[319] Black drug arrestees are also far more likely than their white counterparts to be prosecuted and incarcerated.[320] This racial disparity then compounds itself in the harms visited on prisoners' families and future prospects.[321] A number of overlapping explanations for these Black/white divides have been proposed, from the greater police presence and visibility of drug behaviors in poor urban neighborhoods and the greater penetrability of downscale drug markets to various forms of individual and institutional bias.[322] Even those who question whether drug enforcement has been racist in the narrow sense of reflecting active hostility or indifference to certain groups on account of their race acknowledge that, at a minimum, "it *looks* racist."[323]

Drug policymaking and drug enforcement are complex phenomena; to recognize that racial biases and disparities suffuse them is not to suggest that the war on drugs can be reduced to race. In addition to concerns related to race and to public health and safety, researchers have documented the persistent influence of forces such as class and religion, as well as more specific material and ideological formations such as the pharmaceutical industry, the medical establishment, Cold War geostrategy, and state and federal law enforcement lobbies.[324] Kathleen Frydl, notably, has argued that a "perspective informed by historical materialism, giving primary attention to economic interests, has more to offer in clarifying causality" than does a focus on race per se.[325] Further complicating any simple assessment of racism's role in the war on drugs, scholarship by James Forman Jr. and Michael Javen Fortner has shown how Black politicians and civic leaders provided crucial support for draconian drug reforms throughout the 1970s and 1980s, reforms that they hoped would restore law and order to their communities.[326] Scholars also continue to explore the precise mechanisms by which racism has shaped drug policy development. George Fisher, for instance, has recently argued that the early drug bans were enacted by lawmakers not so much to control racial minorities as for the flip side of that white supremacist project, "to protect the morals of their own racial kin."[327] As in other fields, the character of racism in drug prohibition has evolved over time as well, with subtler and less self-conscious forms of discrimination gradually displacing the most explicit admissions of bias over the course of the twentieth century.

All of this historical complexity and academic argument shouldn't obscure a core set of points. The war on drugs may have many inputs and outputs not determined by race. But there is no dispute that racial images have been "powerful foci of debate"[328] during key periods of policymaking or that the "nation's racial hierarchy helps to determine which drugs will be considered dangerous and which will be accepted as a normal part of society, regardless of their cost in death and disability."[329] Nor is there any dispute that the drug war has had the effect of propping up that hierarchy and perpetuating racial subordination.

The constitutional question all but asks itself: is this consistent with the guarantee of equal protection of the laws?

PROVING RACIAL DISCRIMINATION

The Equal Protection Clause did little to advance racial equality in the first half of the twentieth century. Employing doctrines such as "separate but equal," the Supreme Court allowed racial segregation to reign throughout much of the country in law and in fact. But then came an epoch-making shift. During the chief justiceship of Earl Warren, from 1953 to 1969, the Equal Protection Clause became the centerpiece of a new liberal jurisprudence and a key resource for dismantling Jim Crow. The canonical case from this period is *Brown v. Board of Education*, in which the Court struck down racial segregation in public schools.[330] Other cases relied on equal protection to invalidate poll taxes,[331] interracial marriage bans,[332] and racially exclusionary policies in a wide range of public institutions.[333] "The clear and central purpose of the Fourteenth Amendment," the Court reaffirmed throughout these rulings, "was to eliminate all official state sources of invidious racial discrimination."[334]

Following *Brown*, federal courts began to scrutinize not only laws that classified people on the basis of their skin color or ancestry but also laws that made no mention of race. To root out invidious discrimination, judges in the late 1960s and early 1970s became increasingly attentive to the effects of facially neutral policies across racial groups. Some viewed disparate racial impacts as presumptive evidence of impermissible discriminatory motive. Others suggested that such impacts might violate equal protection in themselves.[335] The Supreme Court, in 1971, took a similarly expansive approach to interpreting the federal statute barring race-based discrimination in employment, holding that "practices, procedures, or tests neutral on their face, even neutral in terms of intent, cannot be maintained if they operate to 'freeze' the status quo of prior discriminatory employment practices."[336]

In the 1976 case *Washington v. Davis*, however, the Court pulled back from this approach. Going forward, the Court ruled, plaintiffs alleging an Equal Protection Clause violation in the absence of an explicit racial classification would have to do more than prove a disparate racial impact, even a very large one. They would have to prove that the government acted with discriminatory intent.[337] Not only that, the Court clarified three years later in *Personnel Administrator v. Feeney*, but they would have to demonstrate that the government acted with a specific sort of intent—that the relevant officials "selected or reaffirmed a particular course of action at least in part 'because of,' not merely 'in spite of,' its adverse effects upon an identifiable group."[338] In other words, it wouldn't be sufficient to show that the decisionmakers knew a certain policy would have harmful consequences for a certain minority and adopted or maintained the policy anyway. After *Feeney*, one had to show that the decisionmakers actively *sought* those harmful consequences, a form of discriminatory intent "tantamount to malice."[339]

Why did the Court adopt the discriminatory-intent requirement in *Davis* and then define it so narrowly in *Feeney*? The justices gave hardly any explanation. The main reason to prioritize intent over impact, *Davis* suggested, was that allowing disparate racial effects to trigger equal protection liability "would raise serious questions about, and perhaps invalidate, a whole range of . . . statutes that may be more burdensome to the poor and to the average black than to the more affluent white."[340] If there was a deeper legal or moral basis for focusing on intent—for instance, some notion that intentional discrimination is especially wrongful—the Court did not name it. What quickly became apparent was that the Court's own intent was to rein in judicial oversight of racial discrimination claims brought under the Equal Protection Clause. "Minorities and civil rights advocates have been virtually unanimous in condemning *Davis* and its progeny," Charles Lawrence observed in 1987, both because it proved almost impossible to satisfy their standard without a flagrant admission of bigotry and because an intent-centered inquiry misses the point insofar as "the injury of racial inequality exists irrespective of the decisionmakers' motives."[341]

Subsequent decisions only expanded *Davis*'s reach. Of particular note, the Court has refused to allow litigants to bring claims of unconstitutional racial bias in law enforcement under the Fourth Amendment, insisting that the Equal Protection Clause is the proper vehicle.[342] And a long line of cases has applied "ordinary equal protection standards"—which is to say, the standards set out in *Davis* and *Feeney*—to claims of bias in prosecution decisions, sentencing patterns, police behaviors, and virtually every other part of the criminal system.[343]

A CURIOUS ABSENCE

The late 1960s and early 1970s, then, turned out to be the most favorable period in U.S. history for bringing claims of unconstitutional racial discrimination. This was the exact same period in which litigants brought a "tidal wave" of constitutional challenges to prohibitory drug laws.[344] Criminal defendants and civil liberties organizations attacked these laws again and again under the First Amendment, the Eighth Amendment, the Due Process Clause, and the Equal Protection Clause itself (when alleging that drugs had been misclassified). But they hardly ever attacked them for being enacted or enforced in a racially discriminatory manner.

In 1979, the same year that the Court handed down *Feeney*, the *American Law Reports* compiled opinions in which a state or federal court had considered the constitutionality of criminal penalties for personal possession or use of marijuana.[345] The compilation included over one hundred cases. None featured a claim of racial discrimination. The leading academic analyses in the 1970s of the constitutional issues raised by drug prohibition—analyses that were exceptionally thorough and openly critical of the legal status quo—likewise made no mention of possible issues related to race.[346]

Isolated references to racial discrimination did appear in the case law, but they were the exceptions that proved the rule. In 1973, for instance, the federal district court in New Mexico declined to review allegations that state law enforcement officials had violated equal protection by "systematically and deliberately arresting and trying Spanish surnamed individuals for the offenses of possession and distribution of heroin."[347] In 1974, two defendants charged with cocaine distribution under the CSA alleged that the Harrison Act was "racially motivated" and that Congress, by "redefining cocaine as a narcotic in the 1970 Act . . . without questioning the basis for that definition," had "continued to perpetuate the 'racial myths' of bygone days."[348] The federal district court in New Jersey was unmoved:

> Defendants' third contention, that the 1970 Act as it relates to cocaine is racially discriminatory . . . is without basis. There is not the least showing, even assuming arguendo that the passage of the Harrison Act in 1914 was racially motivated, that the 1970 Act which supersedes the 1914 Act was based on any such invidious motives or prejudices. Further, it is not contended nor is there a showing that the 1970 Act is directed at or enforced mainly against racial minorities. Therefore, the contention must be rejected.[349]

In a challenge to the marijuana provisions of the CSA filed by NORML in 1973 and resolved in 1980, NORML's lawyers claimed, as a backup to their principal arguments about privacy and rationality, that these provisions were racially discriminatory. The final ruling against NORML by a three-judge panel of the federal district court in the District of Columbia was approximately thirteen thousand words long. In one footnote, the court addressed this claim and, citing *Davis*, dismissed it as "meritless" because "Congress passed the CSA to promote the public health and welfare, and there is no discriminatory intent."[350] This was the entirety of the court's analysis on race. In a 1976 ruling that had no precedential effect, a Massachusetts trial judge remarked in passing that cocaine's initial classification as a narcotic under state law was partly the result of "blatantly racist attacks on cocaine users," before deeming the classification unconstitutional on other grounds.[351]

And that's about it. Not a single precedential ruling from the 1960s or 1970s appears to have found a prohibitory drug law to be unconstitutionally racially discriminatory, either in general or as applied, or even to have taken this possibility seriously. Nor did the drug laws' many critics in the legal profession press this argument in any sustained fashion.

This absence seems especially puzzling given that most of the cases challenging the drug laws involved criminal defendants, who had little to lose from raising any and all nonfrivolous arguments against their prosecutions. The racist origins of these laws had already been documented—Bonnie and Whitebread's 1970 article on marijuana prohibition, for example, contained multiple lengthy sections on this topic[352]—and complaints about selective enforcement were already long-standing. Moreover, as chapter 2 described, dozens upon dozens of lawsuits alleged that the classifications of cannabis and cocaine were so inconsistent with the medical evidence as to fail even rational basis review. Well, why had the government classified cannabis and cocaine as the most dangerous of drugs if the science indicated otherwise? Allegations of racial discrimination could have helped answer that question and thereby shored up allegations of irrationality. And indeed, both of the state court opinions that found cocaine's classification as a narcotic to be irrational adverted to the racist origins of cocaine prohibition.[353]

It is impossible to know for sure why claims of racial discrimination remained so marginal throughout the 1960s and 1970s. Some plausible, non-mutually-exclusive explanations include that the main drugs at issue in the constitutional litigation, cannabis and cocaine, were increasingly coded as "white" during these years, while the drug war writ large was ambiguously raced on account of Vietnam, hippies, and the collegiate counterculture;[354] that the Black community was increasingly internally fractured over whether to support or oppose punitive drug policies;[355] that leading advocacy groups such as NORML and the ACLU believed that nonracial arguments about privacy, liberty, and so forth would be more persuasive to a predominantly white judiciary;[356] that systematic data collection on drug use and enforcement patterns had only just begun to emerge;[357] and that throughout this period state and federal controlled substance laws were being revised, and in many instances relaxed as to possession offenses, with public health arguments in the foreground and few if any lawmakers making overtly racist remarks. The dismissive response to claims of racial discrimination by the two federal district courts quoted above gives some indication of how obvious it seemed to many legal elites that laws like the CSA had shed whatever racist taint their predecessors might have had.[358]

The sidelining of racial discrimination claims may have made sense within this cultural context. But it certainly looks like a lost opportunity in hindsight. Never before or since has there been such an intensive campaign against the constitutionality of prohibitory drug laws. And never before or since have challenges to facially race-neutral laws that perpetuate racial subordination fared so well under the Equal Protection Clause.

THE CRACK/POWDER CRACKUP

Race-based challenges to the war on drugs took off only after the crack scare of the late 1980s elicited an extraordinary legislative response. Crack is a cheap, smokeable, fast-acting form of cocaine, made by cooking cocaine powder with baking soda and water. Beginning in the early 1980s, crack spread across the United States. Beginning in the summer of 1986, it became the subject of a media frenzy, unprecedented in its share of national news coverage.[359] The *Washington Post* alone ran 1,565 stories about crack and other illegal drugs from October 1988 to October 1989, according to the newspaper's ombudsperson, many of which "created the false and hurtful impression that the drug problem is essentially a 'black problem.'"[360] Powder cocaine continued to be associated with white professionals. Crack was associated with gang violence, maternal addiction ("crack babies"), and the Black urban underclass.

The racialized media panic quickly became a bipartisan policy panic. Congress ratcheted up drug penalties and enforcement budgets in the Anti-Drug Abuse Act of 1986 and then again in the Anti-Drug Abuse Act of 1988. The 1986 act drew a sharp distinction between crack and powder cocaine. For powder, possession with intent to distribute five hundred grams carried a five-year mandatory minimum prison sentence. For crack, the same sentence attached to just five grams.[361] The 1988 act extended this penalty to simple possession of five grams.[362] A dozen-odd states soon followed Congress's lead and enacted harsher penalties for crack offenses than for powder offenses.[363]

The racial implications of these developments were impossible to miss. The "Black" version of cocaine was now being punished one hundred times more severely by weight than the "white" version, whose relatively upscale users rarely got busted anyway. With the stakes so high and these implications so salient, race-based equal protection challenges finally came to the fore. Many Black defendants challenged the 100:1 ratio in the 1986 statute, while others challenged the U.S. Sentencing Commission's adoption of this ratio in its 1987 sentencing guidelines or Congress's and the Commission's subsequent refusals to change course as evidence of racially disparate consequences mounted.[364] The gravamen of the challenge, in all instances, was that such an extreme asymmetry in the government's treatment of two forms of the same drug, combined with such an extreme focus on Black users in legislative deliberations and enforcement patterns, amounts to invidious racial discrimination in violation of the Equal Protection Clause.

The federal appellate courts rejected these arguments "unanimously" and "unequivocally."[365] Under *Davis* and *Feeney*, defendants had to show that the 100:1 ratio was "selected or reaffirmed . . . at least in part 'because of,' not merely 'in spite of,' its adverse effects upon an identifiable group."[366] It wasn't hard to show that racially coded language permeated the media coverage and policy discourse on crack, or that the crack laws were being applied overwhelmingly against Black individuals. The Sentencing Commission's 1992 annual report, for instance, indicated that 91.5 percent of the past year's federal crack defendants were Black, even though a majority of crack users nationwide were white.[367] But it didn't necessarily follow that Congress chose the 100:1 ratio in order to harm the Black community, as *Feeney* required. A majority of the Congressional Black Caucus supported both the 1986 and 1988 Anti-Drug Abuse Acts, as did many Black civic and religious leaders. On the floor of the House, Black liberal Democratic representatives Alton Waldon and

Charles Rangel described the crack problem as "the worst oppression we have known since slavery" and urged their colleagues to "crack down on crack."[368]

The judicial opinions rejecting equal protection challenges to the 100:1 ratio followed a simple line of argument. The legislative history of the 1986 Anti-Drug Abuse Act disclosed that, as compared to powder cocaine, Congress believed crack cocaine to be relatively potent, addictive, cheap, accessible to children, and connected to violence. However empirically questionable or racially freighted some of those beliefs may have been, their very existence dispelled any whiff of discriminatory intent. "[B]ecause reasons exist, other than race, for enhanced penalties for [crack] offenses," the U.S. Court of Appeals for the Tenth Circuit wrote, defendants cannot "demonstrate that Congress or the Sentencing Commission had a discriminatory purpose in enacting [these laws] or in leaving them intact."[369] True, some judges acknowledged, "Congress must have known that . . . a disproportionate number of poor people in general, and blacks in particular, would be sentenced under the harsh 'crack' penalty structure."[370] But that's not enough under *Feeney*. "Even conscious awareness on the part of the legislature that the law will have a racially disparate impact does not invalidate an otherwise valid law," the U.S. Court of Appeals for the Third Circuit explained, "so long as that awareness played no causal role in the passage of the statute."[371] And no defendant could convince an appellate court that Congress created the 100:1 ratio "for the discriminatory"—indeed sadistic—"purpose of punishing blacks more than whites for similarly culpable conduct."[372] Likewise, no defendant could convince the courts that other drug laws with disparate racial impacts, such as sentencing enhancements for distributing a controlled substance near a public housing facility or a public school, violated equal protection.[373]

Even while upholding crack convictions, numerous judges expressed discomfort with the 100:1 ratio and called on Congress to reconsider it. One apologized to the defendants as he sentenced them to at least thirty years in prison under a law he had described as treating African Americans "unfairly."[374] Another wept in the courtroom at the "grave miscarriage of justice" he was carrying out.[375] Still another wrote in a 1994 opinion, "Federal judges appear to be uniformly appalled by the severe crack cocaine punishments, particularly as compared with the more moderate punishments mandated for transactions in ordinary, powdered cocaine." Yet given the impossibility of proving that legislators had adopted these punishments because of racial bias, this judge followed the sentencing guidelines, sentenced a Black man convicted of selling crack to 170 months in prison, and expressed "hope for a reversal" that never came.[376]

By 1993, some fifty senior federal judges were reportedly refusing to take drug cases. A few judges resigned. Others, as the *Wall Street Journal* chronicled at the time, engaged in a "low-key rebellion" by "devising ways to get around the rules in their own cases."[377] Most of these creative maneuvers were reversed on appeal. None resulted in the invalidation of a statutory provision or set any broader precedent. There was, it seemed, simply no way around *Davis* and *Feeney*.

RUSSELL AND CLARY

Except that the Minnesota Supreme Court and a federal district judge in Missouri demonstrated how it could be done. The Minnesota justices went first. In *State v. Russell*, they were confronted with a state statute, enacted in 1989, that punished crack cocaine more severely than powder cocaine. A group of Black defendants faced up to twenty years in prison for possession of three or more grams of crack; had they been caught with the same amount of powder, they would have faced a maximum sentence of five years. The defendants alleged that the law's differential treatment of the two substances was racially discriminatory, given that 96.6 percent of those charged with crack possession in Minnesota in 1988 had been Black. The *Russell* majority agreed, declaiming, "There comes a time when we cannot and must not close our eyes when presented with evidence that certain laws, regardless of the purpose for which they were enacted, discriminate unfairly on the basis of race."[378]

But the court did not strike down the law on this ground. Rather, the court reasoned that a "stricter standard of rational basis review" is appropriate under the *state* constitutional guarantee of equal protection "where the challenged classification appears to impose a substantially disproportionate burden on the very class of persons whose history inspired the principles of equal protection."[379] The court then found that the crack/powder differential was not justified by sufficient evidence of crack's greater dangerousness. Expressing puzzlement that the majority could reach this result in the absence of any determination of discriminatory intent, the dissent would have applied federal equal protection doctrine and upheld the law as "a commendable, concerted, and reasoned good faith effort to address a serious social problem."[380]

While the *Russell* majority found an innovative way to sidestep the discriminatory-intent issue, by departing from the U.S. Supreme Court's approach to rational basis review, Judge Clyde Cahill of the Eastern District of Missouri found an innovative way to conceptualize discriminatory intent. By 1994, the judicial response to challenges to the federal 100:1 ratio had become boilerplate. Judge Cahill's passionate, plainspoken novella of an opinion attempted to rouse the judiciary from its complacent slumber.[381] The opinion's analytical engine was the concept of "unconscious racism." Drawing on Charles Lawrence's famous article on the subject, Judge Cahill argued that even though "most Americans have grown beyond the evils of overt racial malice," many of our decisions about race-related matters remain influenced by "outlooks, stereotypes, and fears of which we are vastly unaware."[382]

The crack legislation therefore must be seen in a new light. It may not have been the product of conscious racial malice. Few policies are anymore. But the racially laden language that coursed through the congressional debates—all the news stories entered into the record depicting "crack dealers as black youths and gangs," all the "stereotypical images" of lawless "ghettos," all the fear over the "prospect of black crack migrating to the white suburbs," all the "frenzied" haste—now looked more constitutionally relevant.[383] When combined with evidence of the racist history of cocaine prohibition, the systemic inequalities that helped explain crack's concentration in predominantly Black neighborhoods, and the extreme racial skew in the enforcement of the crack laws, a picture of discriminatory intent came into focus: un-self-aware, perhaps, but no less harmful for it. "Without consideration of the influences of unconscious racism, the standard of review set forth in *Washington v. Davis* is a crippling burden of proof," Judge Cahill acknowledged.[384] With such consideration, he showed, this standard can accommodate a subtle and sweeping inquiry into the racialized dimensions of contemporary policymaking.

Russell and especially *Clary* have become something of cult classics among constitutional scholars who wish to loosen the limits imposed by *Davis* and *Feeney* and reorient equal protection law around the value of antisubordination. Within the judiciary, however, they blazed a path to nowhere. No state court followed *Russell's* lead. No federal court followed *Clary's*. Judge Cahill was overruled in a perfunctory manner. Rejecting his reliance on unconscious racism, the appellate panel stated that his "reasoning . . . simply does not address the question whether Congress acted with a discriminatory purpose."[385] This statement is absurd; Judge Cahill's reasoning addresses the question of discriminatory purpose in great depth. The real problem, as even Cahill's supporters had to admit, was that the theory of unconscious racism "is a poor fit with the Supreme Court's narrow concept of racist intent."[386]

Within the academy, too, *Russell* and *Clary* generated significant resistance. *Russell* was criticized for purporting to apply rational basis review while employing something closer to strict scrutiny.[387] *Clary* was criticized for ignoring arguments advanced by Black members of Congress while emphasizing depictions of crack in the media.[388] Above all, both opinions were criticized for failing "to recognize and respect the genuine and important differences between crack and powder cocaine"[389]—not in their (very similar) chemical composition or physiological effects but in their class-conditioned "sociologies of use and distribution"[390]—and for failing to recognize and respect the Black community's need for protection from the crack trade.[391] The most forceful articulation of these criticisms came from Harvard law professor Randall Kennedy, "probably the most influential African-American legal scholar" of the era, whose writings on the topic drew widespread praise from defenders of the constitutional status quo.[392]

That status quo remains in place. Congress reduced the 100:1 ratio to 18:1 in 2010, but not on account of pressure from equal protection doctrine.[393] *Davis* and *Feeney* are still good law. Unconscious bias still plays no role in ordinary equal protection analysis—consciously, at least.[394] Nor do the structural legacies of racism that Judge Cahill emphasized. Nor do the racist remarks made by supporters of drug laws that have since been superseded.[395] Nor do theories of intent that would hold lawmakers responsible for the foreseeable racial disparities caused by their decisions. Outside the courts, "the discriminatory nature of prior crack sentences is no longer a point of legitimate debate."[396] Inside the courts, the "illegitimate" counterview continues to govern.

CANNABIS REPARATIONS AND
THE COLORBLIND CONSTITUTION

What has changed in equal protection jurisprudence since the 1970s is a growing skepticism about policies that take race into account in order to *protect* racial minorities. The prevailing view of *Davis* and *Feeney* at the time, as Reva Siegel has shown, was that the Court was turning over the project of racial repair to the other branches of government.[397] The new focus on discriminatory intent would make it harder for courts to compel racial integration, but elected officials would largely remain free to attack racial segregation and subordination as they saw fit. In the years that followed, however, the Supreme Court began to ratchet up its oversight of "affirmative action" programs that refer to race with such goals in mind, eventually landing on strict scrutiny as the standard of review a decade after *Feeney*.[398] The Court justified this approach by appealing to the colorblind Constitution, or the notion that all laws that classify people on the basis of race are equally suspect under the Equal Protection Clause, whether intended to preserve white supremacy or dismantle it. As Chief Justice John Roberts summarized this stance in 2007, "The way to stop discrimination on the basis of race is to stop discriminating on the basis of race."[399]

Until quite recently, debates over the constitutionality of affirmative action had little overlap with debates over the constitutionality of drug policy. Drug laws were in the business of racial oppression, not racial redress. And they never referred to race as such. But as more and more states have begun to legalize marijuana, more and more reformers have begun to insist that some of the licenses to run dispensaries should be reserved for minority-owned businesses. Such "cannabis equity" programs respond both to the disproportionate costs that prohibition has imposed on communities of color and to the disproportionate benefits that legalization has yielded for white entrepreneurs, whose access to capital has helped them dominate the multibillion-dollar industry. A 2016 report on "America's whites-only weed boom," for instance, estimated that only 1 percent of the country's storefront dispensaries were owned by Black people.[400] Ohio became the first state to adopt a race-conscious cannabis equity program later that same year, setting aside 15 percent of medical marijuana licenses for entities owned and controlled by "Blacks or African Americans, American Indians, Hispanics or Latinos, and Asians."[401]

The explicit reference to race ensured that this program would draw strict scrutiny, no matter how worthy—or substantively egalitarian—the legislature's aims. Two companies that did not receive licenses sued the Ohio Department of Commerce for discriminating against white applicants, and won. The trial court ruled that the state had not sufficiently explored race-neutral alternatives and had not sufficiently established a pattern of discrimination against racial minorities in the medical marijuana industry—no easy task, given that the industry had just been created.[402] Maryland's medical marijuana commission, meanwhile, abandoned its plan to adopt a similar program after the state attorney general's office advised that it would violate equal protection.[403] The Ohio ruling seems to have deterred many regulators from following suit.[404] Going forward, states with licensing schemes that give any sort of preference to minority-owned businesses or in-state residents can expect to face vigorous constitutional challenges.[405] Under the colorblind Constitution, cannabis equity policies have a far better shot at being upheld if they say nothing about race and instead look to correlated variables such as an applicant's prior criminal convictions or a neighborhood's socioeconomic status.

For those who believe that the Equal Protection Clause ought to be interpreted to protect historically disadvantaged groups, this doctrinal architecture looks upside-down. Not only has equal protection law failed for many decades to offer racial minorities a shield against punitive drug policies; it now offers whites a sword with which to attack policies designed to help minorities share in the windfall of drug legalization. Drug policy is not unique in undergoing this inversion. The evolution of equal protection law from a tool of racial integration into something closer to the opposite is a large phenomenon that cuts across many fields. But the consequences have been particularly stark in the drug context, given the enormous volume of arrests and prosecutions, the oligopoly profits that accrue to authorized drug suppliers, and the persistent racial disparities across both sides of the licit/illicit divide. Congress has enacted antidiscrimination statutes that protect against extreme racial disparities in certain areas, such as housing and employment.[406] These statutes do not apply to the criminal system, though, leaving the Constitution as the only potential legal safeguard.

The litigation over crack cocaine penalties could have been an inflection point. This was the first moment when a large number of judges openly wrestled with the adequacy of the post-1970s equal protection paradigm for responding to contemporary racial inequities. It was also the last such moment. The *Clary* district court introduced the idea of unconscious racism into equal protection jurisprudence, while the *Russell* court introduced a new approach to calibrating the standard of review. And plenty of judges expressed concern over the apparent invulnerability of the 100:1 crack/powder sentencing ratio under controlling precedent. In the end, however, the crack cases resoundingly ratified the prevailing paradigm and supported, rather than subverted, the demise of disparate-impact liability and the rise of the colorblind Constitution.

These cases may well have come out the other way in the late 1960s or early 1970s. By the time critics of the war on drugs had amassed irrefutable evidence of enforcement disparities and converged on a view of the war as a project of racial control, the doctrinal ship had already sailed. The best these critics can hope for now from the Equal Protection Clause is that it won't take down too many cannabis equity initiatives. If reformers manage in the coming years to transform drug policy into any sort of force for racial reparations or minority empowerment, it will be in spite of, not because of, constitutional law.

CHAPTER 4

. . .

Humane and Proportionate Punishment

As chapter 1 explained, jurists and scholars have long debated whether Americans have any sort of constitutional right to take or make drugs and, if so, where in the Constitution this right resides. Yet even if no such entitlement exists, Americans have an undisputed right not to be penalized for their drug crimes in certain ways. The Constitution's Eighth Amendment expressly forbids "excessive fines" and "cruel and unusual punishments." The federal government has been bound by these guarantees since the amendment's adoption in 1791. The state governments have been bound by the Cruel and Unusual Punishment Clause since the Supreme Court "incorporated" it against them in 1962.[407] (The Excessive Fines Clause wasn't incorporated until 2019.)[408] And virtually every state constitution contains its own prohibition on cruel and unusual punishment.[409]

For most of U.S. history, the Eighth Amendment provided minimal protection for drug offenders, or anyone else. The first time the Supreme Court turned its attention to the Cruel and Unusual Punishment Clause, in 1878, the justices unanimously approved

The Constitution of the War on Drugs. David Pozen, Oxford University Press.

execution by firing squad.[410] Most lawyers understood the clause to address barbaric modes of punishment, not prison sentences that fail to fit the crime. And defendants who raised Eighth Amendment claims almost always lost.[411] In the 1910 case *Weems v. United States*, however, the Court wrote that the amendment "may acquire meaning as public opinion becomes enlightened by a humane justice" and seemed to endorse the Massachusetts Supreme Court's view that incarceration " 'for a long term of years might be so disproportionate to the offense as to constitute a cruel and unusual punishment.' "[412] The next time the Court invalidated a punishment under the Cruel and Unusual Punishment Clause, in 1958, Chief Justice Warren declared that the Eighth Amendment "must draw its meaning from the evolving standards of decency that mark the progress of a maturing society."[413] Four years later, in *Robinson v. California*, the Court issued its boldest Eighth Amendment opinion yet, striking down a California law that criminalized addiction to narcotics.[414]

By the 1970s, Eighth Amendment attacks on drug laws were ubiquitous. Some of these challenges relied on *Robinson* and contended that if it's cruel to punish someone for being a drug addict, it must likewise be cruel to punish them for procuring or consuming the drug to which they're addicted. Other challenges relied on *Weems*'s principle of proportionality and contended that lengthy prison sentences for drug crimes are grossly excessive, especially for low-risk drugs such as marijuana and low-level offenses such as possession. Each line of attack produced significant victories at the state and federal levels. "Of all the constitutional objections to the [drug] laws," one commentator opined in 1968, "the eighth amendment prohibition against cruel and unusual punishment may provide the greatest chance for success," as it offers a "middle-of-the-road approach" for courts concerned about draconian drug penalties but unwilling to demand decriminalization.[415]

In what will now be a familiar pattern, such predictions flowered and then fell apart as judges moved to minimize doctrinal openings for reasons both internal and external to constitutional law. Drug defendants thus entered the 1980s as they had entered the 1960s—with effectively zero protection from the Eighth Amendment.

AN ADDICTION EXCEPTION?

The Eighth Amendment story differs from the others in one important institutional respect. The U.S. Supreme Court never directly ruled on the constitutional challenges to the drug laws explored in the previous chapters, based on substantive due process and equal protection. It preferred to let the lower courts handle them. For challenges based on the Cruel and Unusual Punishment Clause, by contrast, the Supreme Court both initiated and terminated the litigation explosion of the 1960s and 1970s. More than any other case, the Court's 1962 ruling in *Robinson v. California* reawakened the movement for constitutional drug rights after a half-century of dormancy.

Robinson had strange facts. When Los Angeles police officers stopped the car in which Lawrence Robinson was riding for an unilluminated license plate, they found "numerous needle marks" on his arm, a "tell-tale" sign of intravenous drug use.[416] Robinson promptly admitted to having shot heroin in the recent past. But he was prosecuted and sentenced to ninety days under a statute that, according to the California courts, made it a misdemeanor to "be addicted to the use of narcotics" regardless of whether one had acted on the addiction.[417] The justices agreed to hear Robinson's appeal even though it lacked all the usual indicia of a Supreme Court case: there was no split among the federal or state courts, no federal law had been struck down, and no prominent law firms or advocacy groups were backing the appeal. Stranger still, neither the justices nor the attorneys realized that Robinson had died of an overdose in August 1961, more than eight months before the Court held oral arguments in his case.[418]

Across the legal and medical professions, authoritative voices were becoming increasingly insistent at the turn of the 1960s that drug addiction is best seen as an illness, not a voluntary choice, and that accordingly it is best treated through medical means, not criminal sanctions. The year before *Robinson*, a joint committee of the American Bar Association and the American Medical Association published a report, *Drug Addiction: Crime or Disease?*, which strongly suggested the latter answer to its titular question. All of the committee's recommendations "emphasize[d] the medical rather than the punitive approach."[419] The *Robinson* majority embraced the ABA/AMA stance that "narcotic addiction is an illness," "[i]ndeed . . . an illness which may be contracted innocently or involuntarily," as when it results "from the use of medically prescribed narcotics" or when a mother's drug habit leaves an infant "a narcotics addict from the moment of his birth." "To be sure," Justice Stewart acknowledged in his opinion for the Court, "imprisonment for ninety days is not, in the abstract, a punishment which is either cruel or unusual. But the question cannot be considered in the abstract. Even one day in prison would be a cruel and unusual punishment for the 'crime' of having a common cold."[420]

Six of the eight justices participating in *Robinson* seemed to think it plain that the statute violated the Eighth Amendment, but they had trouble explaining why.[421] Justice Stewart expressed dismay at the criminalization of "the 'status' of narcotic addiction," which he likened to an "attempt to make it a criminal offense for a person to be mentally ill, or a leper, or to be afflicted with a venereal disease."[422] In Stewart's papers, there is evidence that he reached out before the case was decided to the chief resident of a local children's hospital for "recent medical articles on drug addiction in newborns," suggesting that he knew how he wanted to rule and believed the possibility of "born addicts" would be seen as a compelling point in his favor.[423]

Missing from Stewart's opinion was any analysis, even a single sentence, about the meaning of the Eighth Amendment. In a concurring opinion, Justice Douglas analogized the California statute to sixteenth-century English practices of punishing the mentally insane, while likewise failing to draw a clear connection to the Eighth Amendment's text, history, or case law.[424] None of the justices in the majority had an answer for Justice White's charge that "this application of 'cruel and unusual punishment' " was "so novel" that it would be impossible "to find a way to ascribe to the Framers of the Constitution the result reached today."[425] If *Robinson* had reached the Court after *Griswold*, it likely would have been resolved on substantive due process grounds. Justice Clark telegraphed as much in dissent when he criticized the majority's understanding of "ordered liberty" and its "due process" holding.[426] With substantive due process still in disrepute in 1962, the *Robinson* majority instead invented a new theory of cruel and unusual punishment.

The thinness and novelty of *Robinson* generated confusion over what the opinion stood for. A narrow reading would condemn only those laws that criminalize the status of being an addict (or catching a cold) in the absence of an affirmative act. So construed, *Robinson* would "be little more than a ticket good for this day and train only."[427] Broader readings might condemn other status offenses attributable to illness, or status offenses attributable to conditions beyond an individual's control, or perhaps "involuntary" offenses of any kind.[428] Even though Justice Stewart went out of his way to assert that the Court was not calling into question a state's authority to proscribe the "manufacture, prescription, sale, purchase, or possession of narcotics within its borders,"[429] the reasoning of his opinion, as Justice White pointed out in dissent, "bristles with indications of further consequences."[430] Why should a heroin addict's daily fix trigger criminal liability if it's merely a symptom or expression of an illness? Justice Stewart's catalogue of behaviors that states may continue to criminalize notably failed to include *use* of narcotics—an omission that, as Justice White further pointed out, could not possibly have been "inadvertent."[431] For all of these reasons, *Robinson* "was widely seen as casting a shadow on a variety of criminal drug statutes, including laws barring possession and use."[432]

In short order, courts started building on *Robinson*. A few states had laws on the books that mirrored the offending provision in *Robinson*; these laws were summarily dispatched.[433] A New York trial judge held that drug addicts may not be subject to criminal sanction for escaping from civil commitment, as doing so would "impose vengeance upon sickness" in contravention of *Robinson*.[434] The U.S. Court of Appeals for the Ninth Circuit stated in dicta that an Eighth Amendment attack on the criminalization of compulsive use of narcotics "would be worthy of serious consideration."[435] The U.S. Court of Appeals for the Seventh Circuit and the Idaho Supreme Court disapproved of probation conditions requiring alcoholics to refrain from drinking.[436] And in a pair of celebrated decisions, the federal appellate courts for the D.C. Circuit and the Fourth Circuit ruled that chronic alcoholics could no longer be prosecuted for being drunk in public.[437] If this sounds picayune, consider that one-third of all arrests made in the United States in 1965 were for public intoxication.[438]

Beyond the field of drug control, enterprising lawyers began to enlist *Robinson*'s notion of involuntariness to attack laws criminalizing homelessness, vagrancy, cross-dressing, homosexual sex, and more. Although these efforts generally failed, and although the vast majority of drug laws continued to be upheld, *Robinson* seemed destined to spawn a long line of cases.[439] By the time the Supreme Court agreed in 1967 to hear a public intoxication appeal, *Powell v.*

Texas, many in the legal community had "little doubt" that the Court would continue the progressive doctrinal development and rule for the defendant.[440]

The Court defied such predictions. Although they splintered on the rationale, five justices refused to extend *Robinson* to most cases of public intoxication. *Powell*'s formal holding was ambiguous. Its practical impact was to crush the incipient project of identifying certain crimes as categorically cruel and developing special protections for addiction in Eighth Amendment law.

Writing for Chief Justice Warren, Justice Black, Justice Harlan, and himself, Justice Thurgood Marshall did not dispute that Leroy Powell was an alcoholic. That would have been hard to do, given that Powell had been convicted of public intoxication approximately one hundred times in the past two decades.[441] Nor did Justice Marshall deny that "[t]he picture of the penniless drunk propelled aimlessly and endlessly through the law's 'revolving door' of arrest, incarceration, release and re-arrest"—a picture exemplified by Powell—"is not a pretty one."[442] But Marshall refused to accept the trial court's finding that chronic alcoholism is a disease that robs people of their willpower to stop drinking. It is still unclear exactly how alcoholism works, he protested. And regardless, *Robinson* prohibits punishments for the *status* of being an addict, or what Justice Black termed "pure status crimes,"[443] whereas public intoxication involves "antisocial *conduct*."[444] Acknowledging that his interpretation of *Robinson* "brings [the] Court but a very small way into the substantive criminal law," Marshall argued that such minimalism is necessary in this domain to preserve "[t]raditional common-law concepts of personal accountability and essential considerations of federalism."[445]

The fifth vote to uphold Powell's conviction was supplied by Justice White, who concurred with Justice Marshall's plurality opinion only in the result. White opened his opinion with a stunning concession to the other side. "If it cannot be a crime to have an irresistible compulsion to use narcotics," he volunteered, "I do not see how it can constitutionally be a crime to yield to such a compulsion. . . . Similarly, the chronic alcoholic with an irresistible urge to consume alcohol should not be punishable for drinking or for being drunk."[446] Even though he had dissented in *Robinson*, Justice White felt bound by the logic of precedent to reject the plurality's "pure status" reading of the decision. The more principled way to cabin *Robinson*, White contended, is to allow addicts to be punished for the choice to use drugs *in public*. Leroy Powell's conviction wasn't cruel, on this account, because he could have arranged to drink at home. A chronic alcoholic who lacks a home, on the other hand, must be allowed to drink on the streets.[447] The four dissenting justices rejected White's public/private line but otherwise advanced a congruous interpretation of *Robinson*, which they distilled into a general maxim: "Criminal penalties may not be inflicted upon a person for being in a condition he is powerless to change."[448] The dissenters also indicated strong support for the medical model of regulating addictive drugs, observing that the criminal approach is not just morally dubious but an exercise in "futility."[449]

Powell is now "understood to have all-but-overruled *Robinson*."[450] This understanding was far from inevitable, however. For one thing, it wasn't clear whose opinion was controlling, Justice Marshall's or Justice White's. Justice Marshall received three more votes. But in a situation where "a fragmented Court decides a case and no single rationale explaining the result enjoys the assent of five Justices," the Court advised in a 1977 case called *Marks v. United States*, "the holding of the Court may be viewed as that position taken by those Members who concurred in the judgments on the narrowest grounds."[451] And

Justice White sided with Texas on the narrow ground that this particular defendant failed to show he couldn't have gotten drunk at home. If White's opinion is controlling, then *Powell* protects drug addicts from punishment not only for having an addiction but also for "yielding" to it. Alternatively, many judges and scholars assumed before *Marks* that in the absence of a Supreme Court majority, none of the opinions carries precedential force.[452] Under this assumption, *Powell* created no Eighth Amendment law at all.

There is sufficient ambiguity in both the *Marks* rule and its application to *Powell* that the "debate over how to read *Powell*" has been described as "undeniably inconclusive."[453] Judges on the D.C. Circuit continued to dispute this matter into the 1970s, noting that "there exists a sharp split of opinion throughout the legal profession concerning the meaning of *Powell*" and that "'*Powell* has left [the] matter of criminal responsibility, as affected by the Eighth Amendment, in a posture which is, at best, obscure.'"[454] In the immediate aftermath of the decision, the Minnesota Supreme Court drew on Justice White's "deciding vote" in refusing to apply a criminal ban on drunkenness to chronic alcoholics.[455] The Pennsylvania Supreme Court declared that *Powell* "unequivocally holds that to the extent certain behavior is a 'characteristic part' of a disease . . . such behavior cannot be criminally proscribed," given that "Mr. Justice White was, in a very real sense, the 'swing man' in this case."[456] The D.C. Circuit suggested in dicta in 1970 that an addict "whose acquisition and possession of narcotics is solely for his own use" should be able to make out a claim of "constitutional defectiveness."[457] And President Nixon's attorney general, John Mitchell, characterized *Powell* in a 1971 speech as holding that "alcoholism in itself is involuntary and therefore is not a legal offense in the ordinary sense."[458]

None of these authorities treated Justice Marshall's opinion as controlling. Even if they had done so, his analysis left wiggle room to argue, among other things, that demonstrably involuntary behaviors are covered by *Robinson*, that certain drug behaviors are involuntary in the relevant sense,[459] and that punitive drug laws may not reach all the way into the home.[460]

By the early 1970s, however, judges and scholars had largely abandoned such arguments and settled on the view that *Powell* eviscerated *Robinson*. From the outset, most lower courts treated the *Powell* plurality opinion as controlling and interpreted it to forbid only pure status crimes, without grappling with the complexities of *Powell* or the status/conduct distinction. The Second Circuit, for example, dismissed the notion that *Robinson* protects anything more than "the mere status of narcotics addiction" as unworthy of "serious consideration."[461] Many judges simply asserted that under *Powell*, the government may punish drug-related "acts."[462] The most significant holdout from this emerging consensus was the D.C. Circuit, but by 1973 it too had fallen into line and repudiated its prior suggestion that nontrafficking addicts must be spared punishment for possessing drugs to satisfy their addiction.[463] Although it continues to be "of great theoretical interest," criminal law scholars would soon conclude, *Robinson* "has no practical importance today. Nothing has come of it."[464]

SLIPPERY SLOPES, REAL AND IMAGINED

Why did so little come of *Robinson*? The timing is hard to square with an account of declining sympathy for drug addicts. Richard Nixon became president in 1969 and made four Supreme Court appointments in the four years following *Powell*. But the restrictive reading of *Powell* had already won out by the time these appointees assumed the bench. Three of the four replaced justices who had joined the plurality in *Powell*, and the fourth, Harry Blackmun, would go on to lambaste a Veterans' Administration rule that attributed all cases of alcoholism to "willful misconduct."[465] Nixon, moreover, was careful in the early years of his presidency not to demonize drug addicts, a group that had become associated with the Vietnam War. Although the Nixon administration opposed decriminalization of marijuana, it supported a range of harm reduction initiatives, including methadone clinics for heroin users.[466] The ABA continued to insist in 1972 that "federal, state, and local governments must discard their current law enforcement-oriented strategy toward addiction control and adopt a policy which places primary emphasis on the treatment of addiction."[467] The president's commission on drug abuse issued a second report in 1973, following its blockbuster marijuana report of the year before, echoing the ABA's approach.[468] And Congress increased the budget for drug treatment and prevention by an order of magnitude during Nixon's first term while reducing penalties for simple possession offenses, in line with the prevailing "conception that narcotic addiction is a disease which explains, [even if] it does not excuse, the conduct of defendants."[469]

In their opinions, the judges who refused to extend *Robinson* beyond pure status crimes focused less on the culpability of addicts than on the unacceptable consequences that might follow. Drug addiction is just one of many possible sources of compulsion, after all, and drug use is just one of many possible compulsive behaviors. "If Leroy Powell cannot be convicted of public intoxication," Justice Marshall argued, "it is difficult to see how a State can convict an individual for murder, if that individual . . . suffers from a 'compulsion' to kill." Applying *Robinson* to crimes such as public intoxication without applying it to murder or drunk driving would be "arbitrary," a "limitation by fiat."[470] Not only that, the D.C. Circuit asserted, but "any new limits . . . would soon fall by the wayside and the Court would be forced to hold the States powerless to punish any conduct that could be shown to result from a 'compulsion,' in the complex, psychological meaning of that term."[471] These results, warned a

chorus of jurists and scholars, would be nothing less than "revolu-
tionary,"[472] leading to "virtual abandonment" of criminal punishment if not "the demise of the criminal law."[473]

These arguments were remarkable for their hyperbole. Judges
draw arbitrary lines all the time as they elaborate and refine legal
principles in a common-law fashion. And virtually every legal principle, if taken to the extreme, could lead down a slippery slope toward unpalatable outcomes. In his *Powell* dissent, Justice Abe Fortas
wrote that punishment should still be allowed "for criminal conduct
which is not a characteristic and involuntary part of the pattern of the
disease."[474] Judge Skelly Wright of the D.C. Circuit proposed that
"the addiction defense" apply only to those acts that "are inseparable
from the disease itself and, at the same time, inflict no direct harm
upon other members of society."[475] Both of these tests would have
extended *Robinson* to certain cases of drug purchase, possession,
and use—and not necessarily any further. Drug manufacturing and
trafficking could still be punished. The use of nonaddictive drugs
could still be punished. And as *Robinson* itself had made clear, any
number of "nonpunitive" sanctions, including compulsory medical
treatment and civil commitment, could still be applied to addicts.[476]

Even so, implementing any version of the Fortas or Wright test
would have been a fraught endeavor. The tests turn on a series of undefined and contested concepts. Defendant after defendant would
have sought to prove the "involuntary" or "inseparable" nature of
their conduct. Courts would have had to delve into the details of
addiction science as well as issues of criminal responsibility that are
better illuminated by "moral philosophy, criminology, and other
nonlaw disciplines" than by anything in the constitutional text.[477]
Throughout the 1960s, legislatures were experimenting with new
approaches to addiction while expert commissions were undertaking
comprehensive criminal law reform projects.[478] Against this backdrop, the plurality opinion in *Powell*, authored by none other than

liberal icon Thurgood Marshall, struck many as a model of realism over idealism, judicial restraint over judicial activism.[479] Extending *Robinson* to personal possession offenses would have had one relatively concrete consequence. In the field of property, it is a commonplace that "possession is nine-tenths of the law."[480] The same could be said of illicit drugs, for a very different reason. Prosecutors often find it easier to charge suspects for possession than for distribution—and then to pressure those suspects into becoming witnesses or informants.[481] The ability to extract "cooperation" from low-level addicts has been one of law enforcement's most potent weapons in the war on drugs. Building out *Robinson*'s theory of criminal culpability would not plausibly have led to murderers or drunk drivers going free. But it would have made the job harder for prosecutors as well as judges.

QUESTIONING SEVERE SENTENCES

There was another, more straightforward way the Cruel and Unusual Punishment Clause might have restrained the drug war. Even if it is not categorically unconstitutional to punish addicts for feeding their habits, it may nonetheless be "cruel and unusual" to punish drug offenders with excessive severity. As early as 1910, recall, the Court had intimated that a prison sentence could be "so disproportionate to the offense as to constitute a cruel and unusual punishment."[482] The Court had never actually overturned a sentence on this ground. But before *Trop v. Dulles* in 1958, the Court had never committed to the "evolving standards of decency" test for identifying impermissible punishments,[483] and before *Robinson* in 1962, it had never found a category of crime to be unpunishable. The Eighth Amendment was finally beginning to come to life. State courts, moreover, could always interpret their own constitution's cruel-and-unusual-punishment clause to go further than the federal version.

"Disproportionality" challenges to drug sentences began to heat up in the late 1960s, just as "involuntariness" challenges began to cool off. For the latter, hard drugs like heroin were best for defendants. The more physically addictive the substance you were caught with, the stronger your claim to an uncontrollable compulsion. For disproportionality challenges, on the other hand, soft drugs like marijuana were superior, as the practical and philosophical justifications for their punishment were understood to be weaker.

Penalties for both hard-drug and soft-drug offenses had increased "drastically" in the 1950s at the state and federal levels.[484] Initially, judges took it for granted that these penalties raised no Eighth Amendment problem. Most appellate courts adhered to the common-law rule that, with limited exceptions, sentences within statutory limits are unreviewable.[485] When they did review drug sentences, courts invariably found them not "so out of proportion to the crime committed that it shocks a balanced sense of justice."[486] Marijuana received no special solicitude. In 1960, for instance, the U.S. Court of Appeals for the Ninth Circuit upheld a mandatory minimum prison sentence of five years for bringing pot into the country in "view of the moral degeneration inherent in all aspects" of drug crime.[487] Another panel of the Ninth Circuit brushed off an Eighth Amendment challenge to a forty-year sentence for the sale of marijuana as having "no merit,"[488] while the Texas Court of Criminal Appeals upheld sentences of thirty years for the gift of a single joint and life imprisonment for first-offense possession as matters "we must necessarily leave to the wisdom of the Legislature and the jury which tried the case."[489] Disproportionality claims had no hope under this jurisprudence of permission.

This jurisprudence came under "unprecedented" assault in the late 1960s and early 1970s.[490] For many of the advocates and academics

leading this assault, drug sentences stood out as paradigms of punitive excess, especially when they involved marijuana and mandatory
minimums. Bonnie and Whitebread's 1970 article on the history of
marijuana regulation documented growing "disgust" within the
legal profession at such sentences and urged that "even if marijuana
use is an appropriate matter for criminal legislation," the Cruel and
Unusual Punishment Clause "should prohibit imprisonment for violation of that legislation, even for five minutes."[491] A 1972 article in
the *Stanford Law Review* declared that the "drug laws—especially
those pertaining to marijuana—comprise the clearest case requiring
present application of the proportionality limitation."[492] By 1977,
these arguments had gained so much traction that the National
Governors' Conference could put out a report, published by the U.S.
Department of Justice, stating that "long terms of confinement for
simple possession" of marijuana would "certainly" be "unconstitutionally excessive."[493]

That "certainly" was itself excessive, at least as a description of
the case law, but disproportionality doctrine had made enormous
strides since the decade's start. The leading case in this line was
People v. Lorentzen, decided by the Michigan Supreme Court on
the same day in 1972 as the *Sinclair* case discussed in chapter 1.
Although the Michigan justices fractured over the various constitutional claims raised in *Sinclair*, in *Lorentzen* they voted unanimously
to strike down a state law mandating at least twenty years' imprisonment for the sale of "narcotics," defined to include marijuana, under
the federal and state constitutional prohibitions on cruel and unusual
punishment. The *Lorentzen* opinion began by noting the rigidity as
well as the severity of the law, "equally applicable to a first offender
high school student as . . . to a wholesaling racketeer." The opinion
then tested the law for "excessiveness" against other criminal laws
in Michigan, against the drug laws in other states, and against "the
goal of rehabilitation"—and found it wanting on all fronts. The

twenty-year mandatory minimum was harsher than the penalties imposed in Michigan for many violent crimes; harsher than the penalties imposed in every other state save Ohio for sale of marijuana; and harsher than appropriate for the goal of rehabilitation, which, according to "[e]xperts on penology and criminal corrections," can in most cases "best be reached by short sentences of less than five years' imprisonment." On all of these levels, the court concluded, a "compulsory prison sentence of 20 years for a non-violent crime imposed without consideration for defendant's individual personality and history is so excessive that it 'shocks the conscience.' "[494]

Elements of *Lorentzen*'s multifactor test traveled widely. The U.S. Court of Appeals for the Sixth Circuit applied an identical analysis in 1975 to strike down an Ohio law imposing minimum sentences of twenty years for sale of marijuana and ten years for possession-for-sale—the first time a federal court ever found a statutory sentence to be cruel and unusual based on its length.[495] Both before and after *Lorentzen*, numerous state appellate courts found ways to reduce sentences for marijuana crimes without making an Eighth Amendment holding. In a decision that Bonnie and Whitebread hailed as a "landmark," for instance, the New Jersey Supreme Court in 1970 suspended all prison sentences for first offenders convicted of marijuana possession.[496] Less than a month later, the Oklahoma Court of Criminal Appeals determined that a sentence of seven years for possession of pot was "excessive."[497] On at least two different occasions, the same court later found sentences of one year to be excessive and reduced them to two months.[498] In the mid-1970s, the California courts held that drug sentences precluding the possibility of parole for a minimum period qualify as cruel or unusual punishment under the state constitution. This conclusion was "strengthen[ed]," the California Supreme Court said, by the recommendations against mandatory minimums made by expert commissions throughout the 1960s.[499] The Alaska Supreme

Court not only cited those same recommendations but also, in 1974, expressly "adopted . . . the American Bar Association's view that 'except for cases involving particularly serious offenses, dangerous offenders and professional criminals, maximum prison terms ought not to exceed 5 years.'" Pursuant to this view, the Alaska high court repeatedly overturned drug sentences, including some with prison terms well under five years.[500]

These cases varied in many particulars, but they shared the premise that the length of a sentence alone, if sufficiently disproportionate to the gravity of the crime, could violate a defendant's rights. And they suggested that drug laws were the first place to look for such violations. Even if one excludes the numerous cruel-and-unusual-punishment victories that were overturned on appeal,[501] defendants won more than a dozen disproportionality challenges to their drug sentences in the 1970s—after winning zero such challenges, as far as I can tell, in all the decades prior to 1970.

ROCKEFELLER'S REVENGE

This movement began to stall out right around the time the National Governors' Conference predicted it would accelerate, at least for cannabis crimes. The key cases came out of New York. In the spring of 1973, Governor Nelson Rockefeller signed "the nation's most consequential and devastating narcotics control legislation,"[502] defying the trend toward reduced penalties for possession and imposing mandatory maximum life sentences for more than thirty different drug offenses.[503] Whereas the federal reforms of the late 1960s and early 1970s had taken a mixed criminal-medical approach to the problem of substance abuse, the New York legislation all but abandoned the goal of rehabilitation in response to a perceived crisis of heroin addiction in New York City and the perceived failure of drug treatment programs.[504] If a meaningful jurisprudence of proportionality was going to take hold, it would have to rein in the Rockefeller drug laws.

Eighth Amendment litigation got off to a promising start. In 1974, a state trial judge ruled that a mandatory maximum life term for sale of a narcotic violates the state and federal constitutional prohibitions on cruel and unusual punishment.[505] Three years later, a federal district judge issued an analogous ruling.[506] Both opinions employed the *Lorentzen* methodology of comparing these sentences to the sentences meted out for nondrug offenses within the state, to the sentences meted out for drug offenses in other states, and to the gravity of the offenses at issue—not "petty" but "not crimes of violence" either—and determined that the New York laws "do not comport with prevalent moral notions of what constitute just, temperate, and appropriate punishments."[507]

Both opinions were overturned on appeal. In *People v. Broadie*, New York's highest court conceded that the Rockefeller drug laws were exceptionally severe and inflexible by any comparative metric. But this alone did not make the laws unconstitutionally excessive, Chief Judge Charles Breitel reasoned, because the legislature had concluded "that rehabilitation efforts had failed" and "that the epidemic of drug abuse could be quelled only by the threat of inflexible, and therefore certain, exceptionally severe punishment." Furthermore, life imprisonment is not necessarily out of proportion with a minor drug sale, for

the Legislature could reasonably have found that drug trafficking is a generator of collateral crime, even violent crime. And violent crime is not, of course, the only destroyer of men and the social fabric. Drug addiction degrades and impoverishes those whom it enslaves. This debilitation of men, as well as the disruption of their families, the Legislature could also lay at the door of the drug traffickers.[508]

This rhetoric was straight out of the Federal Bureau of Narcotics's midcentury propaganda. Chief Judge Breitel did not provide any empirical support for these claims, and it was unclear how a defendant could refute his metaphors of destruction and enslavement. Three years later, in *Carmona v. Ward*, the U.S. Court of Appeals for the Second Circuit praised Breitel's "penetrating," "scholarly," and "thorough" opinion and adopted it wholesale.[509]

The only opinion in these cases with a scholarly sensibility was, in fact, the dissent in *Carmona*. Judge James Oakes countered the majority's quasi-religious fervor with cool rationalism, observing that the New York City Bar Association had found the Rockefeller laws to have "no real deterrent effect on drug abuse," that the defendants (one of whom had sold a single dose of cocaine for $20) were "not major traffickers or hardened criminals," and that "New York's drug problem is a socioeconomic phenomenon or set of phenomena attributable to a great many factors with which the [defendants] have had nothing whatsoever to do." For good measure, Oakes also penned a lengthy appendix on "The Origin and Meaning of the Eighth Amendment."[510] The Supreme Court declined to review *Carmona*, over the dissent of Justices Marshall and Powell. Reverting to liberal-lion mode after his plea for minimalism in *Powell*, Justice Marshall associated himself with Judge Oakes's analysis. Marshall emphasized, in particular, that the effort to "rationalize petitioner's sentences by invoking all evils attendant on or attributable to widespread drug trafficking is simply not compatible with a fundamental premise of the criminal justice system, that individuals are accountable only for their own criminal acts."[511]

The Court's refusal to review *Carmona* foreshadowed a more definitive series of decisions soon to come. Over the course of the

1970s, the justices became increasingly enmeshed in the most controversial Eighth Amendment issue of all: capital punishment. The Court yoyoed from striking down every existing death penalty law in 1972, to reinstating the death penalty in 1976 after these laws had purportedly been made less arbitrary and discriminatory, to ruling that imposition of the death penalty for the rape of an adult woman is cruel and unusual in 1977.[512] The plurality opinion in that last case looked like it might be a valuable resource for drug offenders.[513] In the 1980 case *Rummel v. Estelle*, however, the Court upheld a mandatory life sentence under a Texas recidivist statute for a man who had committed minor financial crimes. Writing for the majority, Justice Rehnquist explained that the Court's cruel-and-unusual-punishment decisions in capital cases are "of limited assistance" in noncapital cases and that, outside the death penalty context, findings of gross disproportionality "have been exceedingly rare."[514]

Having tacked back toward this restrictive posture, the Court closed the door on drug defendants two years later in *Hutto v. Davis* and then again, even more firmly, in 1991 in *Harmelin v. Michigan*. The defendant in *Hutto* was sentenced to forty years in prison for possession and distribution of approximately $200 worth of marijuana. Both the district court and the U.S. Court of Appeals for the Fourth Circuit found this sentence grossly disproportionate to the crime. The Supreme Court reversed without holding oral argument. In a brief unsigned opinion described by the dissenters as a "patent abuse of our judicial power," the Court accused the Fourth Circuit of "having ignored, consciously or unconsciously, the hierarchy of the federal court system" by flouting *Rummel*'s command "that 'successful challenges to the proportionality of particular sentences' should be 'exceedingly rare.'"[515] The Court surprised many by siding with such a challenge the following term, in *Solem v. Helm*, a case in which a habitual offender had been sentenced to life without possibility of parole for passing a bad check.[516] *Solem* has never been overruled, and it supplies a slender reed of hope for nonviolent defendants facing long prison terms. In the next case in this line, however, the *Harmelin* Court upheld the same sentence for a first-time offender convicted of possessing 672 grams of cocaine. Justice Scalia argued that the Eighth Amendment contains no proportionality requirement whatsoever in noncapital cases.[517] Justice Kennedy's controlling opinion declined to go that far, but it emphasized that the proportionality principle is a "narrow" one. Given the "momentous" nature of this defendant's crime, Kennedy maintained, his sentence could be sustained without any need to compare it to other sentences in Michigan or elsewhere.[518]

And that's essentially where the doctrine still stands. As long as the defendant is not a minor and the punishment is not death, it is hard to imagine how a drug sentence could qualify as grossly disproportionate under the logic of *Harmelin* and follow-on cases. It "seems to be the Supreme Court's current view," Judge Richard Posner observed in 1996, that "a state can with constitutional impunity sentence" a first offender "to life imprisonment without possibility of parole for the sale of one marijuana cigarette."[519] A few state courts have tried to fill this Eighth Amendment hole with more expansive readings of their state constitutional prohibitions on cruel and unusual punishment. The year after *Harmelin*, the Michigan Supreme Court invalidated the same statutory provision that the U.S. Supreme Court had just upheld.[520] At least two other state courts have likewise struck down mandatory life sentences for drug offenders,[521] and the Louisiana appellate courts have struck down a number of less severe sentences as well.[522] These cases are outliers, though. The "overwhelming majority" of state courts have followed federal precedent and rejected virtually all disproportionality challenges to drug penalties since the 1970s.[523]

CIVIL FORFEITURES AND EXCESSIVE FINES

The one aspect of Eighth Amendment jurisprudence that has
grown slightly more favorable to drug defendants since the 1970s involves the amendment's separate prohibition on "excessive fines."
In the Comprehensive Drug Abuse Prevention and Control Act of
1970, Congress authorized the government to seize drug-related
property even in situations where no criminal case is brought or
where the owner is charged and acquitted. Congress steadily expanded this authority over the course of the next two decades,
both by allowing more types of assets to be seized and, after 1984,
by allowing state and local police departments to keep most of
the proceeds. Compared to a defendant in a criminal forfeiture
or prosecution, defendants in these "civil forfeiture" suits—which
are technically brought against the property itself—enjoy few procedural protections. There is no presumption of innocence, for
example.[524]

Given the relative ease of bringing civil forfeiture actions and
the financial rewards, drug enforcers unsurprisingly gravitated toward this tool, collecting hundreds of millions of dollars in revenue
per year by the 1990s.[525] Critics decried an exploitative regime of
"policing for profit." Defendants began to argue that the Excessive
Fines Clause ought to constrain civil forfeitures even if various procedural safeguards don't. In 1993, the Supreme Court ruled unanimously that civil forfeitures under the federal drug laws are subject
to this clause, while punting on the question of how to determine
"excessiveness."[526] Five years later, the Court adopted the "gross
disproportionality" standard from its cruel-and-unusual-punishment
jurisprudence for *criminal* forfeitures but left it unclear whether all
civil forfeitures, or just some "punitive" subset, are subject to this
proportionality principle.[527] In the 2019 case *Timbs v. Indiana*, the

Court incorporated the Excessive Fines Clause against the states without addressing this question.[528]

Most disproportionality challenges fail under the Excessive Fines Clause, as they fail under the Cruel and Unusual Punishment Clause. There are significantly more examples since 1993 of courts finding an asset forfeiture to be inconsistent with the Eighth Amendment, however, than of courts finding a criminal sentence to be inconsistent with the amendment. In *Timbs* itself, the Indiana Supreme Court ruled on remand in 2021 that the forfeiture of the defendant's Land Rover, which he had used to deal heroin, violated the Excessive Fines Clause.[529]

During the *Timbs* oral argument, Justice Alito scoffed at the possibility that "six years' imprisonment is not an Eighth Amendment violation, but a fine of $42,000 is an Eighth Amendment violation."[530] That asymmetry now seems to be our legal reality. Under the Court's precedents, it is inconceivable that six years in prison would be deemed an excessive punishment for the sale of any amount of heroin, whereas the seizure of an automobile from the seller might well be deemed—and just recently *was* deemed—an excessive fine. Commodity fetishism has been elevated in this realm to the status of supreme law. The owner's property receives more Eighth Amendment protection than the owner herself.

"SOMETHING THAT LOOKS AND FEELS LIKE LEGAL ANALYSIS"

In the end, the judicial experiment in policing the proportionality of drug sentences both started and ended in the 1970s, just as the experiment in developing minimum conditions of culpability did in the 1960s. The stage was thus set for the government to ramp up drug penalties in the 1980s, and for state and federal prison populations to explode, without Eighth Amendment limit. Mounting antidrug

hysteria, along with the general turn in penology away from the rehabilitative ideal, are evident on the face of some of the key decisions,
such as the New York rulings upholding the Rockefeller drug laws
and Justice Kennedy's opinion in *Harmelin*. But the effective erasure
of the Cruel and Unusual Punishment Clause in this area predates
the rise of Reaganism, the collapse of the welfare state, the crack
cocaine panic, the unraveling of the bipartisan consensus against
mandatory minimums, and other extrajudicial developments that
reconciled many legal elites to draconian drug penalties. The Eighth
Amendment story cannot be neatly explained by shifts in modes of
governance or the politics of addiction.

Criminal law scholars have pointed to two doctrinal dynamics
that seem to have reinforced judges' reticence to police the proportionality of drug sentences. First, as Rachel Barkow has detailed, the
Supreme Court demands a far more robust and resource-consuming
form of proportionality review in capital cases than in the 99.999 percent of other criminal cases, on the ground that "death is different."[531]
Barkow posits that the justices created this two-track system in part
to placate critics of the death penalty while soothing their own con-
sciences about the executions that go forward. Drug defendants are
just one (large) category of losers in this quixotic quest for closure
on capital punishment.

Second, beginning with the Warren Court, the justices have
issued many more, and more liberal, rulings on questions of how
crimes may be investigated and prosecuted than on questions of
how they may be defined and punished.[532] Here too, it has been
suggested that a hydraulic effect may be at work, whereby the Court
skimps on substance so that it can splurge on procedure. But if a
trade-off must be made, why not do the reverse? As William Stuntz
laid out in a classic article on the topic, "substantive criminal law
could be constrained quite easily under the authority of the Due
Process Clause and the Eighth Amendment," likely with much

greater benefits for defendants. The "real difficulty," however, is that when judges regulate substantive criminal matters—unlike when they regulate procedure—there is "no way to get to sensible bottom lines by something that looks and feels like legal analysis. Whether proportionality review is lodged in appellate or trial courts, the only way to do it is . . . to decide that this sentence is too great but not that one."[533]

The judges who have voted to uphold extreme penalties for drug offenders have stressed this very point. The *Hutto* majority warned that "the line-drawing process" in criminal punishment is unsuitable for courts.[534] The *Rummel* majority despaired of "the complexities confronting any court" attempting to compare the severity of sentences within or across jurisdictions.[535] When the Alabama Court of Criminal Appeals took the rare step of striking down a mandatory life sentence for an addicted first offender convicted of selling $200 worth of morphine, one of the dissenters admonished the majority for making "decisions based on emotion," while the other asked, "What will the majority do in the next case, which will surely come, where relief from a sentence of life imprisonment without parole is sought by a person . . . whose overall situation in life does not pull quite so strongly on a sensible person's heartstrings?"[536] When the California Supreme Court began to push back against mandatory minimums for drug offenders in the mid-1970s, a dissenting judge implored his colleagues to tell him "just where is the breaking point. Ten years is too much says the Supreme Court. The same court says that three years may not be. How about two years, six and one-half months? Or four years, seven months and twenty-nine days? Or three years, two months and eighteen days?"[537] Proportionality review with any bite, on these accounts, is so deeply and inescapably arbitrary that it doesn't even look and feel like legal analysis. Better to stick with an uncompromising formalism.

The irony is that in the quarter-century since Stuntz called attention to this dynamic, constitutional courts and international tribunals across the globe have converged on a model of rights review known as *proportionality*. Even as American jurists have insisted that scrutinizing the severity of prison sentences is an invitation to lawlessness, the rest of the world has determined that a significantly more ambitious and demanding version of proportionality—one that eschews categorical rules in favor of structured balancing—is a foundation stone of the rule of law. Applying this version of proportionality, apex courts in Africa, Asia, Europe, North America, and South America have limited the penalties that may be applied to a growing set of drug users. In the concluding chapter, I will return to these cases and to the question of what they might teach the United States.

CHAPTER 5

· · ·

Freedom of Speech and Religion

WE COME TO the final set of constitutional arguments that lawyers in the 1960s and 1970s pressed against prohibitory drug laws. Invoking the First Amendment's guarantee of "free exercise" of religion, some drug defendants argued that they have a right to use illicit substances for sacramental or spiritual purposes. Invoking the First Amendment's guarantee of "freedom of speech," others argued that they have a right to use illicit substances to access new modes of cognition and perception, express dissent, and govern their minds.

A different class of drugs featured in this litigation. Whereas marijuana drove the liberty and rationality challenges, cocaine drove the racial equality challenges, and heroin drove the involuntariness challenges, the "classical psychedelics"—mescaline, psilocybin, ayahuasca, and LSD—were at the center of the First Amendment fight. The demographic composition of these cases differed as well, with Native Americans playing a leading role on the religious freedom front. And unlike the other constitutional arguments explored in the book thus far, the free speech arguments never quite made the jump from respected law journals to judicial rulings.

The Constitution of the War on Drugs. David Pozen, Oxford University Press.
© Oxford University Press 2024. DOI: 10.1093/oso/9780197685457.003.0006

The First Amendment advocacy story nonetheless traces a familiar arc, from dramatic early success to subsequent retrenchment and repudiation over the course of the 1970s. Here as well, it is instructive to identify the plausible constitutional paths not taken and to consider where they may have led us. In their heyday, the free exercise attacks on drug prohibition suggested what it might look like to flip the traditional religious opposition to illicit drug use on its head, while the free speech attacks suggested what it might look like to foreground freedom of thought as a constitutional value. The First Amendment jurisprudence that emerged instead from these struggles, as this chapter will show, trivializes the expressive, epistemic, and psychic harms of the war on drugs while subsidizing the speech of licit drugmakers.

THE FREE EXERCISE CLAUSE AND PEYOTE PREFERENTIALISM

For many decades, the Free Exercise Clause was understood to protect only religious beliefs, not religious acts. "However free the exercise of religion may be," the Supreme Court explained in the late 1800s, "it must be subordinate to the criminal laws of the country."[538] Otherwise, the clause would "in effect . . . permit every citizen to become a law unto himself."[539] Claims for religion-based exemptions from drug control laws, or from any other laws with a secular purpose, were nonstarters under this approach. Thus, when a member of the Native American Church (NAC) challenged his conviction for possession of peyote in the mid-1920s on the ground that NAC members used peyote exclusively "for sacramental purposes . . . in the worship of God," the Montana Supreme Court dismissed the challenge as "idle" under long-standing precedent.[540]

The U.S. Supreme Court began in the 1940s to move away from this belief/act binary and to suggest that the First Amendment will sometimes require special accommodations for religion.[541] In the 1963 case *Sherbert v. Verner*, the Court set out a strict scrutiny framework, according to which laws burdening free exercise must be justified by a "compelling state interest" that cannot be adequately achieved through less religion-restrictive means.[542] This doctrinal shift coincided with significant shifts in religious practice throughout the 1960s and 1970s. As part of what the Court described in 1965 as "the ever-broadening understanding of the modern religious community,"[543] an array of influential Judeo-Christian thinkers advanced "radically new views of God" along with nontheistic programs of social reform.[544] Mainline denominations lost ground. Among the churches and sects cropping up across the country, a small but visible subset—including Timothy Leary's League for Spiritual Discovery and Arthur Kleps's Neo-American Church—embraced illicit substances like LSD as an aid to mystical experience and self-actualization.[545] American religious life was becoming more pluralistic, personalistic, and psychedelic, at least in the younger age brackets. All of these developments, as one legal scholar observed at the time, tended "to erode the distinction between the sacred and the secular, between religion and culture."[546]

These shifts in law and society fueled an explosion of free exercise challenges to prohibitory drug laws. In 1960, an Arizona judge became the first to find that such a law unconstitutionally restricts religious freedom, in another case involving an NAC member convicted of possessing peyote.[547] Because this Arizona ruling contained no doctrinal analysis and was never published in a case reporter, the California Supreme Court's comparable ruling four years later in *People v. Woody* immediately supplanted it as the leading decision. *Woody*, too, involved Native American members of the NAC convicted of peyote possession. The California justices first determined that the state's peyote ban "most seriously infringes" upon the religious practices of the NAC, whose ceremonies revolve around the sacramental use of the mescaline-rich cactus and whose theology "combines certain Christian teachings with the belief that peyote embodies the Holy Spirit and that those who partake of peyote enter into direct contact with God."[548] The California attorney general had conceded as much. The justices then turned to the state's allegedly compelling interests in enforcing the ban: that peyote consumption threatens NAC members' health, "obstructs enlightenment," and "shackles the Indian to primitive conditions," while granting the NAC an exemption would invite fraudulent claims of religious immunity and enfeeble enforcement of the drug laws.[549] Each of these arguments, the justices found, rested on "untested assertions" and Eurocentric biases rather than credible evidence.[550] As applied to the defendants, the state's peyote policy therefore failed the *Sherbert* test.

Woody sparked nationwide reconsideration of bans on ceremonial peyote use. On the same day that it handed down *Woody*, the California Supreme Court granted a writ of habeas corpus to a "self-styled 'peyote preacher'" and remanded his case to the lower court to ascertain whether he consumed peyote "in connection with bona fide practice of a religious belief."[551] The Arizona Court of Appeals elected to follow *Woody* in a 1973 case with "startlingly similar" facts, as did the Oklahoma Court of Criminal Appeals in 1977.[552] Broader change came at the legislative level. Inspired in part by *Woody*, some two dozen states created exemptions from their controlled substances acts for religious use of peyote.[553] The federal government did so as well when it first banned peyote in the Drug Abuse Control Amendments of 1965, and then again with the Controlled Substances Act of 1970.[554] These initial federal bans were passed in an atmosphere of alarm over peyote's growing popularity in bohemian circles, which were sharply distinguished from Indigenous communities in the regulatory discourse.[555] In the quarter-century following *Woody*, the "clear trend" across the country was to pair general peyote prohibitions with religious carveouts oriented around the NAC.[556]

While these special legal protections for peyotism and the NAC became increasingly entrenched, attempts to extend *Woody* to other drugs and groups became increasingly hopeless. Drug offenders raised "*Woody* defenses" in a wide variety of contexts. They asserted free exercise rights to use LSD, magic mushrooms, marijuana, and more, in cases involving formal religious organizations whose dogma prescribed a certain mode of drug use and in cases involving unaffiliated individuals who took drugs for idiosyncratic spiritual reasons. Judges responded to these free exercise arguments with a wide variety of legal rationales. The one constant, as scholars of marijuana law quipped in 1970, was the result: victory for the government.[557]

Some courts resurrected the old act/belief distinction and refused to consider the free exercise claim in any depth.[558] Some courts found that the defendant had not used drugs pursuant to a genuine religious belief, either because their church was a sham[559] or because their drug use reflected a "personal philosophy and way of life" rather than a collective creed.[560] Some courts reasoned that the defendant's drug taking was not "indispensable" or "intrinsic" to their religion,[561] even though it was becoming increasingly accepted elsewhere in free exercise law that judges are not supposed "to question the centrality of particular beliefs or practices to a faith."[562] And many courts, including the vast majority of federal courts, ruled that however burdened the defendant's free exercise of religion might be, the state's interest in drug enforcement trumps.[563] *Woody*, it turned out, was easy to distinguish from other factual scenarios because of the defining role of peyote in the NAC's theology; the highly circumscribed, ceremonial manner in which peyote is used by NAC members; the church's relatively long institutional history (dating back to the 1910s) and prominent place in Indigenous culture; the special status of Native peoples in American law; and the relatively low risk of drug diversion to the general public, given both the geographic isolation of certain tribes and the minuscule commercial demand for peyote compared to the demand for a drug such as marijuana. Whereas the DEA had seized less than twenty pounds of peyote from 1980 to 1987, the government liked to point out in every marijuana case after that point, it had seized more than 15 million pounds of pot.[564]

Litigants had a little more success arguing that efforts to confine exemptions exclusively to the NAC, or to Native American members of the NAC, would violate principles of religious equality and the First Amendment's separate prohibition on "an establishment of religion."[565] But none of these rulings resulted in other groups being given permission to use a controlled substance. Courts largely followed the federal executive branch in characterizing the NAC's relationship to peyote as "sui generis."[566] Within the NAC, moreover, this emerging jurisprudence of exception "decisively shift[ed] the balance of power" toward those who opposed a more ecumenical and "racially inclusive approach to peyotism," further narrowing the impact of the one religious accommodation to the drug laws that had been granted.[567]

It was therefore of limited practical significance for the war on drugs when the Supreme Court stunned the legal community by ruling, in the 1990 case *Employment Division v. Smith*, that strict scrutiny is no longer the test for free exercise claims brought against neutral laws of general applicability. In line with *Woody*, the Oregon Supreme Court had held that a state law prohibiting sacramental use of peyote violated the free exercise rights of NAC members, as did a state law denying unemployment benefits to NAC members fired for such conduct.[568] The U.S. Supreme Court reversed. Justice Scalia, writing for the majority, argued that the Court's prior decisions invalidating or restricting the reach of generally applicable laws under the Free Exercise Clause were distinguishable because they had involved not just that clause but other constitutional rights as well; a peyote ban, by contrast, "does not present such a hybrid situation."[569] The dissenting justices accused the majority of "mischaracterizing" key precedents and effectuating "a wholesale overturning of settled law concerning the Religion Clauses of our Constitution."[570]

The irony of this accusation was that even when the Court had applied strict scrutiny in free exercise cases following *Sherbert*, the government almost always prevailed.[571] Outside the specific context of the NAC and peyote, *Smith* didn't change the outcomes in criminal cases so much as the manner in which they were reached—allowing judges to reject religious liberty defenses without purporting to demand that the state show a compelling interest or narrowly tailored means. The *Smith* test, as an Ohio appellate court remarked shortly after the decision came down, reduces free exercise attacks on drug laws "to a puff of smoke."[572]

STATUTORY SALVATION?

Smith stirred elected officials into action. The Oregon legislature quickly codified a religious-use defense to peyote prosecutions.[573] With the support of a broad coalition of religious and civil liberties groups, Congress went further and enacted the Religious Freedom Restoration Act (RFRA) in 1993 with the explicit aim of reinstating the *Sherbert* test that *Smith* had displaced.[574] The facts of *Smith* were ignored in the legislative debates, lest RFRA "become known as 'a drug bill.'"[575] One year later, however, Congress amended the American Indian Religious Freedom Act of 1978 to protect "the use, possession, or transportation of peyote by an Indian for bona fide traditional ceremonial purposes in connection with the practice of a traditional Indian religion."[576] This reform echoed the approach that Congress had taken nearly sixty years before when it exempted the sacramental use of wine by Roman Catholics, Jews, and others under the National Prohibition Act.[577]

In 1997, the Supreme Court reentered the picture and declared RFRA unconstitutional as applied to state and local laws. RFRA exceeds the scope of Congress's power to enforce the Fourteenth Amendment, according to the majority in *City of Boerne v. Flores*, because it attempts to effect "a substantive change in constitutional protections" rather than remedy or prevent conduct already deemed unconstitutional.[578] The message was clear: the Court, not Congress, gets to decide what the Constitution means. But RFRA remained intact at the federal level, so litigants could still invoke its compelling interest test when fighting federal drug charges. And the Court's decisions in *Smith* and *City of Boerne* led numerous states to enact their own "mini-RFRAs."[579] By the turn of the millennium, then, something approximating the pre-*Smith* approach to adjudicating claims of religious exemption had been cobbled together under a mix of federal statutes, state statutes, and state constitutional analogues to the Free Exercise Clause.

In this regime as in the pre-*Smith* regime, the vast majority of drug claims continued to lose. Following the template developed in the late 1960s and 1970s, some courts held that the defendants' drug-related beliefs were not religious in nature,[580] some courts held that the defendants' free exercise rights were not substantially burdened by the laws in question,[581] and some courts held that nothing less than a categorical prohibition could serve the government's compelling interest in drug enforcement.[582] All religious liberty claims involving marijuana failed, whether brought by solitary enthusiasts or by members of a recognized marijuana-centered religion such as Rastafarianism or the Ethiopian Zion Coptic Church.[583] Beyond the drug realm as well, minority religionists rarely prevailed under the federal and state RFRAs, just as they rarely prevailed under the Free Exercise Clause.[584]

These persistent patterns made it all the more noteworthy when the Supreme Court ruled unanimously in favor of a RFRA drug claim in the 2006 case *Gonzales v. O Centro Espírita Beneficente União do Vegetal* (UDV). UDV is a Christian Spiritist sect based in Brazil with a small stateside following. The U.S. government did not dispute that the federal prohibition on dimethyltryptamine, the active ingredient in the ayahuasca (or *hoasca*) used sacramentally by the sect, substantially burdens its sincere exercise of religion. The prohibition may nevertheless be applied to UDV members, the government insisted, because of its compelling interest in protecting their health, preventing the diversion of ayahuasca, and complying with international treaty obligations. These sorts of arguments were familiar in RFRA litigation. What was unfamiliar was the decisive, even disdainful, manner in which the Court rejected them. The alleged health and diversion risks are not only unproven, Chief Justice Roberts wrote, but the "well-established peyote exception also fatally undermines" any broader notion that the Controlled Substances Act requires uniform application.[585] This uniformity argument "echoes the classic rejoinder of bureaucrats throughout history: If I make an exception for you, I'll have to make one for everybody, so no exceptions."[586] But the whole point of RFRA was to make exceptions. And the possibility that the United States would be in breach of the Convention on Psychotropic Substances cannot take precedence over RFRA's commands.[587] As far as the *O Centro* Court was concerned, international law poses no barrier to domestic drug reform.

Many hoped that *O Centro* would invigorate RFRA jurisprudence with respect to psychedelics, if not across the board. Although UDV was an obscure outfit, the Court had portrayed the NAC's peyote exemption in positive terms while showing a new willingness to second-guess government fearmongering. In 2009, the federal district court in Oregon issued a similar ruling in favor of another

Brazil-based ayahuasca church, Santo Daime.[588] But few other litigants profited from *O Centro*. The DEA created a new process for reviewing petitions for religious exemption, only to deny every petition that came in.[589] And "*O Centro* quickly became an outlier rather than a stimulant to a new and tougher reading of RFRA."[590] Just as *Woody* had done a generation before, *O Centro* both catalyzed and constrained the pursuit of religious accommodation for illicit drugs—recognizing the potential sincerity and safety of such drug use, but only when the drug in question grows in the wild, lacks any significant commercial market, and plays a sacramental role in the practices of a church that mixes Christian and Indigenous elements.

The courts' reluctance to recognize additional exemptions to drug bans reflected, in part, their reluctance to recognize religious exemptions of almost any sort. Applying a rigorous compelling interest test to all laws that burden religion, Justice Scalia warned in *Smith*, would be "courting anarchy," given the enormous range of laws that might be implicated and the difficulty of balancing individual religious imperatives against secular policy ends.[591] In the past, such balancing could sometimes be avoided by denying the sincerity of the religious objector. But this tactic fell out of favor after the abolition of the military draft in 1973.[592] Judges forced to apply a compelling interest test since the early 1970s have generally assumed sincerity, and then found other ways to soften strict scrutiny and deny most religious liberty claims.[593]

Religious liberty claims involving illicit drugs were never likely to fare better than the norm. For a legal conservative like Justice Scalia, the anarchic potential of religious exemptions is magnified when the exempted conduct may have unpredictable, ecstatic, mind-altering properties. For evangelical Christians and other morally traditional faith groups, "drug cults" threaten their own exemption requests with taint by association. The leading organizations in the RFRA coalition might have been supportive of rulings such as *Woody* and *O Centro*, but they did not push to expand their reach. Nor have religious liberty claims involving illicit drugs had much success attracting institutional support or judicial solicitude in other countries' constitutional courts.[594]

Woody and the decisions that followed it thus leave an ambiguous legacy. In unusually frank terms, they confirm that prohibitory drug laws can do unjustified violence to religious values and respect-worthy communities. Yet rather than spark a broader reckoning with the costs of prohibition or the legacies of anti-Native racism, *Woody* ultimately led to licit psychedelic drug use being identified with—and confined to—a Christianized corner of "the indigenous realm."[595] In the process, *Woody* was converted from the bane of drug warriors into a public relations boon, allowing judges, legislators, and administrators to demonstrate their reasonableness and restraint while expanding access only to a small set of economically marginal substances. A specific sort of religious liberty claim was vindicated. A larger structure of illiberalism was legitimated.

SYMBOLIC SPEECH AND CHEMICALLY ASSISTED FREE INQUIRY

When Justice Scalia sought in *Smith* to distinguish prior decisions that had granted exemptions to generally applicable laws under the First Amendment, he characterized those decisions as involving "not the Free Exercise Clause alone, but the Free Exercise Clause in conjunction with other constitutional protections, such as freedom of speech."[596] It didn't seem to occur to Scalia that a peyote ban might present just such a "hybrid" situation. Yet as commentators argued throughout the late 1960s and 1970s, prohibitory drug laws may be in significant tension with free speech values.

These arguments came in two main varieties. Some maintained that illicit drug use is protected by the freedom of thought that underwrites the freedom of speech. Others maintained that illicit drug use can itself be a form of symbolic speech. Neither proposition made much headway in the courts, although both drew on growing bodies of free speech doctrine that plausibly pointed in their direction.

As the modern jurisprudence of the First Amendment began to take shape during the mid-twentieth century, its architects repeatedly described the freedom of thought as a fundamental component of, corollary to, or precondition for the freedom of speech. Justice Louis Brandeis, for instance, hailed the "freedom to think as you will and to speak as you think" as "indispensable to the discovery and spread of political truth."[597] Justice Oliver Wendell Holmes wrote that "if there is any principle of the Constitution that more imperatively calls for attachment than any other, it is the principle of free thought."[598] Justice Benjamin Cardozo opined that "freedom of thought and speech . . . is the matrix, the indispensable condition, of nearly every other form of freedom."[599] At points, the Court described the textually enumerated free speech right as "including" a right of free thought and free inquiry.[600] At other points, the Court reversed this relationship and described freedom of thought as "including" freedom of speech.[601]

Of most immediate relevance to critics of the drug laws, the Court's right-to-privacy decisions in the 1960s (discussed in chapter 1) contained strong language about the evils of government thought control. *Griswold* asserted that "the State may not, consistently with the spirit of the First Amendment, contract the spectrum of available knowledge."[602] *Stanley*, which has been described as "perhaps the Supreme Court's most forceful and extended defense of freedom of thought,"[603] explained that it "is now well established that the Constitution protects the right to receive information and ideas . . . regardless of their social worth" and that our "whole constitutional heritage rebels at the thought of giving government the power to control men's minds."[604] Around the same time, a separate line of Supreme Court cases broke new ground by recognizing antiwar activities that blurred the line between speech and conduct, such as the wearing of black armbands in school or the affixing of a peace symbol to an American flag, as protected speech under the First Amendment.[605] At the turn of the 1970s, constitutional doctrine was becoming increasingly attentive to the preverbal and nonverbal dimensions of free expression.

Legal liberals drew on these cases to articulate a new set of constitutional objections to prohibitory drug laws. The argument that drug use amounts to symbolic speech emphasized the *political* connotations of flouting these laws. Communal "pot-smoking," the segregationist senator James Eastland lamented in 1974, has been "embraced as a symbolic rejection of the establishment . . . throughout the American campus community" as well as other sites of social protest and bohemian experimentation.[606] In light of this well-known social fact and the Court's expressive conduct rulings, it became tenable to assert that "marijuana use constitutes symbolic speech because it implicitly expresses a rejection of majoritarian values."[607]

The argument that drug control amounts to thought control emphasized the *perceptual* effects of ingesting illicit substances. It was conventional wisdom within the counterculture that psychedelics and pot could help "free your mind," in the words of the Beatles and Funkadelic, and open "doors of perception," as Aldous Huxley had described his experiences with mescaline.[608] Law journal articles started to suggest in the late 1960s that drug prohibition might offend the Free Speech Clause insofar as it limits "a potentially vast source of information that may be revealed or elicited through [drug] use,"[609] blocking what one scholar called "chemically assisted free inquiry."[610] In the 1978 first edition of his renowned constitutional law treatise, Harvard Law School's Laurence Tribe brought these arguments into the academic mainstream by analogizing bans on psychoactive drugs to bans on "private fantasies" and "certain literary materials"—each of which could, like the anti-obscenity law at issue in *Stanley*, be seen as a "governmental invasion and usurpation of the choices that together constitute an individual's psyche."[611]

Expert witnesses, meanwhile, brought these arguments into the courtroom. During Timothy Leary's trial for marijuana charges, one psychopharmacologist testified that the "primary effect" of LSD, mescaline, and marijuana "is to expand consciousness [and] heighten intellectual activity and sensory awareness."[612] Before the Hawaii Supreme Court, a pair of defendants contended that "smoking marijuana opens up 'new sources of knowledge and information' by allowing an individual to heighten perceptions and sensation" and therefore comes within "the first amendment right to the reception of information and ideas, as conceptualized in *Stanley v. Georgia*."[613]

"GIVING GOVERNMENT THE POWER
TO CONTROL MEN'S MINDS"

Judges brushed off all such arguments. By the second half of the 1970s, few lawyers bothered to raise them. The Hawaii Supreme Court acknowledged in 1975 that the freedom-of-thought claim is "thought provoking," and seemed to imply that a symbolic speech claim might have merit, but it declined to apply First Amendment scrutiny because the U.S. "Supreme Court has never intimated that freedom of speech attaches to chemical substances which physically affect the workings of the brain."[614] This was the most sympathetic judicial discussion of the matter. Other courts asserted without explanation that drugs do "not enjoy the protection of the First Amendment,"[615] or else they invoked footnote 11 of *Stanley*, which cautioned that the Court's ruling on the right to possess obscene materials "in no way infringes upon the power of the State or Federal Government to make possession of other items, such as narcotics, firearms, or stolen goods, a crime."[616] That footnote certainly looked unhelpful for those who wished to build upon *Stanley*. Yet as recounted in chapter 1, the footnote was not legally binding. Nor did it deter legions of drug defendants from enlisting *Stanley* in support of their substantive due process claims. Nor are drugs like marijuana, mescaline, or magic mushrooms "narcotics." Pharmacologically and phenomenologically, they might be better described as euphoriants or "entheogens."[617] Something else must explain why civil libertarian groups such as NORML and the ACLU, reform-minded academics, and criminal defense attorneys invested so much more energy in developing privacy arguments for drug rights than in developing free expression arguments.

The free expression arguments, it seems, struck these lawyers as not only less likely to succeed but also potentially counterproductive. Symbolic speech claims are strongest when the act in question conveys a clear political message to third parties, as with the wearing of antiwar armbands. But the communicative content of drug use is generally far more ambiguous and attenuated, a byproduct rather than the main event. As one student author remarked in 1968, "While drug users may in some sense be trying to tell us something through their actions, the same may be said of virtually every one who does anything."[618] Moreover, constitutional claims that called attention to the public, performative aspects of drug use threatened to undercut privacy advocates' preferred depiction of it as an intensely personal, domestic affair.

The freedom-of-thought version of the free speech argument clashed with privacy advocacy in a different sense. Privacy proponents needed to demonstrate that certain substances can be consumed by adults at home without undue harm to public interests. Proponents of "chemically assisted free inquiry," on the other hand, needed to convince courts of these substances' epistemic or aesthetic *benefits.* The privacy rationale emphasized the risk of government overreach. The freedom-of-thought rationale emphasized the rewards of psychedelic experience. The privacy argument asked for the negative right to be let alone. The freedom-of-thought argument looked like it might press toward a positive entitlement to obtain speech-facilitating resources—just as the Court, in the early 1970s, was moving away from reading the Free Speech Clause to ensure such entitlements.[619] Some bold judges, like Justice Abe of Hawaii, may have been willing to recognize a "liberty to make a fool of [one]self as long as [one's] act does not endanger others."[620] None was willing to recognize illicit drugs as a gateway to "information and ideas."[621] So litigants stuck with privacy and abandoned free thought, even after Justice Scalia opened the door to "hybrid" First Amendment claims in *Smith*.

Yet whereas the symbolic speech argument for drug rights has all but disappeared since the 1970s, the freedom-of-thought argument has acquired a newfound prominence in recent years. Within the academic literature, Seana Shiffrin has put forward an influential "thinker-based" theory of free speech that "takes to be central the individual agent's interest in the protection of the free development and operation of her mind."[622] Although Shiffrin does not draw a connection to drug policy, her theory provides a high-level framework within which to challenge drug bans believed to interfere with this interest. In a similar spirit, Marc Blitz has advanced a sophisticated account of how the First Amendment protects "the power to make autonomous choices about the shape of the self that perceives, learns, archives, and re-imagines the world," including through the use of mind- or mood-altering drugs whose effects are not overly unpredictable or unsafe.[623] Since the 1960s, U.S. constitutional doctrine has taken a step in this direction by endorsing a right to *refuse* the administration of antipsychotic drugs, sometimes on the basis of First Amendment principles of intellectual autonomy as well as substantive due process principles of bodily autonomy.[624] And within the global community of psychedelic law reformers, the "cognitive liberty" case for decriminalization has gained ground alongside arguments focused on spiritual discovery, mental health, and palliative care.[625]

Progressive critics like to point out that contemporary First Amendment law fails to ensure access to many things that facilitate free speech, press, and petition, from education and government-held information to material goods of all sorts.[626] The same holds true for free thought. But these cognitive liberty advocates are not asking that the state supply anyone with magic mushrooms or other allegedly emancipatory technologies. They're asking that the state get out of the way and allow adults to purchase psychedelics on the private market. And as Professor Tribe observed nearly fifty years ago, if the Free Speech Clause entitles adults to consume obscene materials at home—even though obscenity itself is entirely unprotected by the First Amendment—it may seem "bizarre," "offensive," and "a bit preposterous" to criminalize the consumption of drug materials that enable new modes of sensation or cognition.[627]

The main obstacle to the cognitive liberty argument isn't that it is radical in form, then. On the contrary, the structure of the argument is consistent with *Stanley* and the deregulatory thrust of modern free speech law. The main obstacle is that not enough lawyers believe that illicit drugs can safely free your thought, and therefore your speech, in any special sense—although the rapid mainstreaming of psychedelic therapy and the critical success of works like Michael Pollan's *How to Change Your Mind* suggest this could be changing.[628] The architecture of constitutional doctrine remains amenable to this particular claim for drug rights, if and when orthodox legal culture accepts its empirical premises.

PROPAGANDA, PARAPHERNALIA, AND
COMMERCIAL ADVERTISING

This chapter has focused so far on challenges to prohibitory drug laws brought under the First Amendment's speech and religion clauses. At one remove from these direct constitutional challenges, First Amendment doctrine has also shaped and supported the drug war through the different sorts of protections that it has and hasn't bestowed on different categories of drug-related speech. In at least three main respects, the distribution of free speech rights has advantaged prohibitionists over reformers.

First, the many implausible, inflammatory, and inaccurate statements that government officials have made about the dangers of drugs and the track record of prohibition have not been seen to raise any First Amendment problems. The reason is what's known as the government speech doctrine. Initially implied by the Court in the late 1970s, this doctrine holds that "government speech is not restricted by the Free Speech Clause."[629] While the government is supposed to maintain neutrality when regulating the speech of private parties, it may express its own views without fear of First Amendment scrutiny just as long as it doesn't endorse a particular religion (which would bring the Establishment Clause into play). "Were the Free Speech Clause interpreted otherwise," the Court has warned, "government would not work."[630] Propaganda therefore gets a constitutional pass, whether intended to rally support for a conventional war abroad or a drug war at home.[631] The potentially corrosive effects on listeners, democratic deliberation, and the speech system as a whole are irrelevant.

Most constitutional scholars agree that the government needs broad legal latitude to promote its views, including in the form of warnings ("Don't drink and drive!") and urgings ("Talk to your kids about vaping!"). But there is no shortage of theories that would find certain sorts of government propaganda to violate the Free Speech Clause: for instance, when the statements are verifiably false and made with reckless disregard for the truth,[632] when they endorse positions incompatible with full citizenship in a free society,[633] when they manipulate consent on matters of collective self-government,[634] or when they amount to the functional equivalent of censorship.[635] And there is no shortage of examples of government statements about drug prohibition, in a rhetorical lineage dating back over a century, that arguably meet one or more of these criteria.[636] Readers who attended grade school in the United States between 1983 and 2009 may well recall being subjected to the Drug Abuse Resistance Education (DARE) program. DARE's antidrug indoctrination has been shown again and again to trade on spurious claims of harm.[637] No matter how misleading, such programs are immune from First Amendment scrutiny under the government speech doctrine.

Second, the Court has allowed the government to outlaw a wide range of expressive acts that directly or indirectly facilitate drug crimes. Since 1969, First Amendment doctrine has protected adults in most settings from being punished by the state for "mere advocacy" of illegal conduct.[638] In 2002, the U.S. Court of Appeals for the Ninth Circuit held that the First Amendment likewise protects physicians' "recommendations" of marijuana to patients.[639] Beyond that, the doctrine has not prevented school administrators from punishing student speech that could reasonably be viewed as promoting illegal drug use.[640] Nor has it prevented legislatures from criminalizing offers to sell illicit drugs or drug paraphernalia.[641] Nor has it prevented state and local officials from imposing special licensing and registration requirements on businesses that carry items associated with illegal drug use. Although many of these anti-"head shop" ordinances were struck down as unconstitutionally vague or overbroad throughout the 1970s, the case law dried up after the DEA introduced a Model Drug Paraphernalia Act in 1979 and the justices unanimously upheld an Illinois ordinance in 1982, notwithstanding what the appellate court described as "a genuine danger" that it would "be used to harass individuals choosing lifestyles and views different from those of the majority culture."[642]

Had these cases come out the other way, the drug war presumably would have raged on. But student activists, head shop owners, paraphernalia companies, and publications such as *High Times* would have been shielded from such harassment—and a subaltern set of pro-drug institutions would have had legal breathing room to develop into a more potent cultural and commercial force.

Finally, the Court in the late 1970s gave a powerful new First Amendment weapon to the class of companies with the strongest incentive to keep illegal drugs illegal: manufacturers and distributors of legal drugs. Prior to 1976, the First Amendment had been held to have no application whatsoever to "commercial speech." But in the landmark case *Virginia State Board of Pharmacy v. Virginia Citizens Consumer Council, Inc.*, the Court overruled this precedent and struck down a Virginia law that barred pharmacists from advertising prescription drug prices. Writing for the majority, Justice Blackmun emphasized society's "strong interest in the free flow of commercial information."[643] Shortly thereafter, the Court clarified that non-misleading commercial speech about lawful activities would be subject to intermediate scrutiny, meaning that the government must show that any restrictions on it are "narrowly drawn" to advance a "substantial" state interest.[644]

This commercial speech revolution in First Amendment law was launched in a progressive key. Supporters touted it as a means to curb professional monopolies, protect unsophisticated consumers, and bring down prices.[645] By the turn of the century, however, the political valence of commercial speech doctrine had "shifted radically," as conservative lawyers and judges seized on it as a means to attack economic regulation and advance a laissez-faire agenda.[646] In the process, they bore out the prediction of the lone dissenter in *Virginia Pharmacy*, Justice Rehnquist, that the Court's opinion would open the door "not only for dissemination of price information but for active promotion of prescription drugs, liquor, cigarettes, and other products the use of which it has previously been thought desirable to discourage."[647] Active promotion of all these products became pervasive in the early 2000s, from the endless alcohol ads on TV to the "nearly overwhelming ocean of marketing" for prescription drugs like OxyContin at the center of the current opioid crisis.[648] No other country's constitutional law has protected commercial drug advertising to such a degree.[649] And no other country's opioid epidemic has been as severe.[650]

Add up all these points, and it becomes evident that free speech doctrine hasn't just failed to protect drug users. It has also actively shifted power to prohibitionists and pharmaceutical companies and, in so doing, helped make the legal drug market more lethal. Constitutional scholars have chronicled the many ways in which contemporary First Amendment law can be seen as a "new *Lochner*" for its privileging of the economically powerful, disprivileging of vulnerable groups, and undermining of government capacity to regulate in the public interest.[651] The war on drugs has not been part of this conversation. The analysis in this chapter suggests that it should be. Ever since *Virginia Pharmacy*, First Amendment law has been both an engine of deregulation for licit drugs and a tool of entrenchment for the hyperregulation of their illicit counterparts.

CHAPTER 6

· · ·

The Conditions of Constitutional Complicity

THE PRECEDING CHAPTERS focus on constitutional arguments
made to and by courts. Offering a new critical history of drug
doctrine, they explain how lawyers in the 1960s and 1970s (among
other periods) exploited openings in the case law and the culture
to challenge drug prohibition. And they show how judges first facilitated and then foreclosed those challenges, in ways that were
responsive to internal jurisprudential dynamics as well as external
political developments.

This chapter zooms out to consider broader institutional and sociological features of the constitutional order that have constrained
possibilities for resistance to the war on drugs—by determining how
constitutional decisions get made, where they get made, and what
counts as a "constitutional" argument in the first place. Like the interpretive frameworks explored above, these features were promoted
by liberals as much as conservatives over the course of the twentieth
century. While each evolved to serve a rule-of-law function—to promote consistency, stability, and clear lines of authority in the legal
system—they worked in tandem to prop up punitive prohibitionism.

The Constitution of the War on Drugs. David Pozen, Oxford University Press.
© Oxford University Press 2024. DOI: 10.1093/oso/9780197685457.003.0007

In reviewing the case law, my aim has been to canvass every line of doctrine in which constitutional challenges to drug bans made any headway. The question of what to include in this chapter is less straightforward. The U.S. constitutional order comprises many different written and unwritten arrangements, all of which could, conceivably, have been restructured to be more favorable to the claims of drug users.[652] For instance, there could have been a norm on appellate panels of requiring unanimity to uphold criminal convictions or, as in Herodotus's account of the Persians, of taking important decisions once when sober and then again when drunk.[653] But most of these possibilities would strike most lawyers as far-fetched. Rather than aim for any sort of comprehensive catalogue, I focus here on structural features of American constitutional practice that have generated controversy within the legal community, that are not dictated by the Constitution itself, and that have been especially consequential for the war on drugs.[654]

WHAT COUNTS AS A CONSTITUTIONAL ARGUMENT?

To stand a chance of persuading courts to adopt any given reading of the Constitution, litigants have to play by some rhetorical rules. Only certain forms of argument, certain styles of reasoning, are considered legitimate within the legal profession for making claims about the content of supreme law. These argument-forms are known as the "modalities" of constitutional interpretation. They include appeals to the words of the canonical document (textual arguments), appeals to the understandings of its framers and ratifiers (originalist arguments), and appeals to judicial precedent (doctrinal arguments), among others. According to the leading account, the modalities dictate "the way we decide constitutional questions in the American legal culture."[655] They make up "a legal grammar that we all share and that we have all mastered."[656] Although there are endless disputes over how best to specify the modalities and apply them in particular cases, as well as potential shifts over time, there will be broad agreement in any era over the basic outlines of this grammar.[657]

If the modalities mark the boundaries of acceptable constitutional argument, what lies on the other side? Many forms of argument are seen as so irrelevant that they never come up at all—appeals to astrology, say, or to beauty or the tax code. But certain forbidden forms of argument are harder to dispel because they do seem relevant to the controversies that constitutional law is asked to resolve. Adam Samaha and I have described this category of claims that are considered illegitimate in debates over constitutional interpretation, despite being widely employed in nonlegal debates over issues of public policy and political morality, as *anti-modalities*.[658] Some of the anti-modalities involve styles of reasoning that would be dubious in any government decisionmaking context, such as appeals to in-group loyalties (partisan arguments) or to feelings that lack an articulable logical structure (emotional arguments). Other anti-modalities, however, banish from constitutional law sources of information and guidance that responsible regulators might find quite useful. The two most important examples are the norm against "policy arguments," which openly investigate the welfare effects of choosing one course over another, and the norm against "fundamentalist arguments," which draw directly on deep philosophical premises or comprehensive normative commitments.[659]

These are also the two most important anti-modalities for challenging the war on drugs, because they would have revealed its flaws in the harshest light. Under virtually any version of welfarist analysis, punitive prohibitionism has been a spectacular failure. Across time periods and jurisdictions, researchers have found that this regulatory approach yields little benefit for reducing dangerous drug behaviors—and is more often associated with *increases* in such behaviors—while imposing massive costs both in direct financial terms and in terms of fueling crime, corruption, incarceration, and social marginalization.[660] "Were drug laws subjected to the same scrutiny as prescription drugs," one scholar has observed, "those laws would immediately be withdrawn from the marketplace. Such laws cannot be shown to be either safe or effective."[661] The war on drugs likewise looks indefensible under various versions of liberal theory dating back to John Stuart Mill. While Millian or Rawlsian liberalism might allow for bans on substances shown to pose a significant risk of harming third parties or destroying users' capacity for self-rule, our criminal drug laws don't require any such showing to be made, and few of the substances targeted by them appear to meet either standard.[662] Perhaps it would be possible to draw on the perfectionist strand of liberalism, virtue ethics, or some other theory of the good to mount a rigorous defense of actually existing U.S. drug policies. Yet to my knowledge, no scholar has even attempted to do so.[663]

In short, if you were looking to demonstrate that punitive prohibitionism is unwise and unjust, some of your most compelling arguments would enlist cost-benefit analysis and liberal theory. Both sorts of arguments are commonplace in American regulatory debates. And both cannot be made in any straightforward manner in debates over constitutional meaning. The strongest consequentialist and deontological critiques are taken off the table.

This hasn't stopped litigants from bringing aspects of these arguments into the courtroom. As explained in chapters 1 and 2, defendants challenging the classification of marijuana on equal protection grounds have highlighted the perverse nature of these policies, while defendants challenging drug bans on due process grounds have highlighted the paternalistic incursion on their autonomy. Precisely because they are persuasive in other contexts, participants in constitutional debates often try to fold anti-modal considerations into their legal claims. But such efforts tend to be brief and unsystematic; anything more risks inviting accusations of doing policy or philosophy rather than law. The modalities alone determine what is "true from a constitutional point of view."[664] Although drug defendants may allude to the most glaring problems with prohibition, they must ultimately appeal to—and direct the bulk of their attention toward—the language of the constitutional text, judicial precedent, and the like.

In this area as elsewhere, the grammar of constitutional law thus detaches it from what matters to most people. This detachment can be a valuable thing. It can help to channel disagreement, constrain judges, and prevent law from collapsing into politics. Every system of constitutional decisionmaking needs *some* grammatical constraints to maintain its coherence as a discipline. The American constraints are unusually elaborate and abstruse, however.[665] And the costs of detaching constitutional interpretation from ordinary political-moral judgment are unusually high in a system that relies on interpretation to update supreme law, because the constitutional text itself is effectively unamendable.[666] Above all, Samaha and I contend, the prevailing anti-modalities "leave constitutional law without the resources to reckon, seriously and explicitly, with some of the most significant dimensions of social problems."[667] This point is well illustrated by the war on drugs—a set of policies that, by this juncture, no mainstream social scientist will defend and no mainstream constitutional jurist will denounce.

Within the modalities, moreover, still another rule of constitutional grammar prevents drug defendants from making the strongest version of their case: the norm against combining clauses. When litigants assert claims that arise under multiple clauses of the constitutional text, this norm counsels that "the strengths or weaknesses of one clause-specific claim . . . have no official bearing on the strengths or weaknesses of another."[668] A 50 percent persuasive free speech claim, a 60 percent persuasive due process claim, and a 90 percent persuasive cruel-and-unusual-punishment claim don't add up to a 200 percent persuasive juggernaut. They add up to a losing brief. Claims of constitutional rights violations are supposed to be resolved one by one, under whichever rights guarantee seems most relevant, rather than aggregated in any cumulative fashion.

As with the anti-modalities, this norm is fuzzy at the margins, and scholars have identified numerous complications and arguable counterexamples.[669] As with the anti-modalities, this norm is thought to serve rule-of-law values by limiting analytical complexity and judicial discretion. And as with the anti-modalities, this norm has been particularly debilitating for challenges to prohibitory drug laws, which—as the bulk of this book attests—impinge upon myriad rights even if they don't clearly violate any.[670] Challengers must make atomized arguments in court about each of the drug war's harms, when in their lived experience these harms overlap and exacerbate one another.[671]

HOW CAN UNJUST (BUT LAWFUL) PUNISHMENTS BE CHALLENGED?

Judicial doctrine is not the only constitutional mechanism that can protect against unjustified punishment. The U.S. Constitution expressly provides for two mechanisms of particular relevance: a guarantee of a jury trial by ordinary citizens before defendants can be convicted of a crime, plus the possibility of executive clemency afterward.[672] Courts stopped protecting drug defendants under the Cruel and Unusual Punishment Clause by the 1980s, as explained in chapter 4, even in cases where the sentence struck many as excessive. In theory, juries and pardons could have taken up some of the slack. In practice, both institutions collapsed over the late twentieth century.

The jury collapsed on two levels. First, as a large literature has documented, jury trials largely stopped happening. They were replaced, in more than 90 percent of criminal cases, with plea bargains in which defendants waive their right to a trial in exchange for reduced charges or other concessions.[673] The Supreme Court blessed the turn to plea bargaining in 1971, calling it an "essential" and "highly desirable" practice, just as legislatures around the country were beginning to eliminate parole and enact mandatory minimum sentences.[674] These developments greatly enhanced prosecutors' leverage to extract guilty pleas, which in turn greatly enhanced the system's capacity to handle large caseloads. The war on drugs never could have generated so many criminal cases, or produced so many prisoners, if plea bargains hadn't become "the new normal."[675]

Second, when trials did occur, jurors were largely blocked from "nullifying" laws they found unfair. Nullification refers to situations where the jury votes to acquit not out of a belief in the defendant's innocence but out of a disagreement with the law itself or with its application to the accused. Jurors have undoubted power to nullify, in that they deliberate in secret, they cannot be punished for their verdicts, and verdicts of "not guilty" are unreviewable. But under long-standing Supreme Court precedent, trial judges have no obligation to inform jurors that they possess this power.[676] And after defense attorneys started openly seeking nullification for draft resisters and peace activists during the Vietnam War, the judiciary shut down other information pathways as well. By the turn of the millennium, it had become standard procedure to dismiss prospective jurors who expressed openness to, or even awareness of, nullification.[677]

Judicial hostility toward nullification traded not only on perennial concerns about the legal system's consistency and stability but also on the memory of its use by racist white jurors to undermine civil rights statutes in the Jim Crow South. Against these concerns, a growing chorus of scholars and advocates argued that any legal tool can be used for good or for ill; that a popular check on prosecutorial excess is especially valuable in an era of mass incarceration and minimal appellate review of sentence severity; and that, as the U.S. solicitor general recently acknowledged, there is strong evidence that the Constitution's framers intended for the jury "to serve as the conscience of the community," including by "disregard[ing] clearly applicable law with which it disagreed."[678] Widespread nullification of federal liquor laws in the 1920s and early 1930s has been credited with "hasten[ing] the end of the prohibition of alcohol."[679] As Paul Butler suggested in a 1995 law journal article, it might have done something similar for the war on drugs if deployed to acquit Black defendants charged with non-violent drug offenses.[680] Butler's proposal sparked heated debate in the academy but little evident uptake in the courthouse.[681] Any such proposal is likely to remain academic unless and until the Supreme Court gives jury nullification its imprimatur.

If jury verdicts failed to rein in the drug war at the front end of the sentencing process, presidential and gubernatorial pardons failed to do so at the back end. The pardon power is one of the only executive powers in the U.S. system that Congress and the courts cannot restrict. Except in cases of impeachment, the president has virtually "unlimited," "unfettered" authority to pardon federal offenders or to commute their sentences.[682] Presidents may issue pardons for any reason they wish, on a case-by-case or categorical basis. Most state governors have similarly expansive, though somewhat more regulated, powers to grant clemency to state offenders.[683] If the president and all the governors decided to pardon every drug offender tonight, the war on drugs would be a hollow shell tomorrow.

In the final decades of the twentieth century, however, grants of executive clemency became vanishingly rare. Even as the federal and state prison populations soared over the one hundred thousand and one million marks, respectively, the rate of pardons and commutations started to fall during the Nixon, Ford, and Carter administrations and then slowed to a trickle under Presidents Reagan, Bush, and Clinton—averaging fewer than fifty per year across their administrations.[684] A parallel decline occurred at the state level.[685]

The same chief executives who were waging a war on drugs were never likely to dismantle it through their use of clemency. But even a small stream of regular pardons might have sent a cautionary signal to prosecutors and legislators. And certain classes of drug inmates, such as nonviolent first offenders sentenced to decades behind bars for low-level transactions, would have been obvious candidates for clemency in any regime that matched mercy to moral desert. During the 1960s, Presidents Kennedy and Johnson routinely pardoned and commuted mandatory minimum sentences under the Narcotics Control Act of 1956, "laying the groundwork for repeal of mandatory minimum sentencing laws in the 1970s."[686] During the past decade, Presidents Obama and Biden have begun to resuscitate the practice of drug pardons.[687] The political culture of the late twentieth century gave presidents and governors few incentives to do likewise, lest they be portrayed as soft on crime. More than that, chief executives feared being portrayed as arbitrary and abusive in a legal culture that had grown increasingly suspicious of unchecked discretion and increasingly dependent on courts to identify and rectify unfair applications of law.[688] As with the decline of jury nullification, the decline of clemency was enabled by the rise of a process-oriented, court-centric approach to legal decisionmaking that conflated mercy with lawlessness, justice with judicial review.

WHO DECIDES WHAT THE CONSTITUTION MEANS?

The court-centrism of American legal culture insulated the war on drugs from rights-based challenges in other venues as well. Outside the judiciary, even elected officials troubled by the war treated appellate decisions as the last word on its constitutionality rather than push back on their reasoning or advance an alternative constitutional vision. Inside the judiciary, state courts by and large followed the federal courts' interpretive methods and conclusions rather than protect rights more generously under their own constitutions.

Chapters 1 through 5 reviewed challenges to the drug laws on grounds of liberty, privacy, equality, federalism, government rationality, proportionate punishment, free speech, and more. By the 1980s, most of these challenges had lost in court. But their claims were credible at the time they were brought, as evidenced by the support they received from lower court judges and legal scholars. And nothing in the Constitution itself changed to make them any less credible afterward. Sympathetic members of Congress and the executive branch could have continued to press some of these claims in the court of public opinion—insisting, say, that the Fourteenth Amendment really does protect the personal possession of marijuana in the home. They did no such thing. Combing through the past six decades of the Congressional Record and the Federal Register, I have been unable to find any examples outside the religious liberty context of legislative or executive officials attempting to rebut courts' constitutional rulings on drug prohibition, or even engaging with their substance in a serious manner. Of course, many officials may have agreed with many of the rulings, as well as the drug laws themselves, and therefore seen nothing to discuss. But it cannot be the case that every official agreed with every ruling, if for no other reason than that the courts often contradicted one another before the doctrine settled.

To some extent, then, legislative and executive quiescence on drug rights has been the product of *judicial supremacy*, or the practice of treating courts as custodians of the Constitution. Americans today tend to assume that judges have the final say on what the Constitution means. This assumption is not clear from the text, structure, or history of the canonical document, however. Nor is it followed in a growing number of democracies around the globe, which allow their legislatures to reject courts' constitutional rulings under certain conditions.[689] Contemporary legal scholars broadly accept, as a rule-of-law imperative, that properly issued judicial judgments should bind the parties to a dispute.[690] But prominent voices on both the left and the right deny that Congress, the president, and other nonparties should be similarly bound by the courts' constitutional reasoning. Sometimes associated with labels such as popular constitutionalism, political constitutionalism, or departmentalism, the basic idea is that "the people themselves" and their elected representatives must exercise active, ongoing control over the elaboration of constitutional meaning, or else popular sovereignty yields to the dead hand of the past, while democracy devolves into juristocracy.[691]

Exactly when political actors ought to ignore the courts' constitutional pronouncements is a difficult and disputed question. No one disputes, however, that the legislative and executive branches may protect constitutional rights above and beyond what the courts require, provided they don't violate other constitutional constraints in so doing. In a classic article, Lawrence Sager explained that the federal judiciary systematically "underenforces" certain rights, relative to their "full conceptual limits," on account of judges' well-founded anxieties about their democratic authority to boss around elected officials as well as their functional capacity to prescribe enforceable standards.[692] Sager's thesis implies that courts in general, and federal courts in particular, will tend to give short shrift even to the strongest claims for drug rights—not necessarily because these claims are unpersuasive so much as because the judiciary is the wrong institution to vindicate them. Recall from chapter 2 that many of the judges who rejected challenges to marijuana laws in the 1970s went out of their way to acknowledge the laws' absurdity. In Sagerian terms, we might say that these judges were pleading with the legislature to enforce the constitutional guarantee of rational government to a fuller extent than they felt capable of.[693]

It was all too easy for legislators facing pressure to be tough on crime to disregard such pleas, given the norm of judicial supremacy. Inside and outside the halls of government, the major players in drug policy debates treated constitutional enforcement as a matter for the courts. When I asked NORML's former executive director why the organization didn't emphasize its constitutional objections to marijuana bans in public hearings and other venues, he replied that any such strategy was seen as a "nonstarter." Opponents would shoot it down by demanding, "Cite a case!"[694] The Religious Freedom Restoration Act's rebuke of *Smith* (discussed in the previous chapter) provides a partial counterexample from the 1990s. Beyond RFRA, there was no interbranch dialogue on issues relating to drug rights. There was only judicial fiat and legislative fealty.

We can't run the counterfactual to see how much constitutional creativity members of Congress might have mustered on these issues in a more departmentalist system. *Any* amount of independent constitutional thinking would have been higher than the observed total of zero, though. And while a broad-based legislative assault on the doctrine may be hard to imagine in the political climate of the late twentieth century, even the existence of a fringe group of libertarian representatives pushing for decriminalization in explicitly constitutional terms could have kept the idea of "drug rights" alive in the regulatory discourse and the constitutional imaginary.

If members of Congress deferred to the federal courts' constitutional reasoning to a questionable degree, state courts did something similar from within the judiciary. All fifty states in the union have their own constitution. These legal instruments typically contain many of the same rights guarantees found in the U.S. Constitution, along with a slew of others. In our system of federalism, it is uncontroversial that the state courts, when construing their state constitutions, may reach different conclusions from those reached by the federal courts on analogous questions of federal law. Around the time that the movement for constitutional drug rights was stalling out, in the late 1970s, Justice William Brennan famously called on state courts to "step into the breach" left by what he saw as the U.S. Supreme Court's inadequate protection of individual rights.[695] Yet while a cottage industry of "new judicial federalism" scholars echoed this call to protect rights beyond the federal floor, state judges declined to heed it. Instead, they followed in lockstep with their federal counterparts in "the clear majority of cases."[696]

State constitutional jurisprudence on drug prohibition illustrates this dynamic and its drawbacks. The basic pattern of doctrinal development mapped across chapters 1 through 5 is one of federal-state convergence. In the areas of due process, equal protection, cruel and unusual punishment, and free exercise of religion, a small number of state supreme courts issued innovative opinions in favor of drug defendants. Within a few years, however, the federal courts' readings of the federal Constitution's cognate clauses had set the de facto national standard, both in their pro-government bottom line and in their deferential style of review. Such doctrinal lockstepping had some arguable systemic benefits, insofar as it promoted uniformity in the law, allowed state judges to economize on decision costs, and impeded "judicial activism." But lockstepping also limited possibilities for cross-jurisdictional learning and experimentation, as well as potential pathways through which a policy fiasco might be condemned and corrected.

It is striking in this regard how well the leading state court opinions on drug rights—the innovative opinions that ended up as outliers more than trendsetters—have held up from a comparative constitutional perspective. The Alaska Supreme Court's privacy ruling in *Ravin v. State*, the Illinois Supreme Court's rationality ruling in *People v. McCabe*, the Minnesota Supreme Court's racial equality ruling in *State v. Russell*, the Michigan Supreme Court's excessive punishment ruling in *People v. Lorentzen*, the California Supreme Court's free exercise ruling in *People v. Woody*—each engages in a kind of fact-intensive balancing of individual interests and government goals that, as the next chapter explains, has become the dominant method of rights adjudication worldwide. Whether or not these courts' constitutional analyses are fully persuasive, they are at least plausible. And the war on drugs could hardly have gone any worse had more state courts been willing to follow their lead. Lockstepping locked the war's critics into a series of doctrinal deadends. Even as judicial supremacy choked off the development of alternative constitutional approaches in the political arena, federal constitutional hegemony choked off the development of alternative approaches in the judicial arena.

WHICH SORTS OF MOVEMENTS DRIVE
CONSTITUTIONAL CHANGE?

Constitutional change remains possible within these cultural and institutional constraints. The document itself is all but frozen, but new propositions of supreme law are routinely suggested to the federal courts, and occasionally adopted. In the area of civil liberties, the leading examples from the past half-century are the campaigns that led to the decriminalization of same-sex sodomy and recognition of same-sex marriage in *Lawrence v. Texas* and *Obergefell v. Hodges*, and to the recognition of a right to own firearms for self-defense in *District of Columbia v. Heller* and *McDonald v. City of Chicago*.[697] Why did those campaigns succeed so spectacularly while the constitutional campaign for drug liberalization achieved so little?

This discrepancy cannot easily be explained in terms of constitutional text, history, or precedent. As we have seen, state constitutions were widely interpreted in the 1800s to forbid bans on the possession or consumption of intoxicants. In the late 1960s, a generation after a disastrous national experiment with alcohol prohibition, drug-related rights began to gain traction in state and federal courts as well as the academy. By contrast, no judge in the 1960s or 1970s so much as hinted at the idea that the Constitution protects marriage equality or personal gun ownership.[698] The Second Amendment does expressly grant a right "to keep and bear arms." But it was blackletter law throughout the nineteenth and twentieth centuries that this right does not extend beyond the context of organized militias. Former Chief Justice Warren Burger, a Nixon appointee with conservative views on crime, described the emerging individual-rights view of the amendment in 1991 as "one of the greatest pieces of fraud, I repeat the word 'fraud,' on the American public by special interest groups that I have ever seen in my lifetime."[699] The constitutional arguments that would carry the day in *Obergefell* and *Heller* were *way* further out of the legal mainstream in the 1970s than, say, the argument that the right to privacy recognized in *Griswold* encompasses the choice to smoke pot in one's home.

Nor are the discrepant fates of these constitutional movements easily explained in terms of the number of Americans put at legal risk by the status quo ante. The 2007 National Survey on Drug Use and Health found that more than 100 million Americans had tried marijuana in their lifetime, including 25 million who had done so within the past year, and that 36 million Americans had tried cocaine and 34 million had tried hallucinogens such as LSD and Ecstasy.[700] Recreational use of all these drugs was illegal throughout the country. A Gallup survey from the same year found that 28 percent of U.S. adults, or approximately 63 million people, owned a gun—as was lawful to do in some form in every state—while a Williams Institute survey from 2011 found that approximately 9 million Americans identified as lesbian, gay, bisexual, or transgender.[701] These estimates are imperfect, and comparisons across the relevant identity categories and legal regimes are fraught. But even if one adopts the implausible assumption that every single gun owner and every single LGBT person committed gun- or sex-related crimes in the years before constitutional law protected personal firearm ownership and same-sex intimacy, there would still be millions more Americans who risked jail time at some point in their lives for consuming controlled substances. Beyond the historical *pedigree* and doctrinal *plausibility* of arguments for drug rights, the sheer *prevalence* of illicit drug use makes the failure of constitutional reform efforts in this area all the more striking.

Legal scholars who study social movements have identified a number of factors that seem to help explain, in general, why some movements succeed in changing constitutional law while others fail. Derrick Bell, for instance, famously proposed that courts will advance the civil rights of Black people and other marginalized groups only when doing so simultaneously advances the interests of middle- and upper-class whites.[702] Jack Balkin has written that social movements influence constitutional interpretation primarily by influencing the platforms of the major political parties and the values of national elites.[703] David Cole has emphasized the role played by nongovernmental organizations committed to constitutional rights.[704] William Eskridge has highlighted the distinctive strategies and capabilities of "identity-based" social movements.[705] And Reva Siegel has argued that reformers must "justify new constitutional understandings by appeal to older constitutional understandings that the community recognizes and shares," using "the language of a common tradition."[706]

Fully mapping these theories onto the movement for constitutional drug rights would require (among other things) a deep dive into the tactics and theories of the myriad actors who supported and opposed this cause, and therefore another book, but even a brief sketch may shed some light. To begin with, the sort of interest convergence envisioned by Bell never emerged. Although young Black men were arrested and imprisoned in the drug war at uniquely high rates, the Black community's response fractured along socioeconomic lines throughout the 1970s and 1980s, as recounted in chapter 3. Black politicians repeatedly endorsed punitive drug laws during this period *in the name of* civil rights, casting such laws as a means to protect beleaguered neighborhoods.[707] Among middle- and upper-class whites, meanwhile, socially conservative blocs such as religious evangelicals and suburban parents saw drug liberalization as a moral, cultural, and security threat, regardless of the fact that rates of teen marijuana use didn't increase in states that decriminalized in the 1970s any more than in states that retained their bans.[708] These blocs were never likely to join the movement.

More interesting was the refusal of the liberal professional-managerial class to align with subordinated racial minorities after the 1970s in any sort of antiprohibition coalition. The survey data suggest that the overwhelming majority of this class had personally used illicit drugs, especially marijuana, or at least had close friends and relatives who had done so. Recognizing this untapped source of political power, NORML initially "defined its constituency as middle-class college students and professionals" and framed marijuana legalization "as a mission to rescue white victims of the war on drugs."[709] Over the course of the 1970s, myriad establishment groups, including the ABA, the AMA, the American Public Health Association, the National Education Association, the National Student Association, the National Council of Churches, the Central Conference of American Rabbis, the Committee for Economic Development, and the Consumers Union, endorsed some form of marijuana decriminalization and, with it, some sort of broader shift away from punitive approaches to drug control.[710] Why didn't these groups find the drug war's subsequent escalation to be an ever-growing threat to their constituencies? Why didn't they team up and try to convince judges that certain prohibitory drug laws were putting their own children and grandchildren—"good kids"—at risk of unnecessarily harsh punishment?[711]

The hitch, of course, was that these children and grandchildren were not truly at risk of harsh punishment if they were white and well-educated. As scholars of mass incarceration have shown, almost all the growth in the prison population after the 1970s came from people without a college degree. By 2008, the incarceration rate for young male African American high school dropouts had climbed to 37 percent—roughly three times the rate for young male white high school dropouts and orders of magnitude higher than the rate for college-educated whites, which had barely budged since 1980.[712] The war on drugs helped drive the development of what sociologist Loïc Wacquant calls the "centaur state": liberal and humane at the top of the racialized social hierarchy, "brutally paternalistic and punitive" at the bottom.[713] White professionals and others at the top of the centaur state hardly ever served time in prison for nontrafficking drug offenses. If there was interest convergence between white and Black elites on drug doctrine, then, it proved more jurispathic than jurisgenerative, as both groups saw little to gain from new constitutional rights relative to their potential loss in security and status.

THE CONDITIONS OF CONSTITUTIONAL COMPLICITY

Yet while those at the top of the social hierarchy faced much lower odds of criminal punishment for their illicit drug use, no one was entirely in the clear. And prohibition limited their freedom in any number of lesser ways, from drug-testing mandates at work to the specter of humiliating exposure to the denial of access to a safe supply of their preferred intoxicants. Low levels of elite entanglement with the criminal justice system didn't hold back the cause of gay rights or gun rights. Unlike those campaigns, however, the campaign for drug rights lacked both identitarian glue and a mobilizing message that could propel state-level victories and, eventually, federal constitutional change.

The most successful constitutional rights movements of the twentieth century, on Eskridge's account, sought to enhance protections for "discrete and insular minorities" tied together by a shared social "identity."[714] Illicit drug users did not fit this description. Countless drug subcultures continued to exist after the hippies faded from the scene in the mid-1970s: Ecstasy-swallowing ravers, cocaine-snorting financiers, pot-smoking *High Times* readers, and on and on. But as a whole, illicit drug users were not so much a discrete and insular minority as an *anonymous and diffuse plurality* of the population: dispersed throughout all segments of society, poorly organized, largely in the closet.[715]

Nor did legal reformers seek to forge a common identity by depicting drugs as a beneficent force in their users' lives, as opposed to a tolerable vice, an object for "harm reduction," or at best a "recreational" diversion.[716] Such depictions would have been most plausible in the case of physically nonaddictive euphoriants. Recall that the Nixon administration's own health department sponsored a study in 1972 whose primary conclusion was that young people's use of psychedelics can be "highly moral, productive, and personally fulfilling."[717] Notwithstanding a burgeoning body of clinical research suggestive of such conclusions at the turn of the 1970s, liberal elites joined social conservatives in an epistemic contract of responsible-drug-use erasure—denying even the possibility, much less the reality, of prosocial drug taking.

Against this backdrop, the civil society organizations that litigated drug-rights claims, led by NORML and the ACLU, chose to rely almost exclusively on Warren Court cases rather than appeal to what Siegel calls "older constitutional understandings." They portrayed drug prohibition as a threat to privacy rather than a threat to identity, community, the pursuit of happiness heralded by the Declaration of Independence, or the American antipaternalist tradition tested by the temperance movement in the early 1900s but ultimately reinstated—and capital-P Prohibition relegated to the constitutional anticanon—when the Twenty-First Amendment brought booze back. Proponents of the drug war were not shy about demonizing drug users and linking drug use to social degeneracy. Their constitutional critics didn't fight fire with fire. They focused on the flaws of drug prohibition as an authoritarian mode of governance, without offering an account of how drug liberalization could contribute to a shared legal heritage or an attractive mode of living.[718]

The most pointed test of the epistemic contract of responsible-drug-use erasure came near the height of the crack panic, in November 1987, when NPR reported that U.S. Supreme Court nominee and federal appellate judge Douglas Ginsburg had smoked pot while a professor at Harvard Law School in the 1970s and "perhaps" the early 1980s.[719] Ginsburg was an unabashed libertarian. He would go on, in the mid-1990s, to pen a famous article assailing the New Deal settlement for "exiling" classical constitutional precepts of limited government and individual liberty.[720] The NPR disclosure presented the public with an undeniably impressive individual who had used illegal drugs while rising to the top of the legal profession. President Reagan at first stuck by his nominee, stating that Ginsburg was "not an addict" or anything "of that kind," citing his "remarkable credentials," and predicting that the American people would be "compassionate" and "wise" in forgiving him.[721] In a *Newsweek* poll conducted the day after the disclosure, 69 percent of respondents said that Ginsburg's pot smoking should not disqualify him.[722] The day after that, Ginsburg withdrew his nomination after politicians from both parties pointed out the obvious: that this "was not a youthful indiscretion," in Senate Majority Leader Robert Byrd's words, and that Ginsburg's elevation to the high court would fly in the face of the administration's zero-tolerance stance on drugs.[723] A story with no victims and no conflict had become a scandal.

It is at least conceivable, given the measured initial response, that Ginsburg's nomination could have facilitated a cultural shift toward greater differentiation among illicit substances and greater toleration of drug use consistent with mature professionalism. At the same time, Ginsburg's confirmation could have initiated a jurisprudential shift toward greater scrutiny of illiberal drug laws, especially at the federal level. What emerged from the episode instead was a reaffirmation of antidrug ideology, ratification of the "youthful indiscretion" trope as the preferred strategy of evasion for baby-boomer officials, and the rise of drug-related "litmus tests" and "character assassinations" as part of ordinary politics.[724] The Court lost a constitutional critic of paternalistic regulation. The country lost a chance to develop more nuanced norms on acceptable versus unacceptable drug behaviors.

* * *

In almost any system, it will be hard for social movements to change constitutional law. In the late twentieth-century United States, the success conditions for a movement seeking recognition of new substantive rights seem to have included (1) the sustained development of affirmative, identitarian narratives and arguments, (2) allegedly grounded in a shared legal tradition, (3) within a multiracial coalition including white elites whenever issues of racial equality were at stake. It is not at all obvious, as a normative matter, that any of these conditions ought to apply. As a sociological matter, it is hard to deny that they did. For reasons that I have begun to outline but that will need to be explored more fully in future work, the movement for constitutional drug rights failed to satisfy, and perhaps even to see, all three.

CHAPTER 7

. . .

New Directions for Constitutional Reform

LOOKING BACKWARD, THIS book has shown how a profoundly illiberal and moralistic policy regime was assimilated into, and came
to shape, an ostensibly liberal and pluralistic constitutional order.
Scholars of criminal procedure sometimes say that courts have created a "drug exception" to the Bill of Rights, relaxing restrictions on
police and prosecutors when illicit chemicals are at issue.[725] Yet if we
turn our gaze from procedure to substance—from questions about
how criminal laws are enforced to questions about what may be
criminalized in the first place—the drug cases look less exceptional
than representative, and in some areas formative, of the broader
legal landscape. *Most* litigants lose these days when they challenge
criminal statutes on grounds of personal privacy, racial equality, government rationality, proportionate punishment, or the like. Legal
liberalism and punitive paternalism have evolved hand in hand. As
a result, the doctrinal story of drug prohibition doubles as a tour
through some of the key features and failings, compromises and con-
tradictions, of late twentieth-century American constitutionalism.

The Constitution of the War on Drugs. David Pozen, Oxford University Press.
© Oxford University Press 2024. DOI: 10.1093/oso/9780197685457.003.0008

It didn't have to be this way. The very notion of "drug rights" now strikes U.S. lawyers as outlandish, maybe even oxymoronic. But as the book has also shown, many jurists and scholars argued for drug rights of one kind or another in the 1960s and 1970s, as did many jurists and scholars in the late 1800s and early 1900s. These arguments were plausible. They could have won out in this window. Constitutional law could have denied the worst excesses of the war on drugs, instead of becoming ever more defined by them. This study is thus an exercise in constitutional historicism as well as doctrinal realism, in the sense of demonstrating the "contingent character of what is falsely perceived as universal and eternal" and "combatting the fatalistic acceptance of the social order by recovering a sense of possibility that the social world"—the constitutional world—"could be otherwise."[726]

Yet while the country's disastrous experience with punitive prohibitionism invites us to recover a sense of constitutional possibility, the old arguments are unlikely to work, at least for the foreseeable future. The doctrinal doors that were open to litigants in the 1960s and 1970s have been closed; decades of unfavorable precedent stand in the path of those who would push on them now. At the same time, new doors may be opening on account of broad shifts in constitutional law and culture since the 1970s, along with the emergence of a broad consensus that the drug war has failed.

Looking forward, this final chapter briefly considers the two biggest shifts in constitutional practice that may enable challenges to punitive drug laws, before asking whether critics of these laws would do better to abandon the courts, and the Constitution itself, in the pursuit of more humane and effective policies. Reformers have already made significant strides on marijuana, at least, with the Constitution sitting on the sidelines. Do they need constitutional law at all to dismantle the war on drugs?

TURNING BACK THE CLOCK? ORIGINALIST OPTIONS

Within U.S. constitutional jurisprudence, arguably the most important development in recent decades has been the rise of originalism. There are many different strands of originalist theory, but the central claim uniting most of them is that the Constitution's words should be interpreted in accordance with their meaning to the public at the time they were written and ratified. Originalism wasn't a well-developed methodology before the 1980s. Although judges hearing constitutional cases might advert to the framers' intentions or linguistic choices, they drew on numerous other sources of interpretive guidance as well. Across the hundreds of drug decisions reviewed in this book, not a single one investigated the original public meaning of the relevant constitutional clauses in a rigorous fashion, much less took that meaning to be legally dispositive. In recent years, however, more and more judges and scholars have embraced originalism, to the point that it is routinely described as a "dominant" mode of constitutional interpretation.[727] Does this newly prominent approach offer any new resources for those who wish to challenge punitive drug laws?

I see four main possibilities. First, as noted in the previous chapter, scholars have already amassed substantial evidence that the criminal jury guaranteed by the Sixth Amendment was understood by the founding generation to have the right to decide questions of law, as well as questions of fact, and to refuse to apply laws with which it disagrees. In other words, originalism seems to support jury nullification.[728] Even those scholars who have argued against this conclusion acknowledge it to be the "conventional wisdom."[729] Were trial judges to start instructing jurors that they have this right, it hardly follows that the war on drugs would fall, given the eclipse of jury trials by plea bargains, the public's heterogeneous views on drug policy, and the reluctance many jurors may feel about disregarding clearly applicable laws. And for better or worse, the normalization of nullification wouldn't be limited to controlled substance cases. But at a minimum, drug defendants would have one more card to play in challenging harsh sentences and negotiating plea deals.

Second, an originalist approach might invigorate the Eighth Amendment's Cruel and Unusual Punishment Clause. The leading historical scholarship on this clause, by John Stinneford, suggests that it was understood in 1791 to prohibit punishments that are "unduly harsh in light of longstanding prior practice" or the defendant's moral culpability, reflecting the belief that "we most need to worry about cruelty when there is some kind of public panic that has driven the government to feel that it needs to get tough on crime."[730] This reading of the clause would sweep more broadly than the Court's anemic gross-disproportionality test. It might well rule out long prison sentences for low-level drug offenders, perhaps even for all nonviolent offenders.[731] If Stinneford's analysis is sound, faithful originalist judges have no choice but to do precisely what they have sought to avoid doing outside the capital context: scrutinize every criminal conviction to decide, based on legal history and retributive theory, whether "this sentence is too great but not that one."[732]

Third, many originalists believe that Congress's lawmaking authority under the Commerce Clause, and Article I more generally, has swelled beyond what the original understanding would permit. Justice Clarence Thomas, for instance, argued in dissent in *Gonzales v. Raich* (the medical marijuana case discussed in chapter 2) that "the Commerce Clause empowers Congress to regulate the buying and selling of goods and services trafficked across state lines," and no more.[733] Others have argued that the power to "regulate" commerce doesn't include the power to ban products altogether, or to ban products like marijuana that some states wish to allow within their borders.[734] If either position is correct, the federal Controlled

Substances Act needs to be scaled back to some significant degree—and the entire New Deal settlement needs to be rethought. Whereas most contemporary left-liberals would join most right-libertarians in cheering a revival of jury nullification or the Cruel and Unusual Punishment Clause, this reform would be much more controversial among the former group. Along with harsh penal laws like the CSA, such venerated statutes as the Clean Air Act, the Americans with Disabilities Act, and the Civil Rights Act of 1964 might find themselves vulnerable under any originalist rollback of congressional authority.

Fourth, while few originalists would read the Due Process Clause to protect recreational drug use, as advocates urged throughout the 1970s, such protections might be found elsewhere. The most obvious candidate is the right to pursue and obtain happiness, which is expressly guaranteed by most state constitutions, as explained in chapter 1, and which is plausibly one of the privileges or immunities of national citizenship guaranteed by the Fourteenth Amendment. These guarantees have done little doctrinal work in recent decades, and it is not at all clear where an originalist resurrection would lead.[735] Certain originalists contend that the Privileges or Immunities Clause protects against state infringement only those rights enumerated in the U.S. Constitution—leaving drug defendants in the same place they are now—while one historian has mused that the phrase "pursuit of happiness" is "as baffling, as confused, and as interesting an idea as ever appeared in a state paper."[736] Yet like my Columbia colleague Carl Hart, many drug users claim to be pursuing happiness in a eudaimonic (meaning-seeking) or at least a hedonic (pleasure-seeking) sense.[737] And other originalists contend that, together with the Ninth Amendment, the Privileges or Immunities Clause requires judges to safeguard unenumerated substantive liberty interests to a much greater extent than they currently do.[738] Of particular note, Randy Barnett has argued that judges must adopt "the presumption that in pursuing happiness persons may do whatever is not justly prohibited."[739] Drugs could still be restricted on this approach, but only if the government is able to convince courts that particular restrictions on particular substances are necessary to secure the rights of others.[740] Once again, progressives may welcome this doctrinal shift when it comes to criminal drug bans while deploring its deregulatory effects elsewhere.

Originalism, in sum, enables a number of new arguments against punitive prohibitionism. Whether they have any realistic shot at convincing courts in the short to medium term depends on many factors, including the degree to which they receive further academic development and support. But odds seem long at this writing. All of the arguments reviewed above are debatable within the increasingly byzantine terms of originalist theory; the latter two are already hotly contested. As many have chronicled, originalism emerged in the 1970s and 1980s as a partisan project in opposition to the perceived liberal excesses of the Warren Court. And originalism continues to have a strong conservative valence in the courts and in public discourse, even as scholarship on the subject has grown more intellectually sophisticated and ideologically diverse.[741] In practice, the Roberts Court has been highly selective about when it employs this methodology, and when justices in the majority do so, they tend to ignore or discount originalist scholarship that reaches progressive conclusions.[742] Even though opposition to the war on drugs has become mainstream among legal elites, support for decriminalization is much spottier beyond marijuana. The dismissive dicta on drug rights in *Dobbs* suggests that this Court, at least, is more interested in moralizing against illicit drugs than in leading any sort of libertarian vanguard.[743]

At this stage in its theoretical development, originalism is capable of generating many surprising outcomes, including protections for drug offenders. At this stage in its political development, however, originalism remains tied to a conservative movement that has shown little appetite for such surprises—or for drug liberalization.[744] Unless and until this changes, reformers may have more success investing in an interpretive approach that has already taken hold in some U.S. state courts and become the dominant method of rights adjudication outside our borders.

TURNING TOWARD THE WORLD?
PROPORTIONALITY POSSIBILITIES

While the U.S. judiciary was turning toward originalism in recent decades, courts throughout the rest of the world were turning toward proportionality review. As with originalism, proportionality is more a family of principles and practices than a single methodology. The basic idea is that "larger harms imposed by government should be justified by more weighty reasons," and the basic approach is to assess intrusions on rights against the public good they are said to serve.[745] Typically, judges employing proportionality take an expansive view at the outset as to the scope of the relevant right; in one famous case, the German Constitutional Court conceded without discussion that the right to free development of one's personality protected by Germany's Basic Law encompasses the feeding of pigeons in a park.[746] The judges then devote most of their analysis to evaluating, through a structured series of tests, whether the government is pursuing a legitimate objective in a rational and minimally rights-impairing manner and, if so, whether the benefits to the public are sufficient to warrant the cost to the rights-bearer.[747]

Proportionality review is often contrasted with the "categorical" approach taken by U.S. courts, which relies less on balancing competing interests in light of the facts and more on threshold classifications as to what type of right is at issue, what type of regulation, what type of claimant, and so on. This contrast can be overdrawn, as many areas of U.S. constitutional law incorporate elements of proportionality or their functional equivalents.[748] But the contrast helps highlight how, relative to constitutional jurisprudence elsewhere in the world, U.S. jurisprudence lavishes attention on a narrow set of rights while scanting the mine run of liberty and equality claims that don't trigger a heightened standard of review. All such claims get taken seriously under proportionality, though many still lose. Jamal Greene describes proportionality as "a kind of intermediate scrutiny for all," in which a "certain promiscuity in declaring rights to exist is accompanied by a certain austerity in elevating interference with rights into violations of them."[749]

Applying proportionality review, courts in a diverse array of democracies have limited or eliminated criminal penalties for personal possession of marijuana and other substances prohibited under the U.N. drug treaties. In one of the first such cases, the Supreme Court of Argentina invalidated the country's criminal ban on possession of drugs for personal use in 1986, and then did so again in 2009 after reversing course in the interim.[750] Colombia's Constitutional Court followed suit in 1994.[751] Citing this case, the Inter-American Juridical Committee of the Organization of American States has written that "[c]onstitutional courts are increasingly ruling that the decision to use narcotic drugs or psychotropic substances falls within the scope of the moral autonomy of adults and may only be criminalized when such use harms third parties or puts them at serious and immediate risk."[752]

Also in 1994, the German Constitutional Court effectively decriminalized cannabis by holding that criminal penalties may not, "as a general rule," be imposed for behavior that is "merely preparatory to the personal consumption of small amounts" and that "does not pose any danger to third parties."[753] Apex courts in the Eastern Caribbean, Georgia, Italy, Mexico, and South Africa have handed down comparable cannabis rulings over the past decade.[754] Beginning in 2000, Canadian courts have issued a series of decisions protecting the use of marijuana for medical purposes.[755] And any number of appellate tribunals have reduced drug punishments determined to be disproportionate, as when the England and Wales Court of Appeal ruled in 2001 that a twelve-month sentence for a Rastafarian who had pleaded guilty to possession of ninety grams of marijuana with intent to supply was "manifestly excessive."[756]

These rulings—which span five continents—vary in numerous respects. Some apply only to marijuana, while Argentina's and Colombia's apply in principle to any drug. Some consider consequences for religious practice, while most confine the inquiry to secular harms. Some explore evidence on health effects in greater depth than others. What all the rulings share is a commitment to investigating in earnest whether the privacy and autonomy costs of criminal drug bans are justified by the public benefit, not because drug use is "fundamental" or enjoys special status in the constitutional text but simply because the decision to use drugs implicates individual freedom.[757] This approach does a better job of addressing critics' core objection to prohibitory drug laws—that they may limit people's liberty unnecessarily and counterproductively—than do the more categorical analyses performed by most U.S. courts.

It is no coincidence, then, that the leading U.S. decisions finding for drug defendants have broken out of the categorical mold and employed a kind of ersatz proportionality review. Nor is it a coincidence that these decisions come from state courts, which seem to have a greater propensity for proportionality than do their federal counterparts.[758] As chapter 1 highlighted, in *Ravin* the Alaska Supreme Court rejected the U.S. Supreme Court's "two-tier" approach to substantive due process as too "rigid," opting instead to resolve Ravin's privacy claims much like a foreign court would: "by determining whether there is a proper governmental interest in imposing restrictions on marijuana use and whether the means chosen bear a substantial relationship to the legislative purpose."[759] In *Russell*, the Minnesota Supreme Court likewise eschewed both strict scrutiny and traditional rational basis review in favor of something in between, in recognition of the crack cocaine law's "substantially disproportionate burden" on Black residents of the state.[760] In *McCabe*, the Illinois Supreme Court spent no time assessing the meaning of equal protection and many paragraphs assessing "the relevant scientific, medical, and social data" on marijuana.[761] In *Lorentzen*, the Michigan Supreme Court tested the defendant's sentence against the legislature's ostensible goals and found it "in excess of any that would be suitable to fit the crime."[762] In *Woody*, the California Supreme Court "weighed the competing values represented in this case on the symbolic scale of constitutionality."[763] Echoing these themes, some of the most forceful dissents in U.S. drug cases have chided the majority for "not balancing the rights infringed, on the one hand, against the State's interest in the proscription effected by the statute, on the other."[764] Virtually every single time U.S. judges have voted to rein in draconian drug laws, they have been applying the techniques, if not the rhetoric, of proportionality review.

Although proportionality has delivered the most drug-friendly constitutional rulings here and abroad, it has failed to deliver such rulings in many more jurisdictions—and by its nature is incapable of dismantling drug prohibition. Courts applying proportionality review continue to defer to legislatures and administrative agencies on contested empirical questions, perhaps above all on questions of public health and safety.[765] More distinctively, proportionality does not treat constitutional rights as "trumps" that prevail whenever they apply, absent exceptional circumstances.[766] Rather, in Robert Alexy's well-known formulation, proportionality treats most rights as "principles" to be weighed against "competing principles" in light of "what is factually possible."[767] Proportionality, unlike categoricalism, abides by an ethic of balance; it is the antithesis of a winner-takes-all system.

Thus, the German Constitutional Court afforded the legislature what Alexy describes as "empirical epistemic discretion" on the question whether cannabis should be banned, even as it ruled out criminal charges for personal use, while the Alaska Supreme Court limited *Ravin*'s holding to the home and refused to extend it to physically addictive substances like cocaine.[768] And even the most libertarian proportionality rulings have allowed the state to continue to restrict drug production, distribution, and possession with intent to distribute.[769] In all of these jurisdictions, proportionality has yielded what we might call a *harm reduction jurisprudence*, aimed not at maximizing privacy or pleasure but at mitigating the most egregious effects of punitive drug laws for individual users.[770] Those who wish to eradicate such laws will be disappointed. Proportionality is not a recipe for full legalization or penal abolitionism in any country where the elite sees significant competing interests at play in drug policy—which is to say, in every country. Others may welcome the possibility for constitutional compromise, embracing proportionality as a flexible tool for curbing the most destructive drug policies while preserving a large role for the state in safeguarding public health.

Proportionality's potential to serve as such a tool may be limited in the United States, however. As previous chapters have detailed, the U.S. Supreme Court has sought to avoid case-by-case line drawing in favor of relatively rigid formulas across many areas of constitutional review. Most judges here seem content to remain global outliers in declining to adopt proportionality analysis across the board, or to develop anything comparable to a right to free development of personality. In the main line of doctrine that polices proportionality by name, the review of sentences for disproportionality under the Cruel and Unusual Punishment Clause, the Court's decisions have been almost brazen in their vacuity, "messy and complex yet largely meaningless as a constraint."[771] The standard criticisms of proportionality—that it leads to excessive inconsistency and indeterminacy in the law and to insufficient respect for legislatures and for rights themselves—resonate with both American legal liberals and conservatives. The U.S. Constitution's emphasis on negative rights held against the state arguably makes proportionality a poor fit.[772] And at least at the federal level, U.S. courts may not currently be configured to do proportionality well, owing to a lack of "reliable mechanisms for adjudicating empirical disputes over the facts" and a lack of experience with "the kind of remedial discretion that goes hand in hand with treating cases contextually."[773]

American judges are proficient in a specific sort of hermeneutics, focused on excavating meaning from authoritative legal materials. But in proportionality review, as Greene observes, "The question for the adjudicator is not primarily what the rights in the Constitution 'mean.' Rather . . . the question is whether the facts of the particular dispute form a sufficient basis for the government to have acted as it did."[774] To answer this latter question with any rigor, U.S. courts would need to deploy not only relatively unfamiliar styles of justification but also relatively unfamiliar analytical methods and information-gathering procedures.

Drug-rights cases, moreover, present distinctive difficulties for proportionality review both empirically and conceptually. Psychoactive substances come in many varieties—the CSA covers over five hundred at this writing—each class of which might be said to warrant its own fact-intensive analysis, updated on an ongoing basis as new evidence emerges.[775] Different illicit drugs have very different effects on users, and therefore very different implications for third parties and for society at large. Not only that, the *same* drug may have very different effects depending on the user's psychological and physiological makeup and motivation as well as dosage, purity, social setting, and other environmental factors. Across a research domain rife with controversy, perhaps the most fundamental finding about drug outcomes is that they are thoroughly "contingent and situated."[776] In response to the question whether any given psychoactive substance is dangerous or safe, the correct answer always is: both.

None of this is to deny that some drugs are more dangerous than others. As discussed in chapter 2, there is an enormous amount of evidence to suggest that marijuana and magic mushrooms are significantly safer on aggregate than, say, heroin or crystal meth. Although all firearms can kill, courts have little trouble recognizing that handguns are safer than machine guns. The point is that determinations of drug dangerousness are far from straightforward, even assuming mastery of the medical literature, given that no drug is risk-free and that every drug's risk profile varies by context.

The difficulties compound when one considers risks and rewards beyond objective measures of health. Drug law challengers have emphasized the autonomy costs of prohibition, with good cause. But what if a drug turns out to be so debilitatingly addictive that it overwhelms users' moral agency, robbing them of their free will as well as their dignity? In such a case, the value of autonomy may cut both for and against prohibition (though not necessarily for criminalization). Just how small this category of drugs is, and indeed whether *any* widely used drug deserves to be placed in it, presents another contested question mixing descriptive and normative elements.[777]

Beyond asserting their autonomy, proponents of drug rights often contend that illicit substances enable shifts in consciousness or feeling that would be difficult to achieve any other way, that drugs open their hearts and minds to otherwise unattainable perspectives, profundities, and pleasures. These phenomena cannot be measured in a lab. They may not even be fully comprehensible to those who insist on them, especially when they have a mystical or "noetic" aspect.[778] And yet these phenomena cannot be ignored, or else any balancing of the drug user's interest against the public interest becomes lopsided, akin to a cost-benefit analysis in which the hardest-to-quantify benefits are assigned a value of zero. As with certain disputes over religious liberty, the concern that proportionality requires judges to weigh incommensurable factors may have special bite when mind-altering substances are at issue. Some of the core interests at stake in drug prohibition are not just different in kind from one another but difficult to subject to sober analysis—inaccessible to outsiders, ineffable to insiders.

In a phrase, drug disputes may involve not only a clash of research methodologies and cultural sensibilities but also a clash of epistemologies. They pit technocratic expertise, as reflected in the testimony of drug scientists and government officials, against the embodied experience and intuitive knowledge of the drug users themselves.[779] Proportionality review provides a framework in which all sides to these disputes can be heard and, crucially, in which policy failures can be identified and less restrictive options considered. But the disputes cannot be neatly contained within the juridical form. The strongest claims for drug rights strain the bounds of professional legal reason, if not of reason itself.

TURNING AWAY FROM THE COURTS . . . AND THE CONSTITUTION?

Perhaps, then, courts and constitutional law are not the best institutions in which to press the case against punitive drug laws. The doctrinal pathways still open to U.S. lawyers are strewn with obstacles; traveling down them too far could lead to any number of unintended deregulatory consequences as well as judicial aggrandizement in other areas of public health and safety. Outside the courts, meanwhile, drug reform is already underway. More than twenty states have legalized marijuana for adult use over the past decade or so, with the federal government's increasingly explicit consent; federal and state officials are considering approval of psychedelics, including MDMA and psilocybin, for therapeutic applications; and harm reduction policies of various kinds now attract bipartisan support. Litigation has contributed almost nothing to this shift away from criminal regulation.

Against this backdrop, it is unclear whether any significant expenditure of time or money in a constitutional campaign would be a wise investment. There is little risk that such a campaign would backfire in a direct doctrinal sense, given how few favorable precedents remain. On the other hand, there is little reason to expect that the conservative Roberts Court majority would support this struggle. As discussed in chapter 6, the prevailing grammar of American constitutional law doesn't allow litigants to foreground the strongest arguments against punitive drug laws. They have "to scramble around constructing [claims] out of the scraps of some sacred text," as Jeremy Waldron once put it, rather than focus on how these laws do far more harm than good.[780] Launching a constitutional campaign would have opportunity costs, insofar as it diverts scarce resources from other forms of advocacy. It could also have political costs if losses in court are seen to vindicate the status quo or if the legalistic case against drug prohibition distracts policymakers from—or de-radicalizes—the most urgent moral demands for reform.

These sorts of pitfalls to pursuing social change through constitutional litigation generalize well beyond the drug context. They help explain why constitutional law has been on the sidelines of other justice struggles in recent years, from Black Lives Matter and Occupy Wall Street to the Fight for $15 and the Green New Deal.[781] Attorneys who brought test cases against drug laws in the 1960s and 1970s maintained that "the courtroom is a better forum for airing the facts" on politically charged questions, which "may be resolved by the judiciary more quickly and more rationally than by the legislative branch."[782] Yet as a long line of scholars have documented, the ability of courts to bring about social change is significantly hampered by their detachment from mass politics and dependence on the other branches, among other factors.[783] Some scholars on the left go further and suggest that it is not just constitutional litigation but the U.S. Constitution, or constitutionalism writ large, that is anathema to the pursuit of progressive goals.[784] I myself have argued that, as a general matter, we should be looking to narrow the domain of constitutional law—accepting that it is an inherently flawed tool for resolving social controversies and therefore aspiring to reduce the number of questions on which it is expected to provide authoritative answers.[785] Like Bonnie and Whitebread, I "prefer legislative reevaluation" to "judicial invalidation" when it comes to fixing our drug laws, and most everything else that's wrong with our society.[786]

That all said, there are reasons to think that it would be a mistake for drug reformers to give up on the Constitution altogether. For one thing, constitutional arguments can be addressed to audiences other than courts. Just because the judiciary has declined to enforce, say, a right to possess psychedelics or to remove marijuana from Schedule I of the CSA doesn't mean that these rights don't exist. The courts could have misinterpreted the Constitution. Although the parties to these lawsuits may be bound by the courts' judgments, no one in political office has to adopt their analysis. Moreover, courts often choose to "underenforce" substantive rights on account of institutional constraints specific to the judiciary, as chapter 6 explained. It is therefore perfectly possible to insist that the legislature and executive have a constitutional duty to treat drug users or sellers better than the courts require, without insisting that the courts have made any interpretive errors. Constitutional demands on Congress and the DEA need not seek defiance of judicial rulings, just recognition of their inherent limitations in this area.

It is also possible to advance different kinds of constitutional arguments to legislatures and executives. All of the constitutional arguments in U.S. drug litigation have involved claims of a negative right to be spared state coercion. They beseech the government to *punish drug users less.* In other countries, drug reformers have joined these arguments to claims of a positive right to receive state support—typically in the form of guaranteed treatment for addicts who seek it and guaranteed healthcare provision generally.[787] They beseech the government to *help drug users more.*

A right-to-health framework not only deemphasizes criminal responses to drug abuse but also redirects attention toward its most immediate harms and deeper drivers alike. Although there is slim precedent for U.S. courts construing the Constitution to supply such positive rights, Joseph Fishkin and William Forbath have shown that earlier generations of liberal and progressive reformers routinely asserted that the Constitution, taken as a whole, compels the elected branches to meet people's basic social and material needs.[788] If contemporary reformers were to revive this tradition, as Fishkin and Forbath urge, health policy would be a plausible place to start.[789]

There is no assurance that such efforts would succeed, of course, and there is always a risk that they would elicit backlash or crowd out more fruitful strategies.[790] Had judges recognized a limited right to personal drug use a generation ago, it conceivably could have preempted the recent rise of legislative legalization of marijuana, although judicial and legislative reform tended to complement rather than cannibalize each other throughout the 1970s. Figuring out exactly which arguments against the war on drugs to "constitutionalize" is therefore a delicate task, outside the courts as well as inside. Yet given the U.S. culture of constitutional veneration, it seems unlikely that *none* of the arguments merits constitutionalization of any sort. In staying silent about the Constitution in their appeals to legislatures, executives, and the general public, contemporary drug reformers have been ceding the legal and rhetorical high ground to prohibitionists while conceding the norm of judicial supremacy over constitutional meaning that has served similar movements poorly in the past.

The case for reviving constitutional argumentation inside the courts is more straightforward. Despite the policy progress that has been made of late, the war on drugs is still underway. More than 1.5 million drug arrests were made in the United States in 2019, yielding more than 240,000 criminal prosecutions.[791] The lawyers for these defendants have a professional responsibility to be "zealous advocates for their clients."[792] And as their predecessors in the 1960s and 1970s demonstrated, a wide range of colorable constitutional arguments can be mounted against prohibitory drug laws. Of all these arguments, claims based on cognitive liberty and religious liberty may have the best chance of convincing judges in the near term, thanks to the growing recognition among American elites that psychedelics can contribute to both of these interests, as well as the Roberts Court's special solicitude for libertarian claims brought under the First Amendment. Even if few of the old arguments would stand a chance in federal court today, their very existence should remind the defense bar and its civil society allies that such laws have been vulnerable, at times, to constitutional attack. As this chapter has outlined, a new wave of originalist arguments awaits development and deployment in the federal courts (which have become increasingly interested in originalism), while a new wave of proportionality arguments awaits development and deployment in the state courts (which have become increasingly open to the practices of proportionality).

The opportunity costs of turning to the courts can be steep for social movements that aren't already in the day-to-day business of litigating. But with thousands of Americans being prosecuted for drug crimes each week, courts are going to remain intimately involved in supervising drug policy whether reformers appeal to their constitutional conscience or not. Under these conditions, the downside risks of seeking judicial recognition of new constitutional rights are reduced. Lawyers leading such litigation efforts could reduce them further by coordinating with drug policy NGOs, formerly incarcerated activists, and grassroots organizing campaigns to ensure a basic alignment of strategies and priorities. Even if courts cannot solve many aspects of our drug problems, they could at least serve as a brake on overpunishment and force lawmakers to confront the costs of prioritizing criminal prohibition over social provision.

In her much-noted 2019 article "Abolition Constitutionalism," the legal scholar Dorothy Roberts acknowledged that the courts and constitutional law have done little to advance the cause of abolishing prisons, leading many who support the cause to give up on them. Against this defeatist impulse, Roberts recommended that prison abolitionists "use constitutional provisions instrumentally to assert and sometimes win their claims," even as they "imagine a new constitutionalism based on the society they are working to create."[793] This sort of fusion of instrumentalism and idealism may be especially apt for drug war abolitionists, given how many different U.S. constitutional provisions plausibly condemn punitive drug laws and how many different democracies have witnessed successful constitutional campaigns for drug decriminalization in recent years. American drug politics has been characterized by cycles of racialized moral panic and reactionary policymaking, punctuated by periods of liberalization. Now that we find ourselves in another moment when humane, evidence-based drug reform is a realistic possibility, drug reform is a realistic possibility, proponents would do well to entrench as much of it in constitutional law as they can before the next panic arrives.

In the drug policy context, furthermore, court rulings alone might enable the United States to de-carceralize without running afoul of its international treaty commitments. For the world to move fully beyond the war on drugs, the U.N. drug treaty regime will at some point have to be remade. This regime, however, continues to have powerful supporters in the pharmaceutical industry and in the governments of China, Russia, and countries across Africa, Asia, and the Middle East.[794] Comparatively speaking, domestic drug reform is easy. Yet as noted in the book's introduction, the U.N. treaties allow parties to refrain from penalizing illicit substances if their courts determine that such penalization would be unconstitutional. (It is less clear, as a matter of international law, whether a legislative or executive determination of unconstitutionality could trigger these "get-out" clauses.)[795] Those U.S. government officials who wish to decriminalize drugs like marijuana while maintaining compliance with the U.N. treaties should therefore welcome judicial rulings that criminal bans on these drugs violate the Constitution. Such rulings could help solve a thorny problem in international law at the same time that they facilitate and consolidate the ongoing turn toward harm reduction.

* * *

In suggesting all of these ways in which punitive drug laws might be challenged on constitutional grounds, I don't mean to suggest that I know the best way to deal with drug abuse. All I insist is that locking people in cages for nonviolent drug behaviors is a proven failure under any plausible definition of failure. Likewise, I don't mean to suggest that there are clear answers to most of the legal questions explored within these pages. All I insist is that criminal drug bans raise many potential constitutional problems, and that these problems ought to be taken seriously. Whether or not the old litigation campaigns can offer inspiration or ideas for new campaigns, they ought to remind everyone involved in drug policy debates—including scholars, activists, journalists, legislators, and administrators—that punitive drug laws have always been in deep tension with some of our country's deepest normative commitments. Judges are not the only ones who may find this constitutional history lesson instructive.

Acknowledgments

. . .

For years now, I have been struck by the marginal role of "rights talk" in U.S. drug policy debates. Our country is known for constitutionalizing almost every significant social issue. Punitive drug laws threaten a range of individual liberties and collective values. And generations of American lawyers have challenged drug prohibition in court, with some notable successes. What happened to those lines of argument, that mode of advocacy? How did the Constitution fall out of the picture? When Geoffrey Stone invited me to contribute to the Inalienable Rights series, I saw an opportunity to investigate this erasure and what it might teach us about the development of both the war on drugs and our constitutional system.

My first thanks, then, go to Geof for the invitation and for his steadfast support of the project—an unusual one for the series in that it pursues a novel line of inquiry rather than synthesize or expand upon prior work. (Hence the copious endnotes.) This book wouldn't exist without him. Thanks also to Alexcee Bechthold and David McBride at Oxford University Press and to Jubilee James at Newgen, who helped see the manuscript through production.

ACKNOWLEDGMENTS

A remarkable group of Columbia law students served as research assistants for the book. It was a privilege to work with Josh Berlowitz, Ebba Brunnstrom, Julia Fay, Jack Jones, Stephany Kim, Bennett Lunn, Alexandra Nickerson, Jacob Rosenberg, Josceline Sanchez, and Theo Tamayo. For additional assistance in tracking down sources, I thank Columbia Law School librarians Josh Freeman, Samantha Lim, Mariana Newman, Lena Rieke, Hunter Whaley, and Nam Jin Yoon.

Numerous colleagues at Columbia and elsewhere provided helpful feedback on portions of the manuscript. I owe particular thanks to Aslı Bâli, William Baude, Richard Bonnie, Rosalind Dixon, Harold Edgar, Jonathan Gould, Jamal Greene, Olatunde Johnson, Andrea Katz, David Landau, Matthew Lawrence, Youngjae Lee, Daryl Levinson, James Liebman, Robert Mikos, Christopher Morten, Samuel Moyn, Shaun Ossei-Owusu, Kate Redburn, Juannell Riley, Thomas Schmidt, Karen Tani, Caitlin Tully, Katharine Young, and Benjamin Zipursky, as well as workshop participants at Columbia, Fordham, the Knight First Amendment Institute, NYU, Vanderbilt, and a virtual convening hosted by Bijal Shah and Justin Weinstein-Tull. I also thank two former leaders of NORML, Peter Meyers and Keith Stroup, for granting me interviews to discuss the organization's constitutional strategy in the 1970s.

I owe a special debt of gratitude to a clutch of colleagues who engaged with this project in particular depth, over the course of many months and multiple iterations. For their friendship, generosity, and insight, I am immensely thankful to Ashraf Ahmed, Michael Boucai, Josh Chafetz, Jeremy Kessler, Madhav Khosla, Anna Lvovsky, Jedediah Purdy, Aziz Rana, Daniel Richman, Russell Robinson, and Sarah Seo. For his sustaining encouragement as well as many stimulating conversations, Noam Elcott has my deep appreciation.

ACKNOWLEDGMENTS

My most profound gratitude goes to my partner in all things personal and professional, Jessica Bulman-Pozen. In addition to being the love of my life, Jessica is my toughest reader, constant interlocutor, and moral compass. It is my incredible good fortune to share my days with Jessica and our miraculous children, Sam and Clara. I dedicate this book to her.

Notes

. . .

INTRODUCTION

1. In the absence of the war on drugs, these rates conceivably could have gone up even further. But I know of no theory or evidence to support that counterfactual.

2. John F. Galliher, David P. Keys & Michael Elsner, *Lindesmith v. Anslinger: An Early Government Victory in the Failed War on Drugs*, 88 J. CRIM. L. & CRIMINOLOGY 661, 681 (1998) ("[W]hile drug researchers may disagree on the best method of dealing with drug abuse, they nearly all agree that the current policy is an abject failure."); *see also* Mark Kleiman, Book Review, 14 J. POL'Y ANALYSIS & MGMT. 473, 475 (1995) ("[T]he observable costs of U.S. drug control efforts—violence in illicit markets, theft to buy drugs at artificially enhanced prices, and the imprisonment at any moment of some 300,000 people—hugely outweigh the observable damage done by the drugs themselves."). Both of these sources are from the 1990s. Since then, the scholarly consensus on the drug war's destructiveness and futility has only grown stronger.

3. With apologies to Charles Black. *See* Charles L. Black, Jr., *The Lawfulness of the Segregation Decisions*, 69 YALE L.J. 421, 422 n.8 (1960).

4. Marijuana Opportunity Reinvestment and Expungement Act of 2020, H.R. 3884, 116th Cong. (2020). Shortly before the 2022 midterm elections, President Joe Biden pardoned all federal convictions for simple

possession of marijuana and ordered an "expeditious" review of marijuana's scheduling under the Controlled Substances Act. *See Statement from President Biden on Marijuana Reform*, WHITE HOUSE (Oct. 6, 2022), https://www.whi tehouse.gov/briefing-room/statements-releases/2022/10/06/statement-from-president-biden-on-marijuana-reform/ [https://perma.cc/59AT-293M]. That review was still in progress at the time this book went to press.

5. Andrew Jacobs, *The Psychedelic Revolution Is Coming. Psychiatry May Never Be the Same*, N.Y. TIMES (May 12, 2021), https://www.nytimes.com/2021/05/09/health/psychedelics-mdma-psilocybin-molly-mental-hea lth.html [https://perma.cc/W3R5-AVB8].

6. STEVEN WISOTSKY, BEYOND THE WAR ON DRUGS: OVERCOMING A FAILED PUBLIC POLICY 173 (1990).

7. *See* Ely Aaronson, *The Strange Career of the Transnational Legal Order of Cannabis Prohibition, in* TRANSNATIONAL LEGAL ORDERING OF CRIMINAL JUSTICE 176, 194–96 (Gregory Shaffer & Ely Aaronson eds., 2020) (discussing implications of this "issue linkage"); David Bewley-Taylor, *The Creation and Impact of Global Drug Prohibition, in* THE OXFORD HANDBOOK OF GLOBAL DRUG HISTORY 303, 303 (Paul Gootenberg ed., 2022) (describing the "twin reinforcing imperatives" of the U.N. drug treaties).

8. Single Convention on Narcotic Drugs art. 36(1)(a), Mar. 30, 1961, 520 UNTS 151; Convention on Psychotropic Substances art. 22(1)(a), Feb. 21, 1971, 1019 UNTS 175; Convention Against Illicit Traffic in Narcotic Drugs and Psychotropic Substances art. 3(2), Dec. 20, 1988, 1582 UNTS 95.

9. On these constitutional escape clauses, see NEIL BOISTER, PENAL ASPECTS OF THE UN DRUG CONVENTIONS 125–27 (2001). The recent wave of marijuana liberalization measures, together with mounting opposition to the war on drugs from developing countries and from international health and human rights organizations, has thrown the future of the U.N. drug control regime into doubt. For an overview, see Symposium, *Drug Decriminalization, Legalization, and International Law*, 114 AJIL UNBOUND 275 (2020).

10. Richard J. Bonnie & Charles H. Whitebread, II, *The Forbidden Fruit and the Tree of Knowledge: An Inquiry into the Legal History of American Marijuana Prohibition*, 56 VA. L. REV. 971, 976 (1970); *see also Ex parte* Luera, 152 P. 738, 738 (Cal. App. 1915) (reviewing "abundant authority" in support of this proposition); Lindsay Rogers, *"Life, Liberty, and Liquor": A Note on the Police Power*, 6 VA. L. REV. 156, 167 n.23 (1919) (characterizing the legal

literature prior to 1917 as "unanimous in maintaining that constitutional provisions protected possession" of alcohol for personal use).

11. The dozen states were Alaska, California, Colorado, Maine, Minnesota, Mississippi, Nebraska, New York, North Carolina, Ohio, Oregon, and South Dakota. There are many models of drug decriminalization. By "decriminalizing marijuana," I mean that these states eliminated or minimized criminal penalties for possession of small amounts. South Dakota arguably deserves to be dropped from the list because its legislature reversed course before decriminalization took effect. *See* Nev. Legis. Rsch. Div., *Marijuana Penalties* 4 (Background Paper No. 79-8, 1979), https://www. leg.state.nv.us/Division/Research/Publications/Bkground/BP79-08.pdf [https://perma.cc/SUN5-VSLY].

12. Peter G. Bourne, *The Great Cocaine Myth*, 5 DRUGS & DRUG ABUSE EDUC. NEWSL., Aug. 1974, at 5; *see also* DAVID F. MUSTO, THE AMERICAN DISEASE: ORIGINS OF NARCOTIC CONTROL 268 (3d ed. 1999) (discussing the "calm with which experts until the early 1980s viewed cocaine consumption").

13. Among the most influential of these books were RICHARD J. BONNIE & CHARLES H. WHITEBREAD II, THE MARIHUANA CONVICTION: A HISTORY OF MARIHUANA PROHIBITION IN THE UNITED STATES (1974); EDWARD M. BRECHER & EDITORS OF CONSUMERS REPORTS, LICIT AND ILLICIT DRUGS (1972) [hereinafter CONSUMERS UNION REPORT]; LESTER GRINSPOON, MARIHUANA RECONSIDERED (1971); JOHN KAPLAN, MARIJUANA: THE NEW PROHIBITION (1970); DAVID F. MUSTO, THE AMERICAN DISEASE: ORIGINS OF NARCOTIC CONTROL (1973).

14. For a broad historical account of this period, see MUSTO, *supra* note 12, at 230–71. For a summary of the blue-ribbon commissions in the United States, Canada, Great Britain, Australia, and the Netherlands that uniformly "directed strong criticism towards the criminological and medical underpinnings of the prohibitionist approach," see Aaronson, *supra* note 7, at 182–83. *See also infra* notes 232–49 and accompanying text. For a discussion of the antimarijuana parents' movement, see EMILY DUFTON, GRASS ROOTS: THE RISE AND FALL AND RISE OF MARIJUANA IN AMERICA 123–64 (2017). For budgetary data, see KATHLEEN J. FRYDL, THE DRUG WARS IN AMERICA, 1940–1973, at 364 (2013), which describes how federal spending on drug enforcement rose from $3 million in 1968 to $224 million in 1974,

while spending on drug treatment rose from $18 million in 1966 to $350 million in 1975.

15. Mark Soler, *Of Cannabis and the Courts: A Critical Examination of Constitutional Challenges to Statutory Marijuana Prohibitions*, 6 CONN. L. REV. 601, 641 (1974).

16. Bonnie & Whitebread, *supra* note 10, at 1123. "The waste of time, money and other resources of the criminal justice system on enforcement of marijuana laws can no longer be justified," a Michigan appellate judge opined in a representative lament. "Much more significant, however, are the inestimable costs to both individuals and society of making criminals of decent human beings and the encouragement of the citizenry, particularly the young, to disrespect and distrust our laws and those who make and enforce them." Joslin v. Fourteenth Dist. Judge, 255 N.W.2d 782, 787 (Mich. App. 1977) (Burns, J., concurring).

17. People v. Sinclair, 194 N.W.2d 878, 891 (Mich. 1972) (Williams, J., concurring) (joined by Chief Justice Kavanagh).

18. Robinson v. California, 370 U.S. 660 (1962).

19. Leary v. United States, 395 U.S. 6 (1969).

20. HOWARD BROMBERG, MARK K. OSBECK & MICHAEL VITIELLO, CASES AND MATERIALS ON MARIJUANA LAW 55 (2019).

21. "If the legislative process continues to stall," the leading analysts of marijuana law wrote in 1970, "we predict that the judiciary will no longer restrain itself." Bonnie & Whitebread, *supra* note 10, at 1170. Similar predictions appeared in high-level government reports. *See, e.g.*, NAT'L COMM'N ON MARIHUANA & DRUG ABUSE, MARIHUANA: A SIGNAL OF MISUNDERSTANDING app. at 1134 (1972); NAT'L GOVERNORS' CONF. CTR. FOR POL'Y RSCH. & ANALYSIS, MARIJUANA: A STUDY OF STATE POLICIES AND PENALTIES 124 (1977).

22. *See, e.g.*, KAPLAN, *supra* note 13, at xi ("[I]n the long run, the only course of action available within the framework of a democratic society . . . is a liberalization of the marijuana law so extensive as to constitute an abandonment of primary reliance on the criminal law in this area."). A professor at Stanford Law School and a former federal prosecutor, Kaplan was neither an alarmist nor a drug enthusiast. Another Stanford law professor, Herbert Packer, argued in a renowned 1968 book that drug use is categorically unfit for criminalization: "A clearer case of the misapplication of the criminal sanction would be difficult to imagine." HERBERT L. PACKER, THE LIMITS OF THE CRIMINAL SANCTION 333 (1968).

23. *See* AMALIA D. KESSLER, INVENTING AMERICAN EXCEPTIONALISM: THE ORIGINS OF ADVERSARIAL LEGAL CULTURE, 1800–1877, at 8 (2017) ("[I]nternalists insist that legal change is primarily a product of developments internal to law and legal institutions as such . . . . In contrast, externalists believe that law and society are inextricably linked, such that there is no way to understand developments in law without relating them to socioeconomic, political, and cultural change more generally."); *see also, e.g.,* Laura Kalman, *Law, Politics, and the New Deal(s),* 108 YALE L.J. 2165 (1999) (reviewing debates in the legal literature between internalists and externalists in explaining constitutional change during the New Deal).

24. Substantial bodies of scholarship address each of these topics. For an analysis of the drug war's "racial and spatial logics," see Matthew D. Lassiter, *Impossible Criminals: The Suburban Imperatives of America's War on Drugs,* 102 J. AM. HIST. 126 (2015). For an analysis of the 1980s drug panic in historical context, see ERICH GOODE & NACHMAN BEN-YEHUDA, MORAL PANICS: THE SOCIAL CONSTRUCTION OF DEVIANCE 197–217 (2d ed. 2009). For an analysis of the drug war's financial benefits for law enforcement agencies, see Eric Blumenson & Eva Nilsen, *Policing for Profit: The Drug War's Hidden Economic Agenda,* 65 U. CHI. L. REV. 35 (1998).

25. MUSTO, *supra* note 12, at vii.

26. Kenji Yoshino, *The Epistemic Contract of Bisexual Erasure,* 52 STAN. L. REV. 353 (2000).

27. 537 P.2d 494, 512 (Alaska 1975) (punctuation added); *see also* Young v. Hampton, 568 F.2d 1253, 1265 n.17 (7th Cir. 1977) (cataloguing "leading United States agencies and prominent associations recommending the removal of criminal penalties for the private possession and use of marijuana").

28. *Cf.* Michal Buchhandler-Raphael, *Drugs, Dignity, and Danger: Human Dignity as a Constitutional Constraint to Limit Overcriminalization,* 80 TENN. L. REV. 291, 336 (2013) (observing that rights-based claims are rarely made today in the context of drug laws, "in sharp contrast to other areas involving victimless crimes, such as the criminal regulation of sexual practices").

29. 142 S. Ct. 2228, 2258 (2022) (citing Compassion in Dying v. Washington, 85 F.3d 1440, 1445 (9th Cir. 1996) (O'Scannlain, J., dissenting from denial of rehearing en banc)). Justice Alito cited no sources for this assertion apart from a dissent by a contemporary conservative judge. The assertion would be difficult to defend, as the next chapter explains, given both the existence of judicially enforced constitutional limits on alcohol

regulation and the absence of laws restricting other drugs throughout much of the country prior to the 1900s.

30. At this writing, the latest anthology is *The War on Drugs: A History*, published by NYU Press in 2022. Apart from a passing reference to the Eighteenth Amendment, constitutional law does not come up once in this impressive volume's more than three hundred pages.

31. For an accessible summary, see JOANNA R. LAMPE, CONG. RSCH. SERV., R45948, THE CONTROLLED SUBSTANCES ACT (CSA): A LEGAL OVERVIEW FOR THE 118TH CONGRESS (2023).

32. Matthew R. Pembleton, *The Globalization of US Drug Enforcement*, *in* THE OXFORD HANDBOOK OF GLOBAL DRUG HISTORY, *supra* note 7, at 433, 433. There is likewise no consensus on how to define "drugs." *See* Paul Gootenberg, *A New Global History of Drugs*, *in id.* at 1, 12 (calling this the "central puzzle" in the field).

33. Richard Nixon, Remarks About an Intensified Program for Drug Abuse Prevention and Control, PUB. PAPERS 738, 738 (June 17, 1971).

34. *See, e.g.*, ELIZABETH HINTON, FROM THE WAR ON POVERTY TO THE WAR ON CRIME: THE MAKING OF MASS INCARCERATION IN AMERICA 310 (2016) (arguing that the Comprehensive Crime Control Act of 1984 "marked the official beginning of the War on Drugs"); FRANKLIN E. ZIMRING & BERNARD E. HARCOURT, CRIMINAL LAW AND THE REGULATION OF VICE 247 (2d ed. 2014) ("Beginning in 1985 . . . a multi-front 'war on drugs' was launched in the United States that both expanded the total punishment system and increased the share of total prison space attributable to drugs.").

35. *See, e.g.*, FRYDL, *supra* note 14, at 1 ("Between World War II and 1973, the United States transitioned from a regulatory illicit drug regime to a prohibitive and punitive one."); SUZANNA REISS, WE SELL DRUGS: THE ALCHEMY OF US EMPIRE 2 (2014) ("[The Nixon presidency] was not the beginning of the purported war on drugs, but rather the culmination of transformations over the previous three decades . . . .").

36. *See* RUSSELL CRANDALL, DRUGS AND THUGS: THE HISTORY AND FUTURE OF AMERICA'S WAR ON DRUGS 134 (2020); REISS, *supra* note 35, at 197.

37. *See, e.g.*, Craig Reinarman & Harry G. Levine, *Punitive Prohibition in America*, *in* CRACK IN AMERICA: DEMON DRUGS AND SOCIAL JUSTICE 321, 321 (Craig Reinarman & Harry G. Levine eds., 1997) ("Punitive prohibition came into existence in the United States in the 1920s and has been the dominant U.S. drug policy since that time.").

38. Alex Kreit, *Marijuana Legalization and Pretextual Stops*, 50 U.C. DAVIS L. REV. 741, 745 (2016).

39. MICHELLE ALEXANDER, THE NEW JIM CROW: MASS INCARCERATION IN THE AGE OF COLORBLINDNESS (2010); *see also* Kreit, *supra* note 38, at 743 n.14 (collecting sources analyzing the drug war's impact on Fourth Amendment law).

40. Bonnie & Whitebread, *supra* note 10, at 1125.

41. ALEXANDER, *supra* note 39, at 101; *see also* PAUL BUTLER, LET'S GET FREE: A HIP-HOP THEORY OF JUSTICE 50 (2009) ("Here's the problem: drugs are illegal, and they are easy to hide; for police to find them, they have to look hard, which often means they invade the privacy of innocent people."). Over fifty years ago, commentators warned that "[a] disturbingly large number of undesirable police practices . . . have become habitual because of the great difficulty that attends the detection of narcotics offenses," with the burden of enforcement falling "primarily on the urban poor, especially [African Americans] and Mexican-Americans." PACKER, *supra* note 22, at 332–33; *see also* NAT'L COMM'N ON MARIHUANA & DRUG ABUSE, *supra* note 21, at 145 ("Possession of marihuana is generally a private behavior; in order to find it, the police many times must operate on the edge of constitutional limitations. Arrests without probable cause, illegal searches, and selective enforcement occur often enough to arouse concern about the integrity of the criminal process.").

42. *See* MICHAEL TONRY, MALIGN NEGLECT: RACE, CRIME, AND PUNISHMENT IN AMERICA 105–07 (1995); William J. Stuntz, *Race, Class, and Drugs*, 98 COLUM. L. REV. 1795, 1799–815 (1998).

43. On this terminological choice, see *infra* note 314.

44. *See* DOUGLAS A. BERMAN & ALEX KREIT, MARIJUANA LAW AND POLICY 201 (2020); BROMBERG ET AL., *supra* note 20, at 682; JACOB KAPLAN, UNIFORM CRIME REPORTING (UCR) PROGRAM DATA: A PRACTITIONER'S GUIDE § 2.1.3.1 (2023).

45. *See* Ryan S. King & Marc Mauer, *The War on Marijuana: The Transformation of the War on Drugs in the 1990s*, HARM REDUCTION J., Feb. 2006, at 3, 4 ("Our analysis indicates that the 'war on drugs' in the 1990s was, essentially, a 'war on marijuana.'"); Lassiter, *supra* note 24, at 137 ("The perceived marijuana crisis in the white middle-class suburbs guided, and in key ways dominated, the Reagan administration's war on drugs.").

46. Ira Glasser, *American Drug Laws: The New Jim Crow*, 63 Alb. L. Rev. 703, 714 (2000).

47. *See* Amanda Fielding, *Cannabis and the Psychedelics: Reviewing the UN Drug Conventions, in* Prohibition, Religious Freedom, and Human Rights: Regulating Traditional Drug Use 189, 194 (Beatriz Caiuby Labate & Clancy Cavnar eds., 2014) ("Without cannabis, the War on Drugs would collapse . . . ."); Michael Polson, *Cultivating Cannabis, Excepting Cannabis, in* The War on Drugs: A History 92, 92 (David Farber ed., 2022) ("The global War on Drugs could not exist in its broad scale and granular intensity without cannabis.").

48. William J. Chambliss, *Drug War Politics: Racism, Corruption, and Alienation, in* Crime Control and Social Justice: The Delicate Balance 295, 315 (Darnell F. Hawkins, Samuel L. Myers, Jr. & Randolph N. Stone eds., 2003).

49. Steven B. Duke & Albert C. Gross, America's Longest War: Rethinking Our Tragic Crusade Against Drugs 154 (1993).

50. *See, e.g.*, Musto, *supra* note 12, at 254 ("The history of drug laws in the United States shows that the degree to which a drug has been outlawed or curbed has no direct relation to its inherent danger."); Michael Pollan, This Is Your Mind on Plants 81 (2021) ("The war on drugs is in truth a war on *some* drugs, their enemy status the result of historical accident, cultural prejudice, and institutional imperative."); Reiss, *supra* note 35, at 10 ("The historic labeling of a given substance as a 'dangerous drug' was rooted not in scientific objectivity but in the political economy and cultural politics of US drug control . . . ."); Kimani Paul-Emile, *Making Sense of Drug Regulation: A Theory of Law for Drug Control Policy*, 19 Cornell J.L. & Pub. Pol'y 691, 692 (2010) ("[D]rug regulatory decision-making in the United States over the past 150 years has often borne very little relationship to science.").

51. Michael J. Sandel, *Moral Argument and Liberal Toleration: Abortion and Homosexuality*, 77 Calif. L. Rev. 521, 538 (1989).

52. For an important new account of the rise of constitutional veneration in the twentieth century and its costs, see Aziz Rana, The Constitutional Bind: How Americans Came to Idolize a Document That Fails Them (forthcoming 2024). I have voiced my own skepticism about U.S. Constitution worship in David E. Pozen, *Constitutional Bad Faith*, 129 Harv. L. Rev. 885 (2016).

53. *See generally* David T. Courtwright, The Age of Addiction: How Bad Habits Became Big Business (2019). Courtwright coins the term *limbic capitalism* to describe how modern businesses "encourage excessive consumption and addiction" with previously unattainable sophistication and scale "by targeting the limbic system, the part of the brain responsible for feeling and for quick reaction." *Id.* at 6.

54. For a compendium, see Jonathan P. Caulkins, Beau Kilmer & Mark A. R. Kleiman, Marijuana Legalization: What Everyone Needs to Know (2d ed. 2016).

55. *See, e.g.*, Kojo Koram, *The Legalization of Cannabis and the Question of Reparations*, 25 J. Int'l Econ. L. 294 (2022); Jasmin Mize, *Reefer Reparations*, 3 Soc. Just. & Equity L.J., no. 2, 2020, at 1.

56. Its textual basis is a matter of some dispute, but the Supreme Court has described "the constitutional right to travel from one State to another [as] firmly embedded in our jurisprudence." Saenz v. Roe, 526 U.S. 489, 498 (1999) (internal quotation marks omitted). No court has ever understood the right to travel to encompass the right to journey from one state of consciousness to another.

57. Carl L. Hart, Drug Use for Grown-Ups: Chasing Liberty in the Land of Fear 2 (2021); *cf.* Jennifer Oliva, *Coming Out of the Drug-Use Closet*, JOTWELL (Oct. 12, 2021), https://health.jotwell.com/coming-out-of-the-drug-use-closet/ [https://perma.cc/P688-EYEX] (noting that "[f]ew drug policy experts would disagree" with this characterization).

58. *See* Lassiter, *supra* note 24, at 128 (discussing the "cultural and political script of racialized pushers and white middle-class victims"). Lassiter's magisterial book *The Suburban Crisis*, which came out while this manuscript was in production, places additional emphasis on the pharmaceutical lobby's political clout. *See* Matthew D. Lassiter, The Suburban Crisis: White America and the War on Drugs 12 (2023) (arguing that "[e]very major federal and state drug control law during the second half of the twentieth century" had among its main purposes the "preservation of the pharmaceutical industry monopoly to sell therapeutic and often addictive pills to a global market while the U.S. government pledged in vain to eliminate illicit competition").

59. *See* Douglas Husak, Legalize This! The Case for Decriminalizing Drugs 120 (2002) ("[R]eligion plays an absolutely central role in shaping contemporary drug policy."); *see also* David A.J. Richards,

SEX, DRUGS, DEATH, AND THE LAW: AN ESSAY ON HUMAN RIGHTS AND OVERCRIMINALIZATION 193–95 (1986) (arguing that "a formerly religious but now secular ideal of moral perfectionism," which equates drug use with "radical evil" and is "immune to evidence," underwrites U.S. drug policy). 60. *See* Pembleton, *supra* note 32, at 445–46 (summarizing this line of argument). 61. *See generally* CHRISTINA R. JOHNS, POWER, IDEOLOGY, AND THE WAR ON DRUGS: NOTHING SUCCEEDS LIKE FAILURE (1992).

CHAPTER 1

62. Griswold v. Connecticut, 381 U.S. 479, 484 (1965).
63. *See* Joseph R. Grodin, *Rediscovering the State Constitutional Right to Happiness and Safety*, 25 HASTINGS CONST. L.Q. 1, 1 (1997) ("[F]ully two thirds of the state constitutions contain provisions which either declare the right of persons to pursue happiness or . . . to actually 'obtain' it."). As Grodin recounts, the happiness language in the earliest state constitutions likely derived from the Virginia Declaration of Rights, not the Declaration of Independence. *See id.* at 5–8.
64. For a fascinating account of Declarationism's political history, see Ken I. Kersch, *Beyond Originalism: Conservative Declarationism and Constitutional Redemption*, 71 MD. L. REV. 229 (2011). Kersch describes Declarationism as "the view that the Constitution can only be understood and interpreted in light of the principles enunciated in the opening words of the Declaration of Independence, which are held to be the Constitution's beating heart and unshakable foundation." *Id.* at 229–30.
65. Olmstead v. United States, 277 U.S. 438, 478 (1928) (Brandeis, J., dissenting).
66. Andrew Koppelman, *Drug Policy and the Liberal Self*, 100 NW. U. L. REV. 279, 288 (2006).
67. Buchhandler-Raphael, *supra* note 28, at 337; *see also id.* at 337–39 (summarizing prominent liberal theorists' critiques of drug prohibition).
68. Samuel Freeman, *Liberalism, Inalienability, and Rights of Drug Use, in* DRUGS AND THE LIMITS OF LIBERALISM: MORAL AND LEGAL ISSUES 110, 127 (Pablo De Greiff ed., 1999); *see also* Douglas Husak, *Liberal*

Neutrality, Autonomy, and Drug Prohibitions, 29 PHIL. & PUB. AFF. 43, 62 (2000) (explaining that in light of addiction's potential to undermine the conditions of self-governance, the "concept of autonomy can be put to diametrically opposed purposes in debates about the justifiability of drug proscriptions"). Husak and Koppelman offer powerful reasons to doubt that many drugs are in fact sufficiently addictive to warrant proscription on such grounds. *See* Husak, *supra,* at 66–78; Koppelman, *supra* note 66, at 281 & n.14; *see also* HUSAK, *supra* note 59, at 2, 105–06 (arguing that the potential for addiction does not justify punishment of drug users and that drug prohibition was "the worst injustice perpetrated by our system of criminal law in the twentieth century").

69. *See* DUKE & GROSS, *supra* note 49, at 146–59 (detailing "autonomy costs" of drug prohibition).

70. *Cf.* 1 MICHEL FOUCAULT, THE HISTORY OF SEXUALITY 140 (Robert Hurley trans., Pantheon Books 1978) (1976) (coining the term "bio-power" to describe the techniques through which modern states "achiev[e] the subjugation of bodies and the control of populations").

71. *See* WILLIAM J. NOVAK, NEW DEMOCRACY: THE CREATION OF THE MODERN AMERICAN STATE 89–107 (2022).

72. Commonwealth v. Campbell, 117 S.W. 383, 385–87 (Ky. 1909); *see also* State v. Gilman, 10 S.E. 283, 284 (W. Va. 1889) ("The keeping of liquors in his possession by a person, whether for himself or for another, unless he does so for the illegal sale of it, or for some other improper purpose, can by no possibility injure or affect the health, morals, or safety of the public; and, therefore, the statute prohibiting such keeping in possession is not a legitimate exertion of the police power.").

73. *Campbell,* 117 S.W. at 385. As this passage reflects, the "pursuit of happiness" was associated in this line of doctrine with hedonic pleasure and personal autonomy. Some recent scholarship has argued that this phrase was more strongly identified in the eighteenth century with *eudaimonia,* or human flourishing, *see* Carli N. Conklin, *The Origins of the Pursuit of Happiness,* 7 WASH. U. JURIS. REV. 195 (2015), an ideal that would have had more ambiguous implications for the regulation of a drug like alcohol.

74. Beebe v. State, 6 Ind. 501 (1855). *Beebe* has been described as "the philosophical ancestor of all challenges to prohibition of intoxicants— alcohol, narcotics and marijuana." Bonnie & Whitebread, *supra* note 10, at 995 (citation omitted).

75. Herman v. State, 8 Ind. 545, 558 (1855).

76. Ah Lim v. Territory, 24 P. 588, 589, 590 (Wash. 1890). The *Ah Lim* court split 3 to 2. The dissenting justices insisted that while "the habit of smoking opium may be repulsive and degrading," it "is the one great principle of our form of government . . . that the individual right of self-control is not to be limited [except] to that extent which is necessary to promote the general welfare." *Id.* at 171, 174 (Scott, J., dissenting).

77. *Ex parte* Yun Quong, 114 P. 835, 838 (Cal. 1911) (quoting the District Court of Appeal for the First Appellate District).

78. Austin v. State, 48 S.W. 305, 306 (Tenn. 1898), *aff'd*, 179 U.S. 343 (1900).

79. City of Zion v. Behrens, 104 N.E. 836 (Ill. 1914); Hershberg v. City of Bairbourville, 133 S.W. 985 (Ky. 1911).

80. *See* WILLIAM J. NOVAK, THE PEOPLE'S WELFARE: LAW AND REGULATION IN NINETEENTH-CENTURY AMERICA 179–89 (1996); *see also* Rogers, *supra* note 10, at 172–74 (discussing "a number of cases which held that the right to possess intoxicating liquors was not absolute" before 1915, although indicating that these cases were in the minority). The U.S. Supreme Court, meanwhile, repeatedly reaffirmed that the federal Constitution does not bar states from restricting the manufacture and sale of alcohol. *See, e.g.*, Mugler v. Kansas, 123 U.S. 623 (1887); Beer Co. v. Massachusetts, 97 U.S. 25 (1877). During the 1850s, by contrast, judges had struck down state prohibitions on the manufacture and sale of alcohol "with unanimous horror" for violating property and due process rights. Kellen Funk, *Shall These Bones Live? Property, Pluralism, and the Constitution of Evangelical Reform*, 41 LAW & SOC. INQUIRY 742, 749 (2016).

81. *See* Bonnie & Whitebread, *supra* note 10, at 976 (alcohol and narcotics); George Fisher, *Racial Myths of the Cannabis War*, 101 B.U. L. REV. 933, 949 (2021) (marijuana).

82. Pub. L. No. 221, ch. 100, 35 Stat. 614 (1909).

83. Pub. L. No. 63-223, 38 Stat. 785 (1914). I will return to the Harrison Act in the next chapter.

84. The Eighteenth Amendment prohibited the manufacture, sale, transportation, importation, and exportation of intoxicating liquors nationwide, without addressing possession or consumption. It was the first amendment to impose a time limit on state ratification—another instance in which antidrug sentiment fueled constitutional innovation, in this case

outside the courts. *See* David E. Pozen & Thomas P. Schmidt, *The Puzzles and Possibilities of Article V*, 121 COLUM. L. REV. 2317, 2354 (2021).

85. Bonnie & Whitebread, *supra* note 10, at 1005; *see also* Rogers, *supra* note 10, at 156–57 (observing in 1919 that "courts have been sustaining . . . exceedingly stringent laws forbidding the possession and use of intoxicants" which, "even five years ago," "would have been declared unconstitutional").

86. Lee J. Vance, *The Road to Confiscation*, 25 YALE L.J. 285, 299 (1916).

87. 245 U.S. 304, 307–08 (1917); *see also* Minor Bronaugh, *Limiting or Prohibiting the Possession of Intoxicating Liquors for Personal Use*, 23 LAW NOTES 67, 68 (1919) (describing *Crane* as delivering "the death blow to John Barleycorn").

88. RICHARDS, *supra* note 59, at 323.

89. *See, e.g.,* Torres v. Lynch, 578 U.S. 452, 457–58 (2016) ("State legislatures, exercising their plenary police powers, are not limited to Congress's enumerated powers . . . ."); Hodel v. Va. Surface Mining & Reclamation Ass'n, 452 U.S. 264, 311 (1981) (Rehnquist, J., concurring in the judgment) (describing "the reserved police powers of the States" as "plenary unless challenged as violating some specific provision of the Constitution").

90. The canonical initial articulation of this new approach to rights review appeared in footnote 4 of *United States v. Carolene Products Co.*, 304 U.S. 144, 152 n.4 (1938).

91. The Bill of Rights, which comprises the first ten amendments to the Constitution, was originally understood to apply only to the federal government. Beginning in earnest in the 1920s, the Court held over a series of cases that the Fourteenth Amendment's Due Process Clause "incorporates" particular guarantees in the Bill of Rights against the states. Conversely, the Court held in 1954 that the Fifth Amendment's Due Process Clause "reverse incorporates" the Fourteenth Amendment's Equal Protection Clause against the federal government. Bolling v. Sharpe, 347 U.S. 497, 499–500 (1954). The end result was that nearly every right in the Constitution became applicable to the federal government and state governments alike.

92. Griswold v. Connecticut, 381 U.S. 479, 484 (1965).

93. *Id.* at 486 (Goldberg, J., concurring). Long considered one of the Constitution's most enigmatic provisions, the Ninth Amendment instructs

that "[t]he enumeration in the Constitution, of certain rights, shall not be construed to deny or disparage others retained by the people." 94. *Id.* at 500 (Harlan, J., concurring in the judgment) (quoting Palko v. Connecticut, 302 U.S. 319, 325 (1937)). 95. *Id.* at 507 (White, J., concurring in the judgment). 96. *Id.* at 527, 530 (Stewart, J., dissenting) (joined by Justice Black). 97. *Id.* at 482. 98. 198 U.S. 45 (1905). For an overview of *Lochner*'s anticanonical status, see Jamal Greene, *The Anticanon*, 125 HARV. L. REV. 379, 417–22 (2011). 99. 394 U.S. 557, 564 (1969) (citation omitted). 100. 405 U.S. 438, 453 (1972). The full sentence reads, "If the right of privacy means anything, it is the right of the individual, married or single, to be free from unwarranted governmental intrusion into matters so fundamentally affecting a person as the decision whether to bear or beget a child." 101. 410 U.S. 113, 153 (1973). 102. Roe v. Ingraham, 480 F.2d 102, 108 (2d Cir. 1973). 103. NAT'L COMM'N ON MARIHUANA & DRUG ABUSE, *supra* note 21, app. at 1127. 104. *Id.* at 140–42. 105. Tom C. Clark, *Drugs and the Law*, 18 LOY. L. REV. 243, 247 & n.19 (1972). 106. *See, e.g.*, ARTHUR D. HELLMAN, LAWS AGAINST MARIJUANA: THE PRICE WE PAY 13 (1975) ("[I]t can be argued that *Stanley* and *Griswold* in conjunction support the proposition that marijuana possession laws are unconstitutional."); LAURENCE H. TRIBE, AMERICAN CONSTITUTIONAL LAW 910 (1978) ("To be sure, at stake in *Stanley* was the value of preventing government from rummaging through someone's library to discover evidence of his mental and emotional tastes. Yet is it so much less offensive for government to rummage through someone's medicine chest and wine cellar to put together a picture of his oral and chemical predilections?"); Herbert L. Packer, *The Aims of the Criminal Law Revisited: A Plea for a New Look at "Substantive Due Process,"* 44 S. CAL. L. REV. 490, 496 (1971) ("Indeed, the Supreme Court may have already laid the foundation for invalidating criminal laws proscribing the possession of marijuana.").

107. *See, e.g.*, Edgar Paul Boyko & Michael W. Rotberg, *Constitutional Objections to California's Marijuana Possession Statute*, 14 UCLA L. Rev. 773, 792–95 (1967); John F. Decker, *The Official Report of the National Commission Studying Marihuana: More Misunderstanding*, 8 U.S.F. L. Rev. 1, 14–18 (1973); Arden Doss Jr. & Diane Kay Doss, *On Morals, Privacy, and the Constitution*, 25 U. Miami L. Rev. 395, 410–14 (1971); Jeremy Haar, *In Pursuit of Happiness: An Evaluation of the Constitutional Right to Private Use of Marijuana*, 5 Contemp. Drug Probs. 161 (1976); Soler, *supra* note 15, at 696–700; Note, *Substantive Due Process and Felony Treatment for Pot Smokers: The Current Conflict*, 2 Ga. L. Rev. 247 (1968); Michael A. Town, Comment, *The California Marijuana Possession Statute: An Infringement on the Right of Privacy or Other Peripheral Constitutional Rights*, 19 Hastings L.J. 758 (1968).

108. *Decriminalization of Marihuana: Hearings Before the H. Select Comm. on Narcotics Abuse & Control*, 95th Cong. 310 (1977) [hereinafter 1977 Decriminalization Hearing] (statement of Jay A. Miller, ACLU). The ACLU's initial constitutional critique of marijuana prohibition, formulated in the late 1960s, highlighted its privacy costs but placed even greater emphasis on the lack of a legitimate policy rationale. *See, e.g.*, *Controlled Dangerous Substances, Narcotics, and Drug Control Laws: Hearings Before the H. Comm. on Ways & Means*, 91st Cong. 376–84 (1970) (statement of Hope Eastman, ACLU).

109. 1977 Decriminalization Hearing, *supra* note 108, at 292 (statement of Brooksley Elizabeth Landau, ABA); *see also* Musto, *supra* note 12, at 231–34 (discussing the origins of the ABA's opposition to punitive drug policies in the 1950s).

110. Cal. S. Select Comm. on Control of Marijuana, Marijuana: Beyond Misunderstanding 16 (1974).

111. Lydia Saad, *In U.S., 38% Have Tried Marijuana, Little Changed Since '80s*, Gallup (Aug. 2, 2013), https://news.gallup.com/poll/163835/tried-marijuana-little-changed-80s.aspx [https://perma.cc/CRQ8-2K2B].

112. Dufton, *supra* note 14, at 26, 55; *see also* William J. Lanouette, *A Change in Policy on Pot?*, Nat'l Observer, Nov. 30, 1974, at 3 ("More than two million Americans will smoke some marijuana today. Maybe 2,000 of them will be arrested."). Among the 1973 marijuana arrestees, 91 percent had no prior drug convictions. Nat'l Comm'n on Marihuana & Drug Abuse, *supra* note 21, app. at 623.

113. *See* Anthony Ripley, *Spread of Marijuana Creates New Specialist: The Drug Lawyer*, N.Y. TIMES (Sept. 2, 1971), https://www.nyti mes.com/1971/09/02/archives/spread-of-marijuana-creates-new-special ist-the-drug-lawyer.html [https://perma.cc/8UYV-DS3W].

114. DUFTON, *supra* note 14, at 31.

115. *See* Cynthia Cotts, *Our Buds, Ourselves*, VILLAGE VOICE (Oct. 26, 1999), https://www.villagevoice.com/1999/10/26/our-buds-ourselves/ [https://perma.cc/39FT-YY96]; Les Ledbetter, *Rolling Stone Is Tilting Toward the East Coast*, N.Y. TIMES (Sept. 14, 1976), https://www.nytimes.com/1976/09/14/archives/rolling-stone-is-tilting-toward-the-east-coast.html [https://perma.cc/KT2M-LYF6]

116. On the extreme lengths to which the Federal Bureau of Narcotics and its longtime director Harry Anslinger went to propagandize against marijuana and other drugs, see RUFUS KING, THE DRUG HANG-UP: AMERICA'S FIFTY-YEAR FOLLY 161–75 (1972); LARRY "RATSO" SLOMAN, REEFER MADNESS: A HISTORY OF MARIJUANA 29–51, 187–216 (1979); Galliher et al., *supra* note 2.

117. Decker, *supra* note 107, at 8.

118. DOMESTIC COUNCIL DRUG ABUSE TASK FORCE, WHITE PAPER ON DRUG ABUSE 47–52 (1975). The task force rated marijuana "the least serious" illicit drug in terms of adverse consequences. *Id.* at 53.

119. Drug Abuse Message to the Congress, 2 PUB. PAPERS 1400, 1404 (Aug. 2, 1977). All three of Carter's sons had admitted using marijuana, and his oldest son had been dismissed from the U.S. Navy after being caught smoking it. *See* James T. Wooten, *Carter Seeks to End Marijuana Penalty for Small Amounts*, N.Y. TIMES (Aug. 3, 1977), https://www.nytimes.com/1977/08/03/archives/carter-seeks-to-end-marijuana-penalty-for-small-amounts-urges-fines.html [https://perma.cc/2VXK-MWBZ].

120. Bonnie & Whitebread, *supra* note 10, at 1174.

121. Jack Anderson, *Drug Studies Dispute Nixon's Stand*, WASH. POST, Nov. 1, 1972, at C19; *see also Federal Drug Abuse and Drug Dependence Prevention, Treatment, and Rehabilitation Act of 1970: Hearings Before the S. Special Subcomm. on Alcoholism & Narcotics*, 91st Cong. 132 (1970) (statement of Larry Alan Bear, Addiction Services Agency, City of New York) ("[I]t is not difficult to find young people who will talk about their constitutional right to use marihuana . . . .").

122. *See, e.g.*, State v. Adkins, 241 N.W.2d 655 (Neb. 1976) (invalidating such a law); People v. Cressey, 471 P.2d 19, 27–29 (Cal. 1970) (construing such a law to require control of the premises). *See generally* 2 GERALD F. UELMEN & ALEX KREIT, DRUG ABUSE AND THE LAW SOURCEBOOK § 8:21 (2022 ed.). By and large, courts stopped interpreting drug statutes narrowly after the 1970s and the collapse of the constitutional reform movement.

123. 405 U.S. 156, 160, 164 (1972). As Risa Goluboff has documented, Justice Douglas initially drafted an opinion holding that the ordinance violated "the 'liberty' of the individual that is protected by the Due Process Clause," or substantive due process, before switching to a void-for-vagueness rationale at the request of Justice Stewart. The Court's unanimous opinion was nonetheless strikingly bold in its "fervent defense of both physical freedom and cultural nonconformity" and in its "complete rejection of the compromise position—frequently staked out by law enforcement advocates—that gave up social control vagrancy policing but retained vagrancy laws for crime control purposes." RISA GOLUBOFF, VAGRANT NATION: POLICE POWER, CONSTITUTIONAL CHANGE, AND THE MAKING OF THE 1960S, at 313–26 (2016).

124. Leary v. United States, 395 U.S. 6 (1969). In an amicus brief, the National Student Association explained that the case was of special interest to its membership, as students "make up a great percentage of marihuana consumers in the United States today." Brief of *Amicus Curiae* National Student Association at 6, Leary v. United States, 395 U.S. 6 (1969) (No. 65).

125. *See* BROMBERG ET AL., *supra* note 20, at 12 (describing *Leary* as the "tipping point for legal reform"); MICHAEL POLLAN, HOW TO CHANGE YOUR MIND: WHAT THE NEW SCIENCE OF PSYCHEDELICS TEACHES US ABOUT CONSCIOUSNESS, DYING, ADDICTION, DEPRESSION, AND TRANSCENDENCE 58 (2018) (noting that many in the field blame Leary's behavior, "fairly or not," for the suppression of psychedelic research that took hold in the mid-1970s).

126. *See, e.g.*, People v. Fiedler, 31 N.Y.2d 176, 180 (1972) ("It was never contemplated that criminal taint would attach to a family home should members of the family on one occasion smoke marijuana or hashish there."); *see also* Note, *On Privacy: Constitutional Protection for Personal Liberty*, 48 N.Y.U. L. REV. 670, 759 (1973) (observing that although the *Fiedler* court "did not use a privacy rationale, it was clearly concerned with the values underlying the concept of privacy of the home").

127. *See, e.g.*, United States v. Kiffer, 477 F.2d 349, 352 (2d Cir. 1973); Scott v. United States, 395 F.2d 619, 620 (D.C. Cir. 1968) (per curiam); United States v. Maiden, 355 F. Supp. 743, 746–47 (D. Conn. 1973). The U.S. Court of Appeals for the Second Circuit also suggested that the right of privacy may protect patients from having to disclose their prescription drug records to the state. *See* Roe v. Ingraham, 480 F.2d 102, 108–09 (2d Cir. 1973).

128. State v. Kantner, 493 P.2d 306, 308–10 (Haw. 1972).

129. *Id.* at 312 (Abe, J., concurring) (citing State v. Lee, 465 P.2d 573, 578 (Haw. 1970) (Abe, J., dissenting)).

130. *Id.* at 313, 315 (Levinson, J., dissenting).

131. *Id.* at 318–20 (Kobayashi, J., dissenting). The next chapter discusses this line of equal protection attack against drug classifications.

132. State v. Mallan, 950 P.2d 178, 202 (Haw. 1998) (Levinson, J., dissenting). The author of this dissent, Justice Steven Levinson, was a nephew of Justice Bernard Levinson and had clerked for his uncle at the time *Kantner* was decided. Arguably, *Mallan* "left open the question whether possession and use of marijuana *in the home* is protected by the right to privacy." State v. Sunderland, 168 P.3d 526, 537 (Haw. 2007) (Moon, C.J., concurring and dissenting).

133. State v. Renfro, 542 P.2d 366 (Haw. 1975).

134. Brief of *Amicus Curiae* Committee for a Sane Drug Policy at 2, People v. Sinclair, 194 N.W.2d 878 (Mich. 1972) (No. 91-153). Ten organizations submitted "friend of court" briefs to the Michigan Supreme Court, all on Sinclair's side. This level of civil society engagement was extraordinary for its time. I am not aware of any other drug-related case from the 1960s or 1970s that drew half as many amicus briefs.

135. The event was captured on film in the documentary *Ten for Two: The John Sinclair Freedom Rally* (1972), which Lennon and Ono commissioned.

136. People v. Sinclair, 194 N.W.2d 878, 890–91 (Mich. 1972) (opinion of Swainson, J.); *id.* at 895 (opinion of Kavanagh, J.).

137. *Id.* at 887 (opinion of Swainson, J.); *accord id.* at 894–95 (opinion of Williams, J.) (joined by Chief Justice Kavanagh).

138. *Id.* at 905–06 (opinion of Brennan, J.) (joined by Justice Adams); *id.* at 895 (opinion of Kavanagh, J.).

139. *Id.* at 896 (opinion of Kavanagh, J.). Justice Kavanagh did not elaborate on the Big Brother analogy or his unusual capitalization choices.

140. People v. Shackelford, 379 N.W.2d 487, 489 (Mich. 1985) (per curiam).

141. BROMBERG ET AL., *supra* note 20, at 19.

142. Hyman M. Greenstein & Paul E. DiBianco, *Marijuana Laws—A Crime Against Humanity*, 48 NOTRE DAME LAWYER 314, 327 (1972).

143. The Michigan legislature had already passed such a law by the time the *Sinclair* ruling was released, but the law had not yet gone into effect. Justice Swainson's opinion telegraphed that the new law would be upheld. *Sinclair*, 194 N.W.2d at 887 n.36 (opinion of Swainson, J.).

144. State v. Mitchell, 563 S.W.2d 18, 25 (Mo. 1978).

145. Ravin v. State, 537 P.2d 494, 502 (Alaska 1975).

146. *Id.* at 504. Alaska's privacy amendment states simply, "The right of the people to privacy is recognized and shall not be infringed." ALASKA CONST. art. I, § 22.

147. *Ravin*, 537 P.2d at 508–10.

148. *Id.* at 509.

149. State v. Erickson, 574 P.2d 1, 21 (Alaska 1978).

150. *See* Noy v. State, 83 P.3d 538, 542–43 (Alaska App. 2003).

151. Minister of Just. & Const. Dev. v. Prince, [2018] ZACC 30 (CC) (S. Afr.), at paras. 55, 72–75; *see also* Neil Boister, *Decriminalizing Personal Use of Cannabis in New Zealand: The Problems and Possibilities of International Law*, 3 Y.B. N.Z. JURIS. 55, 69 (1999) (noting that, across the globe, *Ravin* "remains" a "land mark case on decriminalization for constitutional reasons").

152. Maccabee v. Comm'r of Police, No. SKBHCV2017/0234 (2019) (E. Caribbean).

153. *See* People v. Aguiar, 257 Cal. App. 2d 597, 603 (1968) (observing, in the course of rejecting a challenge to marijuana prohibition, that "although the state does not now penalize the possession of alcohol acquired through lawful channels, it may do so if it chooses").

154. *See, e.g.*, United States v. Maas, 551 F. Supp. 645, 647 (D.N.J. 1982); NORML v. Bell, 488 F. Supp. 123, 133 (D.D.C. 1980); Laird v. State, 342 So. 2d 962, 965 (Fla. 1977); State v. Murphy, 570 P.2d 1070, 1073 (Ariz. 1977) (en banc); State *ex rel.* Scott v. Conaty, 187 S.E.2d 119, 123 (W. Va. 1972); *Aguiar*, 257 Cal. App. 2d at 605.

155. 262 U.S. 390 (1923) (invalidating a ban on the teaching of foreign languages).

156. 268 U.S. 510 (1925) (invalidating a law requiring children to attend public schools).

157. *See, e.g., Bell*, 488 F. Supp. at 131; *Murphy*, 570 P.2d at 1073; State v. Kells, 259 N.W.2d 19, 23 (Neb. 1977). The U.S. Supreme Court facilitated such readings of its privacy precedents in 1976 when, in rejecting a constitutional challenge to the disclosure of a prior shoplifting arrest, Justice William Rehnquist associated this line of cases with "marriage, procreation, contraception, family relationships, and child rearing and education." Paul v. Davis, 424 U.S. 693, 713 (1976).

158. *See, e.g.*, Marcoux v. Att'y Gen., 375 N.E.2d 688, 692 (Mass. 1978) (quoting Stanley v. Georgia, 394 U.S. 557, 566 (1969)).

159. Stanley v. Georgia, 394 U.S. 557, 568 n.11 (1969); *see, e.g.*, La. Affiliate of NORML v. Guste, 380 F. Supp. 404, 407 (E.D. La. 1974); People v. Shepard, 409 N.E.2d 840, 842 (N.Y. 1980) (per curiam); *Murphy*, 570 P.2d at 1073–74; Illinois NORML v. Scott, 383 N.E.2d 1330, 1332 (Ill. App. 1978). As one commentator observed in 1977, "*Stanley* has often been relied on by litigants urging the invalidity of marijuana and other drug laws and is almost as widely relied on by courts in rejecting such challenges." Thomas L. Hindes, *Morality Enforcement Through the Criminal Law and the Modern Doctrine of Substantive Due Process*, 126 U. PA. L. REV. 344, 351 (1977).

160. *See, e.g., Guste*, 380 F. Supp. at 407; State v. Smith, 610 P.2d 869, 879–80 (1980); *Kells*, 259 N.W.2d at 23–24.

161. Roe v. Wade, 410 U.S. 113, 152 (1973).

162. NORML v. Bell, 488 F. Supp. 123, 133 (D.D.C. 1980); *accord* United States v. Maas, 551 F. Supp. 645, 647 (D.N.J. 1982); Commonwealth v. Leis, Nos. 28841-2, 28844-5, 28864-5 (Mass. Super. Ct. 1968) (unreported decision), *excerpted in* 3 SUFFOLK L. REV. 23, 24 (1968).

163. *Bell*, 488 F. Supp. at 133 (citation omitted); *accord Maas*, 551 F. Supp. at 647; *Marcoux*, 375 N.E.2d at 692.

164. United States v. Kiffer, 477 F.2d 349, 352 (2d Cir. 1973); *see also, e.g., Maas*, 551 F. Supp. at 649; State v. Kantner, 493 P.2d 306, 310 (Haw. 1972).

165. People v. Shepard, 409 N.E.2d 840, 843 (N.Y. 1980) (per curiam).

166. NAT'L COMM'N ON MARIHUANA & DRUG ABUSE, *supra* note 21, at 140–42; *see supra* notes 103–04 and accompanying text.

167. *See, e.g.,* Laird v. State, 342 So. 2d 962, 966 (Fla. 1977) (Adkins, J., dissenting) (contending that *Griswold* and *Roe* are "clearly applicable" to marijuana prohibition "since they establish the individual's right to privacy with regard to [matters that] directly affect the individual's control over his or her bodily functions"). For a later example, see Seeley v. State, 940 P.2d 604, 626 (Wash. 1997) (Sanders, J., dissenting) (contending that marijuana prohibition violates *Roe*'s lesson that "personal choices essential to personal dignity and autonomy, even when those choices are at odds with legitimate state interests, are constitutionally privileged").

168. Joshua D. Hawley, *The Intellectual Origins of (Modern) Substantive Due Process,* 93 Tex. L. Rev. 275, 316–24 (2014).

169. *See* Joel Feinberg, *Autonomy, Sovereignty, and Privacy: Moral Ideals in the Constitution,* 58 Notre Dame L. Rev. 445, 490–91 (1983) (suggesting that the distinction between viewing pornography in one's home and using drugs in one's home is arbitrary from the perspective of privacy or personal sovereignty).

170. *Cf.* Soler, *supra* note 15, at 696–97 (noting that footnote 11 "refers specifically to 'narcotics,'" and "marijuana is not a narcotic").

171. Laurence H. Tribe & Michael C. Dorf, On Reading the Constitution 72 (1991).

172. Paul v. Davis, 424 U.S. 693, 713 (1976) (Rehnquist, J.).

173. Griswold v. Connecticut, 381 U.S. 479, 530 (1965) (Stewart, J., dissenting).

174. Richard H. Fallon Jr., *Some Confusions About Due Process, Judicial Review, and Constitutional Remedies,* 93 Colum. L. Rev. 309, 317–18 (1993) (citations and brackets omitted) (quoting Youngberg v. Romeo, 457 U.S. 307, 320 (1982)). In a recent book, James Fleming details how such balancing continued to occur after the 1970s in scattered cases and argues that the "myth" of two rigid tiers has been perpetuated by opponents of substantive due process looking to restrict its reach. James E. Fleming, Constructing Basic Liberties: A Defense of Substantive Due Process 45–69 (2022).

175. Ravin v. State, 537 P.2d 494, 498 (Alaska 1975).

176. *Compare, e.g.,* Roe v. Wade, 410 U.S. 113, 152 (1973) ("These decisions make it clear that only personal rights that can be deemed 'fundamental' or 'implicit in the concept of ordered liberty' are included in this guarantee of personal privacy." (citation omitted)), *with Griswold,* 381 U.S. at 500 (Harlan, J., concurring in the judgment) ("[T]he proper

constitutional inquiry in this case is whether this Connecticut statute infringes the Due Process Clause of the Fourteenth Amendment because the enactment violates basic values 'implicit in the concept of ordered liberty.'" (citation omitted)).

177. Washington v. Glucksberg, 521 U.S. 702, 722 (1997); *see also* Randy E. Barnett, *Scrutiny Land*, 106 MICH. L. REV. 1479, 1489–93 (2008) (describing numerous ambiguities in the *Glucksberg* test and noting that it "is the approach of those judicial conservatives who . . . want to see no further extension of substantive due process to other [un]enumerated rights").

178. *See, e.g.*, Lawrence v. Texas, 539 U.S. 558 (2003).

179. NORML v. Bell, 488 F. Supp. 123, 133 (D.D.C. 1980).

180. *See* State v. Mallan, 950 P.2d 178, 246–47 (Haw. 1998) (Levinson, J., dissenting) (arguing that a ban on marijuana possession violates the right to be let alone); People v. Shepard, 409 N.E.2d 840, 849 (N.Y. 1980) (Fuchsberg, J., dissenting) (same).

181. RICHARDS, *supra* note 59, at 185–86; *see also* DUKE & GROSS, *supra* note 49, at 152 ("The right to choose which drugs to use, and whether to use them at all, is arguably as fundamental as the right to decide where to live, where to work, whether to marry, whether to have children, how much education to seek, and how to raise one's children."); ROBERT M. HARDAWAY, MARIJUANA POLITICS: UNCOVERING THE TROUBLESOME HISTORY AND SOCIAL COSTS OF CRIMINALIZATION 7 (2018) ("An individual's decision to use drugs is one of these rights that go to the heart of the concept of self-determination."); PHILIP PETTIT, JUST FREEDOM: A MORAL COMPASS FOR A COMPLEX WORLD 66–67 (2014) (suggesting that in the absence of "a threat to public order," the choice to use recreational drugs should be included in "the class of the basic liberties"); ANDREW WEIL, THE NATURAL MIND: AN INVESTIGATION OF DRUGS AND THE HIGHER CONSCIOUSNESS 19 (1998 ed.) ("It is my belief that the desire to alter consciousness periodically is an innate, normal drive analogous to hunger or the sexual drive.").

182. *See generally, e.g.*, DOUGLAS N. HUSAK, DRUGS AND RIGHTS (1992); ROB LOVERING, A MORAL DEFENSE OF RECREATIONAL DRUG USE (2015); THOMAS SZASZ, OUR RIGHT TO DRUGS: THE CASE FOR A FREE MARKET (1992); Eric Blumenson & Eva Nilsen, *Liberty Lost: The Moral Case for Marijuana Reform*, 85 IND. L.J. 279 (2010).

183. Andrew Sherratt, *Alcohol and Its Alternatives: Symbol and Substance in Pre-Industrial Cultures*, in CONSUMING HABITS: DRUGS IN HISTORY AND

ANTHROPOLOGY 11, 33 (Jordan Goodman, Paul E. Lovejoy & Andrew Sherratt eds., 2d ed. 2007); *see also* HUSAK, *supra* note 59, at 128 ("[N]o known societies—except perhaps that of Eskimos—refrain from using drugs for recreational purposes."); Gootenberg, *supra* note 32, at 1 ("Despite their widespread prohibition, illicit drugs such as opiates, cannabis, cocaine, amphetamines, and the myriad of psychedelics and synthetics are fundamental features of the modern world, with historical antecedents in virtually all human societies going back to prehistory.").

184. In rejecting constitutional challenges to marijuana bans, numerous courts drew an analogy to recent litigation against motorcycle helmet mandates. *See, e.g.*, State v. Smith, 610 P.2d 869, 876 (Wash. 1980); Marcoux v. Att'y Gen., 375 N.E.2d 688, 692 (Mass. 1978); Borras v. State 229 So. 2d 244, 246 (Fla. 1969). A minority of courts struck down motorcycle helmet laws in the late 1960s for violating the right to privacy or related reasons, *see* Ravin v. State, 537 P.2d 494, 509 n.59 (Alaska 1975) (collecting cases), but by the end of the 1970s these laws had been almost universally upheld. *See* Melissa Neiman, *Motorcycle Helmet Laws: The Facts, What Can Be Done to Jump-Start Helmet Use, and Ways to Cap Damages*, 11 J. HEALTH CARE L. & POL'Y 215, 236–37 (2008); *see also* J. Harvie Wilkinson III & G. Edward White, *Constitutional Protection for Personal Lifestyles*, 62 CORNELL L. REV. 563, 619 n.263 (1977) (discussing "considerable controversy" created by helmet requirements).

185. State v. Kantner, 493 P.2d 306, 315 (Haw. 1972) (Levinson, J., dissenting) (cited in Amparo en Revisión 237/2014, Primera Sala de la Suprema Corte de Justicia de la Nación [SCJN], 11-04-2015 (Mex.), at p. 41).

186. Anderson, *supra* note 121 (quoting an unpublished study, *Drug Use and the Youth Culture*). Anderson's article also described a second suppressed study that was critical of the government's drug education efforts. I have not been able to track down either study.

187. *See, e.g.*, COMM'N OF INQUIRY INTO THE NON-MEDICAL USE OF DRUGS, CANNABIS 50 (1972), https://publications.gc.ca/collections/collecti on_2018/sc-hc/H21-5370-4-eng.pdf [hereinafter LEDAIN COMMISSION REPORT] ("[M]any users report increased enjoyment of sex and other intimate human contact while under the influence of the drug."); *id.* at 51 ("Increased sensitivity to sound and greater appreciation of the subtleties of music are widely reported by cannabis users."); *id.* at 51 (noting "common reports from cannabis users that taste sensations are greatly enhanced by

the drug"); *see also* Lester Grinspoon, *Learn*, MARIJUANA USES (undated), http://marijuana-uses.com/learn/ [https://perma.cc/69RT-CS7Y] (discussing marijuana's capacity to "heighten the appreciation of music and art" and "deepen emotional and sexual intimacy").

188. *See* CAULKINS ET AL., *supra* note 54, at 69–72 (summarizing purported differences between "straight" and "stoned" ways of thinking).

189. *Cf.* Michael Moore, *Liberty and Drugs, in* DRUGS AND THE LIMITS OF LIBERALISM, *supra* note 68, at 61, 101 ("One has to be high on [drugs] already in order to be able to judge the states induced as any kind of path to profundity or 'authenticity.'").

190. *Kantner*, 493 P.2d at 317 (Levinson, J., dissenting).

191. Kathleen M. Sullivan, *Post-Liberal Judging: The Roles of Categorization and Balancing*, 63 U. COLO. L. REV. 293, 296 (1992); *see also, e.g.*, *Leading Cases*, 106 HARV. L. REV. 163, 211 (1992) ("In an effort to avoid endorsing the untrammeled exercise of judicial power, the Court has tried to fit all of its substantive due process cases into a simple, two-tiered framework.").

CHAPTER 2

192. In its most famous formulation, the harm principle holds that "the only purpose for which power can rightfully be exercised over any member of a civilised community against his will is to prevent harm to others." JOHN STUART MILL, ON LIBERTY 9 (Elizabeth Rapaport ed., Hackett Publishing Co. 1978) (1859). There are endless debates about the persuasiveness, limits, and proper specification of the harm principle. For a flavor, see David Brink, *Mill's Moral and Political Philosophy* § 3, *in* STANFORD ENCYCLOPEDIA OF PHILOSOPHY (Edward N. Zalta ed., 2022), https://plato.stanford.edu/entries/mill-moral-political/ [https://perma.cc/Z6BS-4GYC].

193. *See* Richard Glen Boire, *John Stuart Mill and the Liberty of Inebriation*, 7 INDEP. REV. 253, 253 (2002) (summarizing Mill's views on alcohol and describing *On Liberty* as a "seminal antiprohibition text").

194. NFIB v. Sebelius, 567 U.S. 519, 534 (2012). For an argument that the absence of a federal police power has always been a "fiction,"

see Markus Dirk Dubber, The Police Power: Patriarchy and the Foundations of American Government 86–88 (2015).

195. McCulloch v. Maryland, 4 Wheat. 316, 405 (1819).

196. Pub. L. No. 63-223, 38 Stat. 785 (1914), *amended by* Act of Feb. 24, 1919, Pub. L. No. 65-254, § 1006, 40 Stat. 1057, 1130–31. Violations of the act were punishable by up to five years' imprisonment. *Id.* § 9, 38 Stat. 789.

197. Prosecutions under the Harrison Act led to the Supreme Court's first major ruling upholding criminal strict liability in *United States v. Balint*, 58 U.S. 250 (1922), and the companion case *United States v. Behrman*, 258 U.S. 280 (1922). *See Behrman*, 258 U.S. at 288 ("It is enough to sustain an indictment [under the Harrison Act] that the offense be described with sufficient clearness to show a violation of law . . . . [T]he indictment need not charge such knowledge or intent.").

198. David Herzberg, *Origins and Outcomes of the US Medicine-Drug Divide, in* The Oxford Handbook of Global Drug History, *supra* note 7, at 323, 328.

199. *See* Jason L. Bates, The "Drug Evil": Narcotics Law, Race, and the Making of America's Composite Penal State 140 (Dec. 2017) (Ph.D. dissertation, Vanderbilt University) (ProQuest) (documenting that both the Harrison Act's congressional sponsors and the news media "viewed the Act as a prohibitory measure rather than a tax").

200. Nigro v. United States, 276 U.S. 332, 353 (1928) (citing Child Labor Tax Case, 259 U. S. 20, 38 (1922)).

201. *See* Musto, *supra* note 12, at 186.

202. United States v. Doremus, 249 U.S. 86 (1919).

203. United States v. Daugherty, 269 U.S. 360, 362–63 (1926).

204. *Nigro*, 276 U.S. at 341, 354.

205. *Id.* at 356 (McReynolds, J., dissenting).

206. *Id.* at 358 (Butler, J., dissenting).

207. Pub. L. No. 75-238, 50 Stat. 551 (1937).

208. A. Christopher Bryant, Nigro v. United States: *The Most Disingenuous Supreme Court Opinion, Ever,* 12 Nev. L.J. 650 (2012); *see also id.* at 650 (arguing that *Nigro* "contributed mightily to the demise of the enumerated powers doctrine"); Robert Post, *Federalism in the Taft Court Era: Can It Be "Revived"?,* 51 Duke L.J. 1513, 1567 & n.187 (2002) (depicting *Nigro* as a retreat from the Taft Court's prior determination "to ensure

that federal taxing authority did not become a blank check for federal legislation").

209. *See* United States v. Lopez, 514 U.S. 549, 552–56 (1995) (reviewing this history); *id.* at 568–74 (Kennedy, J., concurring) (same); *id.* at 604–07 (Souter, J., dissenting) (same).

210. MUSTO, *supra* note 12, at 133; Bryant, *supra* note 208, at 651.

211. Pub. L. No. 89-74, 79 Stat. 226 (1965); *see* MUSTO, *supra* note 12, at 239 (identifying the 1965 legislation as the moment when "the constitutional basis for [federal] drug control shifted from the taxing power to interstate and commerce powers").

212. Pub. L. No. 91-513, 84 Stat. 1236 (1970); *see* FRYDL, *supra* note 14, at 355 (describing the 1970 legislation as orchestrating "two shifts" in U.S. drug policy: "from taxing power to the commerce clause, and from state prerogative to national power").

213. *Lopez*, 514 U.S. 549.

214. United States v. Morrison, 529 U.S. 598 (2000).

215. *See* Samuel R. Bagenstos, *Spending Clause Litigation in the Roberts Court*, 58 DUKE L.J. 345, 346 n.1 (2008) (collecting sources from the late 1990s and early 2000s describing these opinions as part of a "federalism revolution").

216. Raich v. Ashcroft, 352 F.3d 1222 (9th Cir. 2003).

217. Gonzales v. Raich, 545 U.S. 1, 18–22 (2005).

218. Justice Scalia's concurrence placed greater emphasis on the Necessary and Proper Clause, which authorizes Congress to "make all Laws which shall be necessary and proper for carrying into Execution" its constitutional powers, but otherwise echoed much of the majority's reasoning. *See id.* at 33–42 (Scalia, J., concurring in the judgment).

219. *Id.* at 43, 46, 57 (O'Connor, J., dissenting).

220. *See, e.g.*, Ryan Grim, *A Guide to Gonzales vs. Raich*, SALON (June 7, 2005), http://www.salon.com/news/feature/2005/06/07/supreme_court_and_pot/ [https://perma.cc/X3MW-L7TM] (suggesting that Justice Scalia sacrificed his jurisprudential "principles" in favor of his desire to "make sure there are no hippies smoking legal marijuana anywhere in his United States").

221. For an example of an especially well-developed intermediate position, articulated after *Raich* had been decided, see Barry Friedman & Genevieve Lakier, *"To Regulate," Not "to Prohibit": Limiting the Commerce*

Power, 2012 Sup. Ct. Rev. 255, 320 (arguing on structural and historical grounds that "Congress's power 'to regulate' interstate commerce does not include the power to prohibit commerce in products or services that the states themselves, or some of them, do not want to prohibit").

222. *See, e.g., Raich*, 545 U.S. at 9 ("The case is made difficult by respondents' strong arguments that they will suffer irreparable harm because, despite a congressional finding to the contrary, marijuana does have valid therapeutic purposes.").

223. Morse v. Frederick, 551 U.S. 393, 448 (2007) (Stevens, J., dissenting). In retirement, Justice Stevens endorsed marijuana legalization. *See* Eyder Peralta, *Retired Justice John Paul Stevens: Marijuana Should Be Legal*, NPR (Apr. 24, 2014), https://www.npr.org/sections/the two-way/2014/04/24/306524864/retired-justice-john-paul-stevens-mariju ana-should-be-legal [https://perma.cc/QUG9-4ENP].

224. Printz v. United States, 521 U.S. 898 (1997); New York v. United States, 505 U.S. 144 (1992).

225. For the leading statement of this position, see Robert A. Mikos, *On the Limits of Supremacy: Medical Marijuana and the States' Overlooked Power to Legalize Federal Crime*, 62 Vand. L. Rev. 1421 (2009). *See also* Erwin Chemerinsky, Jolene Forman, Allen Hopper & Sam Kamin, *Cooperative Federalism and Marijuana Regulation*, 62 UCLA L. Rev. 74, 100–13 (2015).

226. This principle is grounded in the Constitution's Supremacy Clause, which instructs that the federal Constitution "and the laws of the United States which shall be made in pursuance thereof" take precedence over any "contrary" state laws. In practice, federal-state preemption has been rare in the criminal context. *See* Erin C. Blondel, *The Structure of Criminal Federalism*, 98 Notre Dame L. Rev. 1037, 1061–62 (2023).

227. *See, e.g.*, Safe Streets Alliance v. Hickenlooper, 859 F.3d 865, 918– 19 (10th Cir. 2017) (Hartz, J., concurring); Ter Beek v. City of Wyoming, 823 N.W.2d 864, 870–74 (Mich. 2012); Cty. of San Diego v. San Diego NORML, 165 Cal. App. 4th 798, 826–28 (2008). *See generally* Berman & Kreit, *supra* note 44, at 664–81 (reviewing this litigation). Aiding the no-preemption argument, the CSA contains a clause that disclaims any congressional intent to "occupy the field" of drug regulation. 21 U.S.C. § 903.

228. *See* Brief for the United States as *Amicus Curiae*, Nebraska v. Colorado, 577 U.S. 1211 (2016) (No. 144) (successfully urging the Court to deny Nebraska and Oklahoma's motion for leave to file a bill of complaint

against Colorado for adopting marijuana reforms allegedly preempted by the CSA). Since 2014, Congress has bolstered this nonenforcement policy by passing annual appropriations riders that prohibit the Justice Department from expending any funds to prevent states from implementing their own medical marijuana laws. The first such rider appeared in Consolidated and Further Continuing Appropriations Act, 2015, Pub L. No. 113-235, § 538, 128 Stat. 2130, 2217 (2014).

229. The Obama administration's most important statement of its nonenforcement policy came in a document known as the Cole Memorandum. *See* Memorandum from James M. Cole, Deputy Att'y Gen., to U.S. Att'ys (Aug. 29, 2013), http://www.justice.gov/iso/opa/resources/305 2013829132756857467.pdf [https://perma.cc/5WUB-8P57].

230. *See* Ernest A. Young, *The Smoke Next Time: Nullification, Commandeering, and the Future of Marijuana Regulation, in* MARIJUANA FEDERALISM: UNCLE SAM AND MARY JANE 85 (Jonathan H. Adler ed., 2020).

231. It is too early to draw confident conclusions about many aspects of marijuana legalization, which may produce very different results depending on how it is implemented. At this writing, just about the only clear macro-level consequences are a decrease in marijuana-related arrests and an increase in tax revenue. *See* BROMBERG ET AL., *supra* note 20, at 121, 652–53 (reviewing evidence); ANGELA DILLS, SIETSE GOFFARD, JEFFREY MIRON & ERIN PARTIN, CATO INST., THE EFFECT OF STATE MARIJUANA LEGALIZATIONS: 2021 UPDATE (2021), https://www.cato.org/sites/cato.org/ files/2021-01/PA908.pdf [https://perma.cc/9GEB-E532] (same). For a summary of the reforms themselves as of May 2022, see Michael Hartman, *Cannabis Overview*, NAT'L CONF. STATE LEGISLATURES (May 31, 2022), https://www.ncsl.org/research/civil-and-criminal-justice/marijuana-overv iew.aspx [https://perma.cc/4R6W-CGNN].

232. MARIJUANA: REPORT OF THE INDIAN HEMP DRUGS COMMISSION 1893–1894 (Thomas Jefferson Publishing Co. 1969) (1894); MAYOR'S COMM. ON MARIHUANA, THE MARIHUANA PROBLEM IN THE CITY OF NEW YORK (1944). The Panama Canal Zone studies did not result in a single definitive report. For contemporaneous summaries of two studies, see J.F. Siler et al., *Marijuana Smoking in Panama*, 73 MILITARY SURGEON 269 (1933); *Marijuana Smoking Is Reported Safe*, N.Y. TIMES, Nov. 21, 1926, at E3.

233. Allen Ginsberg, *The Great Marijuana Hoax: First Manifesto to End the Bringdown*, ATLANTIC MONTHLY, Nov. 1966, at 104.

234. U.K. Home Off., Advisory Comm. on Drug Dependence, Cannabis 22–23 (1968), https://perma.cc/B8HF-S8XU (punctuation added).

235. *See* LeDain Commission Report, *supra* note 187, at 267 ("On the whole, the physical and mental effects of cannabis, at the levels of use presently attained in North America, would appear to be much less serious than those which may result from excessive use of alcohol.").

236. I have been unable to find an English translation of either commission's report. For a detailed overview, see Peter D.A. Cohen, *The Case of the Two Dutch Drug-Policy Commissions: An Exercise in Harm Reduction, 1968–1976, in* Harm Reduction: A New Direction for Drug Policies and Programs 17 (Patricia Erickson, Diane Riley, Yuet Cheung & Pat O'Hare eds., 1997).

237. *See* Sen. Standing Comm. on Soc. Welfare, Drug Problems in Australia—An Intoxicated Society? 143 (1977), https://parlinfo.aph.gov.au/parlInfo/download/publications/tabledpapers/HPP052016005912/upl oad_pdf/HPP052016005912.pdf ("Cannabis has been in use for centuries and to date no physical ill effects due to its use have been manifest.").

238. *See* Vera Rubin & Lambros Comitas, Ganja in Jamaica: A Medical Anthropological Study of Chronic Marihuana Use 166 (1975) (finding "no evidence" that cannabis causes "mental deterioration, insanity, violence," indolence, poverty, or other negative outcomes). This study contributed to a recommendation two years later by a Joint Select Committee of the Jamaican government that personal use of ganja be decriminalized. *See* Nat'l Comm'n on Ganja, Report of the National Commission on Ganja 2 (2001), https://perma.cc/N7EJ-QFLA (recounting this history).

239. Proceedings of the White House Conference on Narcotic and Drug Abuse 286 (1962).

240. President's Comm'n on L. Enf't & Admin. of Just., The Challenge of Crime in a Free Society 224 (1967). The report further explained that marijuana does not produce physical dependency and is "much less" potent than LSD, before concluding somewhat cagily that "enough information exists to warrant careful study of our present marihuana laws and the propositions on which they are based." *Id.* at 224–25.

241. Nat'l Comm'n on Marihuana & Drug Abuse, *supra* note 21, at 78, 91.

242. Lewis A. Grossman, Choose Your Medicine: Freedom of Therapeutic Choice in America 8 (2021).

243. KAPLAN, *supra* note 13, at 315.

244. Clark, *supra* note 105, at 247.

245. The canonical references here are the 1936 film *Reefer Madness* and the similarly lurid 1937 article *Marihuana: Assassin of Youth*, coauthored by the FBN Commissioner and a pulp crime writer. H.J. Anslinger with Courtney Ryley Cooper, *Marihuana: Assassin of Youth*, AM. MAG., July 1937, at 18.

246. Bonnie & Whitebread, *supra* note 10, at 1169.

247. *See* NAT'L COMM'N ON MARIHUANA & DRUG ABUSE, *supra* note 21, at 86–102 (reviewing allegations); Jerome L. Himmelstein, *From Killer Weed to Drop-Out Drug: The Changing Ideology of Marihuana*, 7 CONTEMP. CRISES 13, 13 (1983) ("In the turbulent debate over marihuana beginning in the 1960s, the Killer Weed claim was abruptly replaced by the virtually opposite assertion that marihuana induced passivity and destroyed motivation.").

248. NAT'L COMM'N ON MARIHUANA & DRUG ABUSE, *supra* note 21, at 65; *see also* Brief of *Amicus Curiae* American Orthopsychiatric Society, Inc. at 3, People v. Sinclair, 194 N.W.2d 878 (Mich. 1972) (No. 91-153) ("Amicus recognizes that there is no proof that marijuana is harmless. There cannot be; no drug is harmless.").

249. United States v. Collier, Crim. No. 43604-73 (D.C. Super. Ct. 1974) (unreported decision), *reprinted in Nomination of an Associate Judge: Hearing Before the S. Comm. on the District of Columbia*, 94th Cong. 866, 872 n.21 (1975).

250. *See* Leary v. United States, 395 U.S. 6, 16 n.15 (1969); Michael P. Rosenthal, *Dangerous Drug Legislation in the United States: Recommendations and Comments*, 45 TEX. L. REV. 1037, 1077 (1967).

251. Pub. L. No. 91-513, § 202, 84 Stat. 1247–49 (1970). The CSA assigns the authority to reschedule drugs to the attorney general, who in turn has delegated it to the Drug Enforcement Administration (DEA). Further enhancing the DEA's control over rescheduling, the act does not define any of the terms quoted in the main text.

252. CONSUMERS UNION REPORT, *supra* note 13, at 525 & n.†.

253. FRYDL, *supra* note 14, at 359.

254. David J. Nutt, Leslie A. King & Lawrence D. Phillips, *Drug Harms in the UK: A Multicriteria Decision Analysis*, 376 LANCET 1558 (2010); *accord* Jan van Amsterdam, David Nutt, Lawrence Phillips & Wim van den Brink, *European Rating of Drug Harms*, 29 J. PSYCHOPHARMACOLOGY 655

(2015). The most comprehensive assessment of marijuana's health effects at this writing is Nat'l Acads. of Scis., Eng'g & Med., The Health Effects of Cannabis and Cannabinoids: The Current State of Evidence and Recommendations for Research (2017). Many proponents and some opponents of legalization have claimed that this report—which found that cannabis has proven therapeutic value for a number of conditions while posing risks for adolescents, pregnant people, and drivers—supports their side. I am not aware of anyone who has claimed that the report supports cannabis's continued classification in Schedule I of the CSA.

255. Skinner v. Oklahoma, 316 U.S. 535, 541 (1942). Scholars and advocates who advanced this argument often simultaneously attacked marijuana prohibition on substantive due process grounds. For representative examples, see 1977 Decriminalization Hearing, *supra* note 108, at 310 (statement of Jay A. Miller, ACLU); Boyko & Rotberg, *supra* note 107, at 785–89; Joseph S. Oteri & Harvey A. Silverglate, *The Pursuit of Pleasure: Constitutional Dimensions of the Marihuana Problem*, 3 Suffolk L. Rev. 55, 77–80 (1968); Soler, *supra* note 15, at 605–40; Roger Allan Glasgow, Note, *Marijuana Laws: A Need for Reform*, 22 Ark. L. Rev. 359, 368–74 (1968); Town, *supra* note 107, at 763; *see also* Bonnie & Whitebread, *supra* note 10, at 1149 (declining to endorse the equal protection argument yet stating that "our central objection to the marijuana laws is of constitutional dimensions[:] We believe that those laws are irrational").

256. McLaughlin v. Florida, 379 U.S. 184, 191 (1964).

257. People v. McKenzie, 458 P.2d 232 (Colo. 1969); People v. Stark, 400 P.2d 923 (Colo. 1965).

258. *McKenzie*, 458 P.2d at 236.

259. State v. Zornes, 475 P.2d 109, 115–16 (Wash. 1970) (en banc).

260. People v. McCabe, 275 N.E.2d 407, 409–13 (Ill. 1971) (per curiam).

261. People v. Sinclair, 194 N.W.2d 878, 887 (Mich. 1972) (opinion of Swainson, J.); *id.* at 894–95 (opinion of Williams, J.) (joined by Chief Justice Kavanagh); *see supra* note 137 and accompanying text. Later that year, the Michigan Court of Appeals stated, technically incorrectly, that in *Sinclair* "the Supreme Court declared that marijuana is improperly classified as a narcotic and held that such classification is unconstitutional." People v. Griffin, 198 N.W.2d 21, 23 (Mich. App. 1972).

262. State v. Kantner, 493 P.2d 306, 352 (Haw. 1972) (Kobayashi, J., dissenting).

263. 286 A.2d 740 (N.J. Super. 1972). Two years earlier, the New Jersey legislature had excluded marijuana from the definition of a narcotic in a reform to its criminal drug laws, *see id.* at 741, but neglected to change marijuana's status under the Motor Vehicle Act.

264. Sam v. State, 500 P.2d 291 (Okla. Crim. App. 1972).

265. English v. Miller, 341 F. Supp. 714, 717–18 (E.D. Va. 1972), *rev'd sub nom.* English v. Va. Probation & Parole Bd., 481 F.2d 188 (4th Cir. 1973).

266. This tactic of judicial resistance was chronicled at the time in Lynn Darling, *The Rape of Mary Jane*, WASHINGTONIAN, Jan. 1975, at 46, 51, and rebuffed in *United States v. Walton*, 514 F.2d 201 (D.C. Cir. 1975), and *United States v. Johnson*, 333 A.2d 303 (D.C. 1975) (per curiam).

267. Soler, *supra* note 15, at 668–69.

268. Commonwealth v. Miller, 20 Crim. L. Rep. 2331, 2331 (Mass. Mun. Ct. 1976). Because municipal court decisions in Massachusetts don't have precedential value, the prosecutor declined to appeal this ruling—presumably for fear that a higher court would ratify its reasoning—or to change his office's enforcement practices. *See Mass. Ban on Cocaine Is Rejected by Judge*, WASH. POST, Dec. 12, 1976, at A26. Reflecting the reform movement's overwhelming focus on the (mis)classification of cannabis, the constitutional law literature appears to have overlooked this case entirely. It is discussed in one sentence in MARTIN TORGOFF, CAN'T FIND MY WAY HOME: AMERICA IN THE GREAT STONED AGE, 1945–2000, at 320 (2004), and Larry I. Palmer, *The Role of Appellate Courts in Mandatory Sentencing Schemes*, 26 UCLA L. REV. 753, 788 (1979).

269. *Challenging the Cocaine Laws*, ANN ARBOR SUN (Sept. 3, 1976), *available at* https://aadl.org/node/201855 [https://perma.cc/7YZK-V356] (quoting Joseph Oteri).

270. People v. McCarty, 418 N.E.2d 26 (Ill. App. 1981), *rev'd*, 427 N.E.2d 147 (Ill. 1981).

271. Steven Schorr, *Judge Voids Cocaine Laws*, HARV. CRIMSON (Dec. 11, 1976), https://www.thecrimson.com/article/1976/12/11/judge-voids-coca ine-laws-pa-massachusetts/ [https://perma.cc/H2J3-LP4P].

272. Trust Territory v. Bermudes, 7 TTR 80, 89 (1974). To my knowledge, no prior work of legal scholarship has cited or discussed this case. I learned of it from the "In the Courts" column of NORML's former newsletter, *The Leaflet*, held at the UMass Amherst Special Collections and

University Archives. *See* Peter H. Meyers, *U.S. Trust Territory Decriminalizes Marijuana After Court Voids Prior Law*, 3 Leaflet, no. 3, 1974, at 5.

273. State v. Gilbert, 44 Fla. Supp. 69, 71 (Fla. Cir. Ct. 1976).

274. State v. Leigh, 46 U.S.L.W. 2425, 2425 (Fla. Cir. Ct. 1978), *rev'd*, 369 So. 2d 947 (Fla. 1979) (per curiam).

275. State v. Anonymous, 355 A.2d 729, 741–42 (Conn. Super. Ct. 1976), *rev'd sub nom.* State v. Rao, 370 A.2d 1310 (Conn. 1976). To similar effect, a Missouri justice opined in 1978: "When one generation irrationally uses the criminal sanction to coerce and intimidate another into rejecting a relatively harmless drug, marijuana, while openly promoting the use of what we know to be relatively harmful drugs, alcohol and tobacco, respect for law and the legal process suffers." State v. Mitchell, 563 S.W.2d 18, 31–32 (Mo. 1978) (Seiler, J., dissenting).

276. United States v. Randall, 104 Daily Wash. L. Rptr. 2249, 2252 (D.C. Super. Ct. 1976); *see also id.* (suggesting that the "right of an individual to protect his body" recognized in *Roe v. Wade* reinforces this conclusion); Dufton, *supra* note 14, at 209–12 (discussing this case and its aftermath); Grossman, *supra* note 242, at 235–41 (same).

277. Opinion and Recommended Ruling, Findings of Fact, Conclusions of Law and Decision of Administrative Law Judge, In the Matter of Marijuana Rescheduling Petition at 26, 58–59, DEA, No. 86-22 (Sept. 6, 1988), *available at* https://perma.cc/DC2H-U6RJ. A longtime administrative law judge who had no evident countercultural leanings but relished his reputation for independence, Young was, unsurprisingly, "treated as something of a pariah within his agency." Michael Isikoff, *DEA Judge's 'Fresh' View on Legal Marijuana Use*, Wash. Post (Sept. 19, 1988), https://www.washingtonpost.com/archive/politics/1988/09/19/dea-judges-fresh-view-on-legal-marijuana-use/2055d246-9003-403d-94a6-69fb9b469a3e/ [https://perma.cc/5SMQ-XFEA].

278. Schedules of Controlled Substances; Scheduling of 3,4-Methyl enedioxymethamphetamine (MDMA) into Schedule I of the Controlled Substances Act, 51 Fed. Reg. 36,552 (Oct. 14, 1986). This was an initial scheduling order, not a response to a rescheduling petition, as MDMA came onto the DEA's radar only in the 1980s.

279. Marijuana Scheduling Petition; Denial of Petition, 54 Fed. Reg. 53,767, 53,782–73 (Dec. 29, 1989).

280. *See* BROMBERG ET AL., *supra* note 20, at 65, 337; *see also* Daniel Richman, *Defining Crime, Delegating Authority—How Different Are Administrative Crimes?*, 39 YALE J. ON REG. 304, 317 (2022) ("Since very significant sentencing consequences follow from the scheduling of a drug at a particular level, the [CSA] comes close to authorizing crime-definition by the very department in charge of prosecutions."). In October 2022, President Biden instructed the secretary of health and human services and the attorney general "to review expeditiously how marijuana is scheduled under federal law." *See supra* note 4. It will be interesting to see whether and how Judge Young's opinion is invoked throughout this review process.

281. People v. Summit, 517 P.2d 850, 853–54 (Colo. 1974) (en banc).

282. State v. Renfro, 542 P.2d 366, 369–70 (Haw. 1975).

283. People v. Schmidt, 272 N.W.2d 732, 736 (Mich. App. 1978).

284. 477 F.2d 349, 356 (2d Cir. 1973).

285. *See, e.g.*, Bourassa v. State, 366 So. 2d 12, 13–19 (Fla. 1978) (Adkins, J., dissenting); State v. Mitchell, 563 S.W.2d 18, 32–36 (Mo. 1978) (Shangler, J., dissenting); People v. Summit, 517 P.2d 850, 854–56 (Colo. 1974) (Lee, J., dissenting).

286. 316 U.S. 535, 541 (1942).

287. 379 U.S. 184, 192–94 (1964).

288. *See supra* notes 255–56 and accompanying text; *see also* State v. Kantner, 493 P.2d 306, 348 (Haw. 1972) (Kobayashi, J., dissenting) (citing *McLaughlin* and *Skinner* to this effect); State v. Zornes, 475 P.2d 109, 116, 119 (Wash. 1970) (en banc) (citing *Skinner* to this effect).

289. *See* Ariela R. Dubler, *Sexing* Skinner: *History and the Politics of the Right to Marry*, 110 COLUM. L. REV. 1348, 1370–73 (2010).

290. United States v. Kiffer, 477 F.2d 349, 356 & n.15 (2d Cir. 1973).

291. NORML v. Bell, 488 F. Supp. 123, 136 (D.D.C. 1980). For similar statements equating uncertainty or disuniformity in expert opinion with policy rationality, see English v. Va. Probation & Parole Bd., 481 F.2d 188, 191 (4th Cir. 1973); State v. Smith, 610 P.2d 869, 875 (Wash. 1980) (en banc); Hamilton v. State, 366 So. 2d 8, 11 (Fla. 1978); State v. Murphy, 570 P.2d 1070, 1074 (Ariz. 1977) (en banc); NORML v. Gain, 100 Cal. App. 3d 586, 594 (1979); State v. Dickamore, 592 P.2d 681, 683 (Wash. App. 1979); Illinois NORML v. Scott, 383 N.E.2d 1330, 1334 (Ill. App. 1978); People v. Schmidt, 272 N.W.2d 732, 735 (Mich. App. 1978).

292. United States v. Castro, 401 F. Supp. 120, 127 (N.D. Ill. 1975); *see also, e.g.*, United States v. Brookins, 383 F. Supp. 1212, 1215–17 (D.N.J. 1974); United States v. DiLaura, 394 F. Supp. 770, 773 (D. Mass. 1974).

293. State v. Kells, 259 N.W.2d 19, 24 (Neb. 1977); *see also, e.g., Bell*, 488 F. Supp. at 137 ("Legislatures have wide discretion in attacking social ills. A State may direct its law against what it deems evil as it actually exists without covering the whole field of possible abuses . . . ." (internal quotation marks omitted)). The German Constitutional Court relied on similar logic in 1994 when it reversed a lower court judgment that criminalizing cannabis, but not alcohol or cigarettes, violates the guarantee of equality before the law. BVerfGE 90, 145, 195–97 (1994). The German court qualified this conclusion, however, by disallowing criminal penalties for personal possession of small amounts of the drug.

294. State v. Rao, 370 A.2d 1310, 1313–14 (Conn. 1976) (ellipsis and parentheses omitted; hyphen added).

295. United States v. Pickard, 100 F. Supp. 3d 981, 1005 (E.D. Cal. 2015) (internal quotation marks and citations omitted); *see also* Meghan Boone, *Perverse & Irrational*, 16 HARV. L. & POL'Y REV. 393, 396 (2022) ("While the proposition that a law is irrational if it results in the opposite outcome from lawmakers' intentions likely strikes most as a fairly obvious contention, the Supreme Court has not interpreted the Constitution to require laws to work in any meaningful way to meet the rational basis threshold.").

296. *See* Sidney A. Shapiro & Richard W. Murphy, *Arbitrariness Review Made Reasonable: Structural and Conceptual Reform of the "Hard Look,"* 92 NOTRE DAME L. REV. 331, 332–48 (2016) (reviewing this history).

297. KAPLAN, *supra* note 13, at 3.

298. Bonnie & Whitebread, *supra* note 10, at 1149, 1154.

299. NAT'L COMM'N ON MARIHUANA & DRUG ABUSE, *supra* note 21, at 8–9.

300. U.S. Dep't of Agric. v. Moreno, 413 U.S. 528, 534 (1973). This proposition has come to be known as the anti-animus principle in equal protection law.

301. Denial of Petition to Initiate Proceedings to Reschedule Marijuana, 81 Fed. Reg. 53,688, 53,693–94 (Aug. 12, 2016) (capitalization altered).

302. Oliva, *supra* note 57 (discussing "anti-pleasure principles" in American antidrug ideology); *cf.* HUSAK, *supra* note 59, at 127–28 (observing that "the decision to use illicit drugs for recreational purposes" is invariably attributed by many to a "pathology," even though "[e]mpirical support for these preconceptions is dubious"); Lisa Scott, *The Pleasure Principle: A Critical Examination of Federal Scheduling of Controlled Substances*, 29 SW. U. L. REV. 447, 449–50 (2000) (detailing ways in which U.S. drug policy assumes that the pursuit of pleasure through drug use is irrelevant "at best . . . and morally condemnable at worst").

CHAPTER 3

303. DAVID GARLAND, THE CULTURE OF CONTROL: CRIME AND SOCIAL ORDER IN CONTEMPORARY SOCIETY 132 (2001); *see also* Ron Harris, *Blacks Bear Brunt of Drug War*, L.A. TIMES (Apr. 22, 1990), https://www.latimes.com/archives/la-xpm-1990-04-22-mn-387-story.html [https://perma.cc/Z7AR-P7SW] ("[A]round the country, politicians, public officials and even many police officers and judges say the nation's war on drugs has in effect become a war on black people.").

304. Deborah Small, *The War on Drugs Is a War on Racial Justice*, 68 SOC. RSCH. 896, 897 (2001).

305. ALEXANDER, *supra* note 39; Glasser, *supra* note 46; Graham Boyd, *The Drug War Is the New Jim Crow*, NACLA REPORT ON THE AMERICAS, July–Aug. 2001, at 18.

306. Lassiter, *supra* note 24, at 127 ("Scholars primarily have analyzed the U.S. drug war as a racial system of social control of urban minority populations . . . ."); *see also* Samuel K. Roberts, *The Impact of the US Drug War on People of Color*, *in* THE OXFORD HANDBOOK OF GLOBAL DRUG HISTORY, *supra* note 7, at 474, 487 ("Since the 1990s, one study after another . . . has accumulated damning evidence about the disproportionate and harmful impact the war on drugs had on communities of color in the United States.").

307. *See* DIANA L. AHMAD, THE OPIUM DEBATE AND CHINESE EXCLUSION LAWS IN THE NINETEENTH-CENTURY AMERICAN WEST 56 (2007) (stating that journalists' pleas for opium regulation "rarely varied" in this period and centered on the desire "to eliminate the drug and its distributors, the Chinese,

from their communities"); ELIZABETH KELLY GRAY, HABIT FORMING: DRUG ADDICTION IN AMERICA, 1776–1914, at 162–69 (2022) (reviewing news stories from the late 1800s that accused Chinese men of "luring white youth to dens" and "giving opium to young girls and then raping them"); Patricia A. Morgan, *The Legislation of Drug Law: Economic Crisis and Social Control,* 8 J. DRUG ISSUES 53, 57–60 (1978) (concluding that the first opium laws in California were motivated above all by hostility toward "the laboring 'Chinamen' who threatened the economic security of the white working class").

308. *Ya-pien,* DAILY EVENING POST, Mar. 1, 1879, at 1, 1. The title of this article is a reference to the Chinese term for opium.

309. *Ex parte* Yung Jon, 28 F. 308, 312 (D. Or. 1886). "True," the judge further acknowledged, "we permit the indiscriminate use of alcohol and tobacco, both of which are classed by science as poisons, and doubtless destroy many lives annually. But the people of this country have been accustomed to the manufacture and use of these for many generations," whereas smoking opium has "little, if any, place in the experience or habits of the people of this country, save among a few aliens." *Id.* at 311–12.

310. CORAMAE RICHEY MANN, UNEQUAL JUSTICE: A QUESTION OF COLOR 60 (1993).

311. MUSTO, *supra* note 12, at 43–44 (quoting Hamilton Wright).

312. *Id.* at 304 n.15 (quoting Edward Huntington Williams, *Negro Cocaine "Fiends" Are a New Southern Menace,* N.Y. TIMES, Feb. 8, 1914, at 12).

313. *See, e.g.,* Bonnie & Whitebread, *supra* note 10, at 1010–62 (documenting this pattern and concluding that the "most prominent" influence on the enactment of marijuana bans in the 1910s and 1920s was "racial prejudice"). *But see* Isaac Campos, *Mexicans and the Origins of Marijuana Prohibition in the United States: A Reassessment,* 32 SOC. HIST. ALCOHOL & DRUGS 6, 7 (2018) (arguing that "the role of Mexican immigrants in the history of U.S. marijuana prohibition has surely been overstated").

314. I employ the term "marijuana" throughout this book not to conjure or condone any negative association with Mexican immigrants, of course, but in recognition of the fact that the term has passed into common parlance and been reappropriated by large swaths of the pro-legalization community since the 1960s. *See* JOHN HUDAK, MARIJUANA: A SHORT HISTORY 23–26 (2d ed. 2020) (reviewing the etymology of "marijuana" in U.S. drug policy discourse and defending its continued use on similar grounds).

Should the social meaning of the term change in the years ahead, I would think it appropriate to reconsider this choice.

315. One of the most inflammatory statements attributed to Anslinger, quoted in dozens upon dozens of articles, books, and websites, is some variant on the following: "Most marijuana smokers are Negroes, Hispanics, Filipinos, and entertainers. Their satanic music, jazz and swing, result from marijuana usage. This marijuana causes white women to seek sexual relations with Negroes." *See, e.g.*, ATT'Y GEN. ALLIANCE, CANNABIS LAW DESKBOOK § 7:2 (2022–2023 ed.); RUDOLPH J. GERBER, LEGALIZING MARIJUANA: DRUG POLICY REFORM AND PROHIBITION POLITICS 9 (2004); PAULA MALLEA, THE WAR ON DRUGS: A FAILED EXPERIMENT 25 (2014); DAVID E. NEWTON, MARIJUANA: A REFERENCE HANDBOOK 163 (2013); Robert Solomon, *Racism and Its Effect on Cannabis Research*, 5 CANNABIS & CANNABINOID RES. 2, 3 (2020); *Cannabis and Racial Justice*, MARIJUANA POL'Y PROJECT (2023), https://www.mpp.org/issues/criminal-justice/cannabis-and-racial-justice/ [https://perma.cc/SZ3F-JYRS]. The spirit and tenor of this statement are indeed Anslingerian. But the Columbia Law School librarians and I have been unable to track down the quotation in Anslinger's papers at Penn State, the record of the hearings where it was allegedly uttered, or anywhere else, and none of the works quoting it provides a citation to the original source—all of which leads me to believe that the statement is apocryphal. I have likewise been unable to track down one of the other outrageous statements most commonly attributed to Anslinger, that "[r]eefer makes darkies think they're as good as white men." *Cf.* Fisher, *supra* note 81, at 935–45 (arguing that, contrary to the conventional wisdom among drug war scholars, Anslinger largely refrained from using "ethnic coding" or "racial imagery" in his public advocacy for marijuana prohibition).

316. *See* DAVID T. COURTWRIGHT, DARK PARADISE: A HISTORY OF OPIATE ADDICTION IN AMERICA 149–60 (2001) (heroin); DORIS MARIE PROVINE, UNEQUAL UNDER LAW: RACE IN THE WAR ON DRUGS 37–62 (2007) (alcohol); andré douglas pond cummings & Steven A. Ramirez, *The Racist Roots of the War on Drugs and the Myth of Equal Protection for People of Color*, 44 U. ARK. LITTLE ROCK L. REV. 453, 460–74 (2022) (Nixon and Reagan administrations).

317. 1977 Decriminalization Hearing, *supra* note 108, at 538 (punctuation altered). This point "gives me some dilemma," Alexander poignantly added, "but it does not prejudice my mind." *Id.*; *see also* Steven Bender, *The*

Colors of Cannabis: Race and Marijuana, 50 U.C. Davis L. Rev. 689, 692–95 (2016) (discussing the "whitewashed" nature of most marijuana law reform campaigns since the 1960s, as well as "the current softening of enforcement response to the epidemic of opiate use among whites").

318. Reiss, *supra* note 35, at 202; *cf.* Naomi Murakawa, The First Civil Right: How Liberals Built Prison America 64 (2014) ("Federal lawmakers launched the 1950s war on drugs to combat 'red' and 'black' threats: red heroin-pushing communists and black heroin addicts.").

319. *See* Am. Civil Liberties Union, The War on Marijuana in Black and White 17–20 (2013), https://www.aclu.org/sites/default/files/field_d ocument/1114413-mj-report-rfs-rel1.pdf [https://perma.cc/YE2C-DJV9]; Hum. Rts. Watch, Decades of Disparity: Drug Arrests and Race in the United States 1 (2009), https://www.hrw.org/sites/default/files/reports/ us0309web_1.pdf [https://perma.cc/SU3L-LL3S]; Nat'l Rsch. Council, The Growth of Incarceration in the United States: Exploring Causes and Consequences 60 (2014); David D. Cole, *Formalism, Realism, and the War on Drugs*, 35 Suffolk U. L. Rev. 241, 247–49 (2001); Michael Tonry & Matthew Melewski, *The Malign Effects of Drugs and Crime Control Policies on Black Americans, in* Thinking About Punishment: Penal Policy Across Space, Time, and Discipline 81, 104–05 (Michael Tonry ed., 2009).

320. *See, e.g.,* Hum. Rts. Watch, Targeting Blacks: Drug Law Enforcement and Race in the United States 16 (2008), https://www.hrw. org/sites/default/files/reports/us0508_1.pdf [https://perma.cc/EST6-XXUF] (finding that in 2003 the total rate of prison admission for drug offenses was ten times higher for Blacks than for whites across thirty-four states); *see also* James Forman, Jr., *Racial Critiques of Mass Incarceration: Beyond the New Jim Crow*, 87 N.Y.U. L. Rev. 21, 46 n.96 (2012) (describing racial disparities in drug-related prison/arrest ratios as "the strongest evidence for disparate treatment in the court system itself").

321. *Cf.* Gabriel J. Chin, *Race, the War on Drugs, and the Collateral Consequences of Criminal Conviction*, 6 J. Gender Race & Just. 253 (2002) (discussing the disparate racial effects of drug convictions' myriad "collateral consequences").

322. *See* sources cited *supra* note 42; *see also* Jamie Fellner, *Race, Drugs, and Law Enforcement in the United States*, 20 Stan. L. & Pol'y Rev. 257, 270–74 (2009) (cataloguing explanations that have been offered for racial disparities in drug arrests); Michael Vitiello, *Marijuana Legalization, Racial*

Disparity, and the Hope for Reform, 23 Lewis & Clark L. Rev. 789, 805–06 (2019) (same).

323. Stuntz, *supra* note 42, at 1798 (emphasis added).

324. *See supra* notes 24, 59–61 and accompanying text.

325. Frydl, *supra* note 14, at 421. Suzanna Reiss similarly argues that economic interests "have historically exerted a commanding influence with regard to establishing the dividing line between legal and illegal . . . drug markets." Reiss, *supra* note 35, at 6–7. David Herzberg has documented the "relentless, profit-driven increase in the potency and availability of addictive [licit] pharmaceuticals" over the course of the twentieth century. David Herzberg, White Market Drugs: Big Pharma and the Hidden History of Addiction in America 282 (2020). Antonia Eliason and Robert Howse describe the pharmaceutical industry as "the elephant in the room" in all conversations about the development or reform of the international drug control regime. Antonia Eliason & Robert Howse, *Towards a Global Governance Regime: The Inadequacies of the UN Drug Control Regime*, 114 AJIL Unbound 291, 291 (2020).

326. James Forman Jr., Locking Up Our Own: Crime and Punishment in Black America (2017); Michael Javen Fortner, Black Silent Majority: The Rockefeller Drug Laws and the Politics of Punishment (2015).

327. Fisher, *supra* note 81, at 933.

328. H. Wayne Morgan, Drugs in America: A Social History, 1800–1980, at x (1981).

329. Provine, *supra* note 316, at 118; *see also* Gray, *supra* note 307, at 7 (explaining that "racism and classism" likewise "shaped dominant American attitudes toward drug use and . . . drug laws and their enforcement" throughout the nineteenth century).

330. 347 U.S. 483 (1954).

331. Harper v. Va. Bd. of Elections, 383 U.S. 663 (1966).

332. Loving v. Virginia, 388 U.S. 1 (1967).

333. *E.g.*, Coleman v. Alabama, 389 U.S. 22 (1967) (juries); Schiro v. Bynum, 375 U.S. 395 (1964) (city auditoriums); Johnson v. Virginia, 373 U.S. 61 (1963) (courtrooms); New Orleans City Park Improvement Ass'n v. Detiege, 358 U.S. 54 (1958) (parks); Gayle v. Browder, 352 U.S. 903 (1956) (buses); Mayor of Baltimore v. Dawson, 350 U.S. 877 (1955) (beaches).

334. *Loving*, 388 U.S. at 10.

335. For a detailed synopsis, see Reva B. Siegel, *The Supreme Court, 2012 Term—Foreword: Equality Divided*, 127 HARV. L. REV. 1, 9–15 (2013); *see also* United States v. Bannister, 786 F. Supp. 2d 617, 664 (E.D.N.Y. 2011) ("Intent was not a clear requirement of Equal Protection violations before the Supreme Court's 1976 decision of *Washington v. Davis.* . . . Pre-*Davis*, some cases indicated that impact alone was sufficient basis for finding a violation."); Michael J. Perry, *The Disproportionate Impact Theory of Racial Discrimination*, 125 U. PA. L. REV. 540, 544 (1977) ("Considerable uncertainty existed prior to [*Davis*] in regard to whether the principal element of a constitutional claim of racial discrimination was discriminatory purpose or simply discriminatory effect.").

336. Griggs v. Duke Power Co., 401 U.S. 424, 430 (1971).

337. 426 U.S. 229, 238–48 (1976); *see also* Village of Arlington Heights v. Metro. Hous. Dev. Corp., 429 U.S. 252, 264–65 (1977) ("Our decision last Term in *Washington v. Davis* made it clear that official action will not be held unconstitutional solely because it results in a racially disproportionate impact. . . . Proof of racially discriminatory intent or purpose is required to show a violation of the Equal Protection Clause." (citation omitted)).

338. 442 U.S. 256, 279 (1979).

339. Reva B. Siegel, *Why Equal Protection No Longer Protects: The Evolving Forms of Status-Enforcing State Action*, 49 STAN. L. REV. 1111, 1113 (1997).

340. *Davis*, 426 U.S. at 248.

341. Charles R. Lawrence III, *The Id, the Ego, and Equal Protection: Reckoning with Unconscious Racism*, 39 STAN. L. REV. 317, 319 (1987).

342. *See, e.g.*, Whren v. United States, 517 U.S. 806, 813 (1996) ("We of course agree with petitioners that the Constitution prohibits selective enforcement of the law based on considerations such as race. But the constitutional basis for objecting to intentionally discriminatory application of the laws is the Equal Protection Clause, not the Fourth Amendment.").

343. Wayte v. United States, 470 U.S. 598, 608 (1985); *see also, e.g.*, United States v. Armstrong, 517 U.S. 456, 465–66 (1996) (selective prosecution claims); McCleskey v. Kemp, 481 U.S. 279, 291–99 (1987) (sentencing discrimination claims).

344. Soler, *supra* note 15, at 641.

345. John C. Williams, *Constitutionality of State Legislation Imposing Criminal Penalties for Personal Possession or Use of Marijuana*, 96 A.L.R.3d 225 (1979).

346. *See generally, e.g.*, HELLMAN, *supra* note 106; KAPLAN, *supra* note 13; Bonnie & Whitebread, *supra* note 10; Soler, *supra* note 15. In 1964, Kaplan had published an influential article arguing that the Equal Protection Clause is specially offended by laws that draw explicit racial classifications—which the drug laws did not do. John Kaplan, *Segregation Litigation and the Schools—Part II: The General Northern Problem*, 58 Nw. U. L. REV. 157 (1964).

347. State v. Tartaglia, 365 F. Supp. 171, 172 (D.N.M. 1973) (dismissing a petition for removal to federal court).

348. United States v. Brookins, 383 F. Supp. 1212, 1214 (D.N.J. 1974).

349. *Id.* at 1217 (citation omitted); *see also* Dennis J. Helms, Thomas Lescault & Alfred A. Smith, *Cocaine: Some Observations on Its History, Legal Classification and Pharmacology*, 4 CONTEMP. DRUG PROBS. 195, 196 (1975) (stating that the "early racial motivations for the regulation of cocaine" were "still smoldering in the minds of the defense lawyers" who litigated *Brookins*). The following year, a district court in Illinois expressly embraced the "reasoning and conclusions" of *Brookins*, without addressing the issue of racial discrimination. United States v. Castro, 401 F. Supp. 120, 125 (N.D. Ill. 1975).

350. NORML v. Bell, 488 F. Supp. 123, 141 n.44 (D.D.C. 1980). NORML did not appeal this ruling.

351. Commonwealth v. Miller, 20 Crim. L. Rep. 2331, 2331 (Mass. Mun. Ct. 1976); *see supra* notes 268–71 and accompanying text (discussing this opinion and a similar one by an Illinois appellate court in 1981).

352. Bonnie & Whitebread, *supra* note 10, at 1010–62.

353. People v. McCarty, 418 N.E.2d 26, 28 (Ill. App. 1981); *Miller*, 20 Crim. L. Rep. at 2331.

354. *See supra* note 317 and accompanying text; *see also* United States v. Clary, 846 F. Supp. 768, 775 (E.D. Mo. 1994) (explaining that in the 1960s and 1970s cocaine "began to move into mainstream society" and "earned the moniker of the 'rich man's drug'").

355. *See supra* note 326 and accompanying text.

356. *Cf.* Lassiter, *supra* note 24, at 133–35 (arguing that the ACLU and NORML framed their marijuana reform campaigns in the late 1960s "as

NOTES TO PAGE 78

a mission to rescue white victims of the war on drugs" and that the "marijuana decriminalization movement of the 1970s revolved around the forthright view that white middle-class Americans should not have their futures ruined by policies designed to protect them"). "The most striking feature of the drug-war consensus from the 1950s through the 1980s," Lassiter reflects in his new book, "involves the almost complete absence of concern for, or even acknowledgment of, racial discrimination in policing and other aspects of the criminal legal system." LASSITER, *supra* note 58, at 11.

357. Gallup first began asking Americans about illegal drug use in 1969, and the U.S. government first began administering the National Survey on Drug Use and Health in 1971. *See* Jennifer Robison, *Decades of Drug Use: Data from the '60s and '70s*, GALLUP (July 2, 2002), https://news. gallup.com/poll/6331/decades-drug-use-data-from-60s-70s.aspx [https:// perma.cc/6GAX-KHQ7]; *What Is NSDUH?*, NAT'L SURVEY ON DRUG USE & HEALTH (2023), https://nsduhweb.rti.org/respweb/homepage.cfm [https:// perma.cc/5LB6-MDTE]. The FBI's Uniform Crime Reports have collected data on the race of arrestees by crime type since the 1930s, although the generally more reliable National Crime Victimization Survey did not begin until 1973. *See* Paul Knepper, *Race, Racism and Crime Statistics*, 24 S.U. L. REV. 71, 86–87 (1996); *see also* Benjamin D. Steiner & Victor Argothy, *White Addiction: Racial Inequality, Racial Ideology, and the War on Drugs*, 10 TEMP. POL. & CIV. RTS. L. REV. 443, 455 n.40 (2001) (arguing, with reference to the war on drugs, that the National Crime Victimization Surveys "present a more accurate and vastly different picture of race and crime" than do the Uniform Crime Reports).

358. In interviews, I asked NORML's former executive director and chief counsel why they did not press claims of unconstitutional racial discrimination more forcefully during the 1970s. Both suggested that, for all the racism involved in the enactment and enforcement of marijuana laws, such claims were seen at the time as off the wall. Telephone Interview with R. Keith Stroup (Dec. 16, 2022); Telephone Interview with Peter Meyers (Dec. 19, 2022). In response to a similar question, another leading criminal defense lawyer from this period, whose Boston-based firm specialized in drug cases, recalled to my research assistant that "the basic legal strategy was to argue that the private possession statutes violated fundamental personal rights . . . . The crack/powder disparity was a decade in the future."

Email from Martin G. Weinberg to Josceline M. Sanchez (Feb. 1, 2023, 10:06 PM).

359. *See* James D. Orcutt & J. Blake Turner, *Shocking Numbers and Graphic Accounts: Quantified Images of Drug Problems in the Print Media*, 40 Soc. Probs. 190, 191–92 (1993) (finding that drug issues consumed nearly 5 percent of national television, magazine, and newspaper news coverage in the late summer and early fall of 1986). For a broad overview of the media frenzy over crack, see Craig Reinarman & Harry J. Levine, *The Crack Attack: Politics and Media in the Crack Scare, in* CRACK IN AMERICA, *supra* note 37, at 18.

360. Richard Harwood, *Hyperbole Epidemic*, WASH. POST (Oct. 1, 1989), https://www.washingtonpost.com/archive/opinions/1989/10/01/hyperb ole-epidemic/82fe62b1-7816-4df1-8080-7027abb6911d/ [https://perma.cc/ C6QE-B2YX].

361. Anti-Drug Abuse Act of 1986, Pub. L. No. 99-570, § 1302, 100 Stat. 3207, 3207–15. The act created another 100:1 ratio in imposing a ten-year mandatory minimum sentence for trafficking crimes that involve either five kilograms of powder cocaine or fifty grams of crack cocaine. *Id.*

362. Anti-Drug Abuse Act of 1988, Pub. L. No. 100-690, § 6371, 102 Stat. 4181, 4370.

363. *See* NICOLE D. PORTER & VALERIE WRIGHT, SENT'G PROJECT, CRACKED JUSTICE 6 (2011), https://www.prisonpolicy.org/scans/sp/Cracked-Justice.pdf [https://perma.cc/AL9Y-G55A].

364. *See* David A. Sklansky, *Cocaine, Race, and Equal Protection*, 47 STAN. L. REV. 1283, 1303 (1995).

365. United States v. Galloway, 951 F.2d 64, 66 (5th Cir. 1992).

366. Pers. Adm'r v. Feeney, 442 U.S. 256, 279 (1979).

367. U.S. SENT'G COMM'N, ANNUAL REPORT 88 tbl.31 (1992); *see also* Dan Weikel, *War on Crack Targets Minorities over Whites*, L.A. TIMES, May 21, 1995, at A1 (relating that in more than half of the federal districts that handled crack cases in 1992, no white individuals were prosecuted for crack offenses). In the 1991 National Household Survey on Drug Abuse, 52 percent of respondents who reported crack use at least once in the prior year were white, as were 65 percent of respondents who reported crack use at least once in their lifetime. *See* U.S. SENT'G COMM'N, SPECIAL REPORT TO THE CONGRESS: COCAINE AND FEDERAL SENTENCING POLICY 38–39 (1995). These survey results indicated that a substantially higher (though still very

NOTES TO PAGES 80–82

low) fraction of the Black population had tried crack, but this racial discrepancy evaporated when researchers controlled for social and environmental conditions. *Id.* at 39–40. Put simply, crack was sold in lower-income urban neighborhoods, and Black people were more likely to live in those neighborhoods.

    368. RANDALL KENNEDY, RACE, CRIME, AND THE LAW 371–73 (2007) (quoting Waldon); 132 CONG. REC. E3515-02 (daily ed. Oct. 9, 1986) (statement of Rep. Charles B. Rangel) (submitting into the Congressional Record an editorial titled *Crack Down on Crack*); *cf.* JOHN H. MCWHORTER, LOSING THE RACE: SELF-SABOTAGE IN BLACK AMERICA 14 (2000) ("Yet how racist can a law be which the Congressional Black Caucus vigorously supported and even considered too weak?").

    369. United States v. Thurmond, 7 F.3d 947, 953 (10th Cir. 1993).

    370. United States v. McMurray, 833 F. Supp. 1454, 1466 (D. Neb. 1993); *see also* United States v. Chandler, 996 F.2d 917, 918 (7th Cir. 1993) ("But awareness of consequences alone does not establish discriminatory intent. In fact, *Feeney* expressly precludes such an inference . . . .").

    371. United States v. Frazier, 981 F.2d 92, 95 (3d Cir. 1992) (citing Pers. Adm'r v. Feeney, 442 U.S. 256, 279 (1979)).

    372. United States v. Bynum, 3 F.3d 769, 775 (4th Cir. 1993).

    373. *See, e.g.*, United States v. Holland, 810 F.2d 1215, 1219–20 (D.C. Cir. 1987) (discussing school cases); State v. Hatton, 918 S.W.2d 790 (Mo. 1996) (public housing).

    374. *See* United States v. Majied, 1993 WL 315987, at *5 (D. Neb. 1993), *rev'd sub nom.* United States v. Maxwell, 25 F.3d 1389 (8th Cir. 1994) (departing from the sentencing guidelines because "members of the African American race are being treated unfairly in receiving substantially longer sentences than caucasian males who traditionally deal in powder cocaine"); *Judge Is Forced to Lengthen Sentences for Crack*, N.Y. TIMES, Nov. 27, 1995, at B5 (describing Judge Lyle Strom's remarks during the resentencing hearing in this case).

    375. Ira Eisenberg, *The One-Size-Fits-All Approach to Justice*, BALTIMORE SUN (Apr. 2, 1993), https://www.baltimoresun.com/news/bs-xpm-1993-04-02-1993092278-story.html [https://perma.cc/AY32-WJAH] (quoting Judge William Schwarzer).

    376. United States v. Conard, 1994 WL 90356, at *1, *5 (W.D. Mo. 1994). This district judge aligned himself with U.S. Supreme Court Justice

Anthony Kennedy, who had testified to Congress a week before, "I simply do not see how the Congress can be satisfied with the results of mandatory minimums for possession of crack cocaine." *Departments of Commerce, Justice, and State, the Judiciary, and Related Agencies Appropriations for 1995: Hearings Before the Subcomm. on the Dep'ts of Commerce, Justice, & State, the Judiciary, & Related Agencies of the H. Comm. on Appropriations*, 103d Cong. 29 (1994).

377. PROVINE, *supra* note 316, at 149–53 (quoting Jonathan M. Moses, *Many Judges, in Low-Key Revolt, Go Around Sentencing Guidelines*, WALL ST. J., May 7, 1993, at B12).

378. State v. Russell, 477 N.W.2d 886, 888 n.2 (Minn. 1991); *see also id.* at 892 (Yetka, J., concurring specially) ("The legislature's power is admittedly broad in this area, but it is not so broad as to allow distinctions that have a harsher impact on minority groups, particularly when those distinctions are based on minimal information."); *id.* at 895 (Simonett, J., concurring specially) ("I conclude a showing has been made that the statute, in its general application, impacts substantially more on black than white defendants.").

379. *Id.* at 889.

380. *Id.* at 903 (Coyne, J., dissenting).

381. United States v. Clary, 846 F. Supp. 768 (E.D. Mo. 1994). Judge Cahill's opinion was over nineteen thousand words long, with seventy-five footnotes. As Doris Marie Provine relates, Cahill had been a distinguished public interest lawyer before becoming the first African American to be appointed to his court. At the time he wrote *Clary*, Cahill was seventy years old, on senior status, and "had plans to retire" (plans that were later scrapped; he stayed on the bench until his death in 2004). *Clary* was to be his "swan song." PROVINE, *supra* note 316, at 22–23.

382. *Clary*, 846 F. Supp. at 779. Lawrence's article on *Reckoning with Unconscious Racism*, published the year after Congress created the 100:1 ratio, did not discuss crack or any other drugs. Lawrence, *supra* note 341.

383. *Clary*, 846 F. Supp. at 783–84.

384. *Id.* at 781 (internal quotation marks and citation omitted).

385. United States v. Clary, 34 F.3d 709, 713 (8th Cir. 1994); *cf.* Christopher J. Tyson, *At the Intersection of Race and History: The Unique Relationship Between the Davis Intent Requirement and the Crack Laws*, 50 How. L.J. 345, 392 (2007) (suggesting that the Eighth Circuit's decision

in *Clary* "ironically reflects the unconscious racism [that] Judge Cahill references").

386. Richard Dvorak, *Cracking the Code: "De-Coding" Colorblind Slurs During the Congressional Crack Cocaine Debates*, 5 MICH. J. RACE & L. 611, 616 (2000).

387. *See, e.g.*, Todd Rakoff, Washington v. Davis *and the Objective Theory of Contracts*, 29 HARV. C.R.-C.L. L. REV. 63, 97 (1994).

388. *See* KENNEDY, *supra* note 368, at 369–77.

389. Sklansky, *supra* note 364, at 1306.

390. Randall Kennedy, *The State, Criminal Law, and Racial Discrimination: A Comment*, 107 HARV. L. REV. 1255, 1263 (1994). On appeal to the Eighth Circuit, both of the organizations that filed amicus briefs in *Clary* argued that crack cocaine is, if anything, *less* potent and addictive than powder cocaine. *See* Brief of *Amicus Curiae* American Civil Liberties Union at 11, United States v. Clary, 34 F.3d 709 (8th Cir. 1994) (No. 94-1422); Brief of *Amicus Curiae* National Association of Criminal Defense Lawyers at 4–7, United States v. Clary, 34 F.3d 709 (8th Cir. 1994) (No. 94-1422).

391. *See* Kennedy, *supra* note 390, at 1261–70; Kate Stith, *The Government Interest in Criminal Law: Whose Interest Is It, Anyway?*, *in* PUBLIC VALUES IN CONSTITUTIONAL LAW 137, 153 (Stephen E. Gottlieb ed., 1993).

392. Paul Butler, *(Color) Blind Faith: The Tragedy of* Race, Crime, and the Law, 111 HARV. L. REV. 1270, 1273 (1998). For prominent rebuttals of Kennedy by legal scholars, see *id.*; David Cole, *The Paradox of Race and Crime: A Comment on Randall Kennedy's "Politics of Distinction,"* 83 GEO. L.J. 2547 (1995).

393. Fair Sentencing Act, Pub. L. No. 111-220, 124 Stat. 2372 (2010); *see also* Kyle Graham, *Sorry Seems to Be the Hardest Word: The Fair Sentencing Act of 2010, Crack, and Methamphetamine*, 45 U. RICH. L. REV. 765 (2011) (discussing the unusual confluence of factors that led Congress to reduce this ratio and highlighting Congress's simultaneous failure to reconsider penalties for methamphetamine offenses). After the 2010 legislation was enacted, a panel of the U.S. Court of Appeals for the Sixth Circuit ruled that equal protection principles compel it to be applied retroactively to convictions under the 1986 law. But this ruling was rejected by every other circuit and overturned en banc. United States v. Blewett, 719 F.3d 482 (6th Cir. 2013), *rev'd en banc*, 746 F.3d 647 (6th Cir. 2013). In 2005, the Supreme Court held that the Sixth Amendment's guarantee of a jury trial requires

the federal sentencing guidelines to be advisory rather than mandatory. United States v. Booker, 543 U.S. 220 (2005). Judges may now impose sentences that are longer or shorter than the guidelines recommend.

394. The Supreme Court did acknowledge that "unconscious prejudices" may contribute to "discriminatory intent" in a 2015 case about the federal Fair Housing Act, Tex. Dep't of Hous. & Cmty. Affs. v. Inclusive Cmtys. Project, Inc., 576 U.S. 519, 540 (2015), but this observation has not similarly informed the Court's equal protection jurisprudence.

395. *See, e.g.,* United States v. Green, 2016 WL 11483508, at *4 (W.D.N.Y. 2016); United States v. Pickard, 100 F. Supp. 3d 981, 1004 (E.D. Cal. 2015); United States v. Heying, 2014 WL 5286155, at *4 (D. Minn. 2014); State v. Bradley, 2018 WL 3117117, at *6–*7 (Conn. Super. Ct. 2018). *See generally* W. Kerrel Murray, *Discriminatory Taint*, 135 HARV. L. REV. 1190 (2022) (explaining that the Court frequently ignores discriminatory predecessors of contemporary policies).

396. *Blewett*, 719 F.3d at 487.

397. Siegel, *supra* note 335, at 20–23.

398. Although the Burger Court invalidated a race-conscious admissions policy in *Regents of the University of California v. Bakke*, 438 U.S. 265 (1978), it wasn't until William Rehnquist's chief justiceship that a majority opinion applied strict scrutiny to an affirmative action or minority set-aside program. *See* Adarand Constructors, Inc. v. Peña, 515 U.S. 200 (1995); City of Richmond v. J.A. Croson Co., 488 U.S. 469 (1989).

399. Parents Involved in Cmty. Schs. v. Seattle Sch. Dist. No. 1, 551 U.S. 701, 748 (2007). Originally conceived as a progressive ideal in the late 1800s, when policies that classified people on the basis of race did so in the service of American apartheid, the conceit of a colorblind Constitution is the textbook example of "ideological drift" in U.S. law. *See* J.M. Balkin, *Ideological Drift and the Struggle over Meaning*, 25 CONN. L. REV. 869, 871–73 (1993); David E. Pozen, *Transparency's Ideological Drift*, 128 YALE L.J. 100, 105–07 (2018); *see also* Kenneth B. Nunn, *Rights Held Hostage: Race, Ideology and the Peremptory Challenge*, 28 HARV. C.R.-C.L. L. REV. 63, 112 (1993) ("The [contemporary] adoption of colorblind constitutionalism . . . clearly furthers the political agenda of the neo-conservative right by defending and preserving white privilege.").

400. Amanda Chicago Lewis, *How Black People Are Being Shut Out of America's Weed Boom*, BuzzFEED (Mar. 16, 2016), https://www.buzzfeedn

ews.com/article/amandachicagolewis/americas-white-only-weed-boom
[https://perma.cc/J9UA-ZS2R].

401. Ohio Rev. Code § 3796.09(C).

402. PharmaCann Ohio, LLC v. Ohio Dep't of Commerce, 2018 WL
7500067 (Ohio Ct. Com. Pl. 2018).

403. *See* ROBERT A. MIKOS, MARIJUANA LAW, POLICY, AND AUTHORITY
522–25 (2017).

404. *See* MINORITY CANNABIS BUS. ASS'N, MCBA NATIONAL CANNABIS
EQUITY REPORT 32 (2022), https://mjbizdaily.com/wp-content/uplo
ads/2022/02/National-Cannabis-Equity-Report-1.pdf [https://perma.cc/
DSX5-GZ7T] ("Ohio's failed attempt to create a social equity program
presented a cautionary tale that wrongfully deterred states' use of race-
based criteria.").

405. Cannabis licensing preferences for in-state residents have
been challenged under the so-called dormant Commerce Clause, which
limits states' ability to restrict interstate commerce through protec-
tionist measures. *See, e.g.,* Ne. Patients Grp. v. United Cannabis Patients
& Caregivers of Me., 45 F.4th 542 (1st Cir. 2022); Variscite NY One, Inc.
v. New York, 2022 WL 17257900 (N.D.N.Y. 2022); *see also* Andrew Kline
& Thomas Tobin, *Cannabis and the Dormant Commerce Clause*, PERKINS
COIE LLP (2022), https://www.perkinscoie.com/images/content/2/5/251
638/Cannabis-and-the-Dormant-Commerce-Clause.pdf [https://perma.
cc/5L2S-PMPG] (providing an overview of recent litigation).

406. Disparate racial impacts may give rise to liability under the Fair
Housing Act and Title VII of the Civil Rights Act of 1964, which regu-
lates employment discrimination. *See* Tex. Dep't of Hous. & Cmty. Affs. v.
Inclusive Cmtys. Project, Inc., 576 U.S. 519, 530–40 (2015).

CHAPTER 4

407. Robinson v. California, 370 U.S. 660, 666–67 (1962). Fifteen years
earlier, the Court had assumed without deciding that the Cruel and Unusual
Punishment Clause applies to the states via the Due Process Clause of the
Fourteenth Amendment. Louisiana ex rel. Francis v. Resweber, 329 U.S.

459, 462 (1947); *cf. supra* note 91 (discussing "incorporation" of the Bill of Rights generally).

408. Timbs v. Indiana, 139 S. Ct. 682, 686–87 (2019).

409. *See* William W. Berry III, *Cruel State Punishments*, 98 N.C. L. Rev. 1201, 1252–54 (2020) (showing that only the Vermont constitution lacks an analogue to the federal Cruel and Unusual Punishment Clause).

410. Wilkerson v. Utah, 99 U.S. 130 (1878).

411. As one commentator observed in 1961, the year before *Robinson*, "Few constitutional guarantees of individual liberty have so often been relied on, to so little avail, as has the eighth amendment." Note, *The Effectiveness of the Eighth Amendment: An Appraisal of Cruel and Unusual Punishment*, 36 N.Y.U. L. Rev. 846, 846 (1961).

412. 217 U.S. 349, 368, 378 (1910) (quoting McDonald v. Commonwealth, 53 N.E. 874, 875 (Mass. 1899)).

413. Trop v. Dulles, 356 U.S. 86, 101 (1958) (plurality opinion). The *Trop* plurality held that denationalization is a cruel and unusual punishment for the crime of military desertion.

414. 370 U.S. 660 (1962).

415. Mark S. Dichter, Comment, *Marijuana and the Law: The Constitutional Challenges to Marijuana Laws in Light of the Social Aspects of Marijuana Use*, 13 Vill. L. Rev. 851, 878 (1968).

416. Robinson v. California, 370 U.S. 660, 661, 666 (1962).

417. *Id.* at 660, 662.

418. *See* Robinson v. California, 371 U.S. 905 (1962) (Clark, J., dissenting from denial of rehearing); *see also* Nancy D. Campbell, OD: Naloxone and the Politics of Overdose 66 (2000) ("[Robinson's] lawyer had either given a very credible performance of not knowing that his client was dead, or was genuinely unaware of that cold fact.").

419. Alfred R. Lindesmith, *Introduction, in* Joint Comm. of Am. Bar Ass'n & Am. Med. Ass'n, Drug Addiction: Crime or Disease? at vii, x (1961). This final report followed the 1958 publication of an interim report that had reached the same conclusions and been subject to "vituperative" and "desperate" attack by the Federal Bureau of Narcotics. Musto, *supra* note 12, at 234. By the time the final report came out, there was "little that [was] new or original" in it. John M. Murtagh, Review, 71 Yale L.J. 363, 363 (1961).

420. *Robinson*, 370 U.S. at 667 & n.9.

421. Justice Felix Frankfurter suffered a stroke shortly before the *Robinson* oral argument and did not participate in the case.

422. *Robinson*, 370 U.S. at 666.

423. Letter from Elizabeth Kenney, secretary to Justice Stewart, to Dr. Frederick Floyds, chief resident of Children's Hospital of the District of Columbia (June 26, 1962), *in* Potter Stewart Papers, Yale University Library Manuscripts and Archives, MS 1367, Box 19, Folder 173 ("Many thanks for your help in digging out recent medical articles on drug addiction in newborns for us."). The phrase "born addicts" comes from a popular article by that title, *Born Addicts*, TIME, May 19, 1958, at 70, which did not make it into Justice Stewart's *Robinson* opinion but was part of his case file. Potter Stewart Papers, *supra*, at MS 1367, Box 19, Folder 172; *see also* Supplementary Memo on *Robinson v. California* from Nathan Lewin, law clerk, to Justice Harlan (undated), *in* John M. Harlan II Papers, Mudd Manuscript Library, Princeton University, Box 149, at 194 (referring to a "clipping sent along by Justice Douglas" that "proves . . . someone may be born an addict").

424. *Robinson*, 370 U.S. at 668–78 (Douglas, J., concurring). Justice Harlan also wrote a concurrence, which added nothing of substance to the majority opinion except the assertion that the California statute was "arbitrary." *Id.* at 679 (Harlan, J., concurring).

425. *Id.* at 689 (White, J., dissenting).

426. *Id.* at 682–83 (Clark, J., dissenting); *see also* Bonnie & Whitebread, *supra* note 10, at 1141 (stating that *Robinson* was "clearly a substantive due process decision cloaked in the protective garb of the eighth amendment"). Technically, any decision invalidating a state law under the Cruel and Unusual Punishment Clause, or any other provision of the Bill of Rights, is a due process decision, in that the Court has applied these provisions to the states through the Fourteenth Amendment's Due Process Clause. But Justice Clark seemed to imply that *Robinson* was a due process ruling in content as well as form.

427. Note, *The Cruel and Unusual Punishment Clause and the Substantive Criminal Law*, 79 HARV. L. REV. 635, 650 (1966) (internal punctuation and quotation marks omitted).

428. *See* Michael R. Asimow, Comment, *Constitutional Law: Punishment for Narcotic Addiction Held Cruel and Unusual*, 51 CALIF. L. REV. 219, 226–27 (1962).

429. *Robinson*, 370 U.S. at 664.

430. *Id.* at 688 (White, J., dissenting). Justice White put this point more forcefully in an uncirculated draft: "The Court goes out of its way to reaffirm the power of a State to attach criminal penalties to use of narcotics, but the opinion bristles with *implications to the contrary.*" Justice Byron R. White, Draft Dissent in Robinson v. California 6 (undated) (emphasis added), *in* Byron R. White Papers, Library of Congress, Box 7, Folder 4.

431. *Robinson*, 370 U.S. at 688 (White, J., dissenting).

432. William J. Stuntz, *The Uneasy Relationship Between Criminal Procedure and Criminal Justice*, 107 YALE L.J. 1, 68 n.234 (1997).

433. Commonwealth v. Hall, 394 S.W.2d 448 (Ky. 1965); People v. Davis, 188 N.E.2d 225 (Ill. 1963); State v. Bridges, 360 S.W.2d 648 (Mo. 1962).

434. People v. Malloy, 58 Misc. 2d 538, 542 (N.Y. Crim. Ct. 1968).

435. Morales v. United States, 344 F.2d 846, 849 n.2 (9th Cir. 1965).

436. Sweeney v. United States, 353 F.2d 10 (7th Cir. 1965); State v. Oyler, 436 P.2d 709 (Idaho 1968).

437. Easter v. District of Columbia, 361 F.2d 50 (D.C. Cir. 1966) (en banc); Driver v. Hinnant, 356 F.2d 761 (4th Cir. 1966). Although the D.C. Circuit case was decided on statutory grounds, the influence of *Robinson* was pervasive.

438. Justin Driver, *The Constitutional Conservatism of the Warren Court*, 100 CALIF. L. REV. 1101, 1145 (2012).

439. Although it has not proved nearly as generative as reformers in the 1960s hoped, *Robinson* continues to anchor attacks on "antihomeless" ordinances, with mixed results. For an overview, see Ryan P. Isola, Note, *Homelessness: The Status of the Status Doctrine*, 54 U.C. DAVIS L. REV. 1725 (2021). For the leading contemporary case in this line, see Martin v. City of Boise, 920 F.3d 584 (9th Cir. 2019).

440. Walter W. Steele, Jr., *The Status of Status Crime*, 52 JUDICATURE 18, 19 (1968); *see also* George F. Bason, Jr., *Chronic Alcoholism and Public Drunkenness*—Quo Vadimus Post Powell, 19 AM. U. L. REV. 48, 50, 63 (1969) (discussing developments that "led so many experts to predict so confidently what the Court would hold in *Powell*" and "the unexpectedness of the result"); Driver, *supra* note 438, at 1141 & nn.238–39 (collecting commentary predicting that the Court would rule for Powell or expressing surprise at the outcome).

441. Powell v. Texas, 392 U.S. 514, 555 (1968) (Fortas, J., dissenting).

442. *Id.* at 530 (plurality opinion).

443. *Id.* at 542–44 (Black, J., concurring).

444. *Id.* at 531 (plurality opinion) (emphasis added); *see also id.* at 535–36 (discussing "the moral accountability of an individual for his antisocial deeds").

445. *Id.* at 533–35.

446. *Id.* at 548–49 (White, J., concurring in the result).

447. *Id.* at 551.

448. *Id.* at 567 (Fortas, J., dissenting).

449. *Id.* at 565 (quoting MANFRED S. GUTTMACHER & HENRY WEIHOFEN, PSYCHIATRY AND THE LAW 319 (1952)).

450. Kate Stith-Cabranes, *Criminal Law and the Supreme Court: An Essay on the Jurisprudence of Byron White*, 74 U. COLO. L. REV. 1523, 1537 (2003); *see also* Sanford H. Kadish, *Fifty Years of Criminal Law: An Opinionated Review*, 87 CALIF. L. REV. 943, 965–66 (1999) (stating that *Powell* "closed the door" on the opening created by *Robinson*).

451. Marks v. United States, 30 U.S. 188, 193 (1977) (internal quotation marks omitted).

452. *See* Richard M. Re, *Beyond the* Marks *Rule*, 132 HARV. L. REV. 1942, 1948 n.28 (2019); Ryan C. Williams, *Questioning* Marks: *Plurality Decisions and Precedential Constraint*, 69 STAN. L. REV. 795, 806 n.44 (2017).

453. H. Jefferson Powell, *Judges as Superheroes: The Danger of Confusing Constitutional Decisions with Cosmic Battles*, 72 S.C. L. REV. 917, 928–29 (2021); *see also* Kent Greenawalt, *"Uncontrollable" Actions and the Eighth Amendment: Implications of* Powell v. Texas, 69 COLUM. L. REV. 927, 927 (1969) (discussing the "inconclusive disposition of *Powell*").

454. United States v. Moore, 486 F.2d 1139, 1239 & n.178 (D.C. Cir. 1973) (en banc) (Wright, J., dissenting) (quoting Watson v. United States, 439 F.2d 442, 451 (D.C. Cir. 1970) (en banc)).

455. State v. Fearon, 166 N.W.2d 720, 724 (Minn. 1969).

456. *In re* Jones, 246 A.2d 356, 362–63 (Pa. 1968).

457. Watson v. United States, 439 F.2d 442, 453 (D.C. Cir. 1970) (en banc).

458. Att'y Gen. John N. Mitchell, "To Heal, and Not to Punish": Address at a Testimonial Dinner Honoring R. Brinkley Smithers 5 (Dec. 9, 1971), https://www.justice.gov/sites/default/files/ag/legacy/2011/08/23/12-09-1971 pro.pdf [https://perma.cc/D3K7-S9QB].

459. *See, e.g.*, United States v. Lindsey, 324 F. Supp. 55, 58 (D.D.C. 1971) ("The [*Powell*] Court seemed to say that to make out a constitutional defense, the defense would have to show both a 'loss of control' once the individual has begun to drink and an 'inability to abstain from drinking in the first place.'").

460. Justice White, recall, argued explicitly that *Robinson* applies to drug use by addicts in their own homes. *See supra* notes 446–47 and accompanying text. Justice Marshall emphasized in dicta that the state of Texas had not "attempted to regulate appellant's behavior in the privacy of his own home," presumably to distinguish the Court's recent ruling in *Griswold*. Powell v. Texas, 392 U.S. 514, 532 (1968) (plurality opinion).

461. Smith v. Follette, 445 F.2d 955, 961 (2d Cir. 1971).

462. *See, e.g.*, People v. Jones, 251 N.E.2d 195, 198–99 (Ill. 1969); Nutter v. State, 262 A.2d 80, 86–87 (Md. App. 1970); Rangel v. State, 444 S.W.2d 924, 926 (Tex. Crim. App. 1969); *see also* Note, *Criminal Law: Demise of "Status"—"Act" Distinction in Symptomatic Crimes of Narcotic Addiction*, 1970 DUKE L.J. 1053, 1055 ("Courts applying criminal sanctions to symptomatic crimes of narcotics addiction since *Powell* have relied heavily upon the Court's distinction between 'status' and 'act' to support their refusal to extend *Robinson*.").

463. *See* United States v. Moore, 486 F.2d 1139, 1209 (D.C. Cir. 1973) (en banc) (Wright, J., dissenting) ("Today this court rejects the *Watson* rationale and holds that a non-trafficking addict is a criminal because he possesses drugs to satisfy his addiction.").

464. PETER W. LOW, CRIMINAL LAW 361 (1990).

465. Traynor v. Turnage, 485 U.S. 535, 552–67 (1988) (Blackmun, J., concurring in part and dissenting in part). Justice Blackmun replaced Justice Fortas, who had authored the dissent in *Powell*. President Nixon's other appointments replaced Justices Black, Harlan, and Warren.

466. *See* CAROLINE JEAN ACKER, CREATING THE AMERICAN JUNKIE: ADDICTION RESEARCH IN THE CLASSIC ERA OF NARCOTIC CONTROL 217–18 (2002).

467. AM. BAR ASS'N, SPECIAL COMM. ON CRIME PREVENTION & CONTROL, NEW PERSPECTIVES ON URBAN CRIME, at i (1972) (punctuation added).

468. NAT'L COMM'N ON MARIHUANA & DRUG ABUSE, DRUG USE IN AMERICA: PROBLEM IN PERSPECTIVE (1973). As the associate director of this commission reflected in 2016, this second report took "what we now would

NOTES TO PAGES 100–101

call a public health approach to drug policy—an emphasis on demand re-duction (particularly the prevention and treatment of addiction)." Richard J. Bonnie, *The Surprising Collapse of Marijuana Prohibition: What Now?*, 50 U.C. DAVIS L. REV. 573, 581 (2016).

469. *Moore*, 486 F.2d at 1174 (Leventhal, J., concurring) (discussing the climate in which the Controlled Substances Act of 1970 was enacted); *see also id.* at 1167 (explaining that the 1960s witnessed "an increasing real-ization and acceptance that the Government could not satisfactorily cope with the narcotic drug abuse problem by concentrating on law enforcement activities"). On the unprecedented growth in federal spending on treatment and prevention during President Nixon's first term, see FRYDL, *supra* note 14, at 339, 364; MUSTO, *supra* note 12, at 250–51; PROVINE, *supra* note 316, at 93–95.

470. Powell v. Texas, 392 U.S. 514, 534 (1968) (plurality opinion).

471. *Moore*, 486 F.2d at 1151–52 (opinion of Wilkey, J.); *see also id.* at 1147 ("The obvious danger is that this defense *will* be extended to all other crimes—bank robberies, street muggings, burglaries—which can be shown to be the product of the same drug-craving compulsion."); Smith v. Follette, 445 F.2d 955, 961 (2d Cir. 1971) ("[I]f every criminal act which was the result in some degree of a socially developed compulsion was beyond society's control, the interests and safety of the public would be seriously threatened.").

472. *Powell*, 392 U.S. at 537, 544, 547 (Black, J., concurring).

473. Herbert L. Packer, *Mens Rea and the Supreme Court*, 1962 SUP. CT. REV. 107, 147 n.144 ("If [the] premise . . . that the legislature may not make it a 'crime' to be 'sick' is to be taken literally, the demise of the criminal law may be at hand."); Note, *supra* note 427, at 654 (stating that acceptance of the "status one cannot change" reading of *Robinson* "would lead to virtual abandonment of the criminal law").

474. *Powell*, 392 U.S. at 559 n.2 (Fortas, J., dissenting).

475. *Moore*, 486 F.2d at 1257 (Wright, J., dissenting).

476. *See* Robinson v. California, 370 U.S. 660, 665 (1962) ("[A] State might establish a program of compulsory treatment for those addicted to narcotics. Such a program of treatment might require periods of involuntary confinement."); *see also Moore*, 486 F.2d at 1170–71 (Leventhal, J., concur-ring) (discussing civil commitment provisions of the federal Narcotic Addict Rehabilitation Act of 1966); *id.* at 1247–48 (Wright, J., dissenting) (same);

JULILLY KOHLER-HAUSMANN, GETTING TOUGH: WELFARE AND IMPRISONMENT IN 1970S AMERICA 40 (2017) ("The exact same ruling [*Robinson*] that decriminalized addiction also enabled the civic subordination of addicts by affirming the states' power to confine them indefinitely."); Alan M. Dershowitz, *Constitutional Dimensions of Civil Commitment, in* 4 NAT'L COMM'N ON MARIHUANA & DRUG ABUSE, *supra* note 468, app. at 397, 449 (concluding in 1973 that "at this moment . . . the weight of authority and history clearly favor the constitutionality of narcotic commitment laws").

477. Joshua Dressler, *Kent Greenawalt, Criminal Responsibility, and the Supreme Court: How a Moderate Scholar Can Appear Immoderate Thirty Years Later*, 74 NOTRE DAME L. REV. 1507, 1517 (1999); *see also* Greenawalt, *supra* note 453, at 956–72 (detailing complications and ambiguities in the limiting principles proposed by the *Powell* dissent).

478. *See* Richard S. Frase, *The Warren Court's Missed Opportunities in Substantive Criminal Law*, 3 OHIO ST. J. CRIM. L. 99–100 (2005) (suggesting that the existence of these contemporaneous reform projects may help explain the Warren Court's reluctance to rein in criminal sentencing).

479. *See* Robert Batey, *The Costs of Judicial Restraint: Forgone Opportunities to Limit America's Imprisonment Binge*, 33 NEW ENG. J. ON CRIM. & CIV. CONFINEMENT 29, 32–33 (2007); Mark Tushnet, *The Warren Court as History: An Interpretation, in* THE WARREN COURT IN HISTORICAL AND POLITICAL PERSPECTIVE 1, 24–26 (Mark Tushnet ed., 1993).

480. *See generally Possession Is Nine-Tenths of the Law*, WIKIPEDIA (2023), https://en.wikipedia.org/wiki/Possession_is_nine-tenths_of_the_law [https://perma.cc/GXD8-656Z] ("*Possession is nine-tenths of the law* is an expression meaning that ownership is easier to maintain if one has possession of something, or difficult to enforce if one does not.").

481. *See* Batey, *supra* note 479, at 35 ("Possession is the basic building block of all drug offenses . . . ."); Daniel Richman, *Informants and Cooperators, in* 2 REFORMING CRIMINAL JUSTICE 279, 282 (Erik Luna ed., 2017) ("Informants are not a unique feature of narcotics investigations, but they are particularly prevalent in that area."); Stuntz, *supra* note 432, at 59 (explaining that prosecutors may use "high mandatory sentences for [drug] possession as a means of punishing distribution without having to prove it").

482. Weems v. United States, 217 U.S. 349, 368 (1910). Eighteen years before *Weems*, Justice Stephen Field had espoused this view in an

influential dissent. O'Neil v. Vermont, 144 U.S. 323, 339–40 (1892) (Field, J., dissenting).

483. 356 U.S. 86, 101 (1958) (plurality opinion); *see also* John F. Stinneford, *The Original Meaning of "Unusual": The Eighth Amendment as a Bar to Cruel Innovation*, 102 Nw. U. L. Rev. 1739, 1749 (2008) ("The evolving standards of decency test, which has dominated the Supreme Court's Cruel and Unusual Punishments Clause jurisprudence over the past fifty years, was first articulated by Chief Justice Warren in *Trop v. Dulles*.").

484. Bonnie & Whitebread, *supra* note 10, at 1133.

485. *See* John J. Michalik, *Review for Excessiveness of Sentence in Narcotics Case*, 55 A.L.R.3d 812 (1974).

486. Gallego v. United States, 276 F.2d 914, 918 (9th Cir. 1960).

487. *Id.* (quoting State v. Thomas, 69 So. 2d 738, 740 (La. 1953)).

488. Anthony v. United States, 331 F.2d 687, 693 (9th Cir. 1964).

489. Garcia v. State, 316 S.W.2d 734, 735 (Tex. Crim. App. 1958) (life imprisonment); *accord* Johnson v. State, 447 S.W.2d 927, 932 (Tex. Crim. App. 1969) (thirty years). For a compendium of cruel-and-unusual-punishment challenges to drug sentences brought during this period, see Michalik, *supra* note 485.

490. Malcolm E. Wheeler, *Toward a Theory of Limited Punishment: An Examination of the Eighth Amendment*, 24 Stan. L. Rev. 838, 838 (1972).

491. Bonnie & Whitebread, *supra* note 10, at 1123, 1153–54.

492. Wheeler, *supra* note 490, at 863.

493. Nat'l Governors' Conf. Ctr. for Pol'y Rsch. & Analysis, *supra* note 21, at 125.

494. People v. Lorentzen, 194 N.W.2d 827, 831–34 (Mich. 1972); *see also* People v. Bruinsma, 191 N.W.2d 108, 115–17 (Mich. App. 1971) (anticipating *Lorentzen*'s Eighth Amendment analysis in dicta); Charles P. Graupner, Note, *Constitutional Law—Eighth Amendment—Appellate Sentence Review*, 1976 Wis. L. Rev. 655, 662–63 (explaining that some state courts used the "shock the conscience" formulation as a shorthand for a finding of gross disproportionality).

495. Downey v. Perini, 518 F.2d 1288 (6th Cir. 1975), *vacated and remanded on other grounds*, 423 U.S. 993 (1975).

496. State v. Ward, 270 A.2d 1, 5 (N.J. 1970); *see* Bonnie & Whitebread, *supra* note 10, at 1123 (describing *Ward* as "a landmark decision" and contending "that the true locus of the opinion," which does not cite the

Constitution, "is the eighth amendment"); *see also, e.g.*, People v. Young, 46 A.D.2d 202, 208 (N.Y. App. Div. 1974) (ordering that a defendant convicted of marijuana possession be released from prison into a residential treatment program); State v. Brennan, 279 A.2d 900, 904 (N.J. Super. Ct. 1971) (extending *Ward*'s "no-jail rule for initial possessors of marijuana" to "a seller-user of that drug under favorable rehabilitative prospects").

497. Hill v. State, 477 P.2d 399, 402–03 (Okla. Crim. App. 1970).

498. Graham v. State, 20 Crim. L. Rep. 2223, 2223 (Okla. Crim. App. 1976); McCarty v. State, 525 P.2d 1391, 1395 (Okla. Crim. App. 1974).

499. *In re* Foss, 519 P.2d 1073, 1081–85 (Cal. 1974) (citing recommendations by the President's Commission on Law Enforcement and the Administration of Justice, the President's Advisory Commission on Narcotic and Drug Abuse, the Advisory Council of Judges of the National Council on Crime and Delinquency, and the American Bar Association Project on Minimum Standards for Criminal Justice). For subsequent drug cases building on *Foss*, see *In re* Grant, 553 P.2d 590 (Cal. 1976); *In re* Williams, 69 Cal. App. 3d 840 (1977); People v. Ruiz, 49 Cal. App. 3d 739 (1975); People v. Thomas, 45 Cal. App. 3d 749 (1975).

500. Salazar v. State, 562 P.2d 694, 697 (Alaska 1997) (quoting Donlun v. State, 527 P.2d 472, 475 (Alaska 1974)); *see also, e.g.*, Wharton v. State, 590 P.2d 427 (Alaska 1979) (invalidating a one-year sentence for possession of cocaine); Huff v. State, 568 P.2d 1014 (Alaska 1977) (invalidating an eight-year sentence for sale of heroin).

501. *See, e.g.*, United States v. Leigh, 46 U.S.L.W. 2425 (Fla. Cir. Ct. 1978), *rev'd*, 369 So. 2d 947 (Fla. 1979) (per curiam) (holding that any criminal sanction for personal possession of marijuana is cruel and unusual); United States v. Grady, 102 Daily Wash. L. Rep. 1161 (D.C. Super. Ct. 1974), *rev'd sub nom.* United States v. Thorne, 325 A.2d 764 (D.C. 1974) (same); *cf.* Watson v. United States, 4 Crim. L. Rep. 3051 (D.C. Cir. 1968), *vacated en banc*, 439 F.2d 442 (D.C. Cir. 1970) (applying a hybrid *Robinson-Weems* analysis to hold that a mandatory ten-year sentence for an addicted narcotics recidivist is cruel and unusual). The next section discusses several other overturned opinions. For a sampling of forceful dissents from the end of the 1970s urging that a drug sentence be deemed unconstitutionally excessive, see Bellavia v. Fogg, 613 F.2d 369, 375–79 (2d Cir. 1979) (Mansfield, J., concurring in part and dissenting in part); State v. Smith, 610 P.2d 869, 884–91 (Wash. 1980) (Dolliver, J., concurring in part and dissenting in part);

State v. Mitchell, 563 S.W.2d 18, 28–32 (Mo. 1978) (Seiler, J., dissenting); State v. Mallery, 364 So. 2d 1283, 1285–90 (La. 1978) (Tate, J., dissenting).

502. FORTNER, *supra* note 326, at xi; *see also id.* at 11 (describing the Rockefeller drug laws as "a critical juncture in the historical development of the carceral state"); KOHLER-HAUSMANN, *supra* note 476, at 29–120 (examining the Rockefeller drug laws' political history and policy legacy).

503. *See* Robert E. Glanville, Note, *Drug Abuse Law Abuse and the Eighth Amendment New York's 1973 Drug Legislation and the Prohibition Against Cruel and Unusual Punishment*, 60 CORNELL L. REV. 638, 639–40 (1975).

504. A large literature examines why penal policymakers began to abandon the rehabilitative ideal in the mid-1970s, pointing to factors such as rising crime rates, economic upheaval, declining faith in public institutions, and growing criticism of rehabilitation programs as ineffective and coercive. *See generally* FRANCIS A. ALLEN, THE DECLINE OF THE REHABILITATIVE IDEAL: PENAL POLICY AND SOCIAL PURPOSE (1981); KOHLER-HAUSMANN, *supra* note 476; Francis T. Cullen, *Rehabilitation: Beyond Nothing Works*, 42 CRIME & JUST. 299 (2013). Perhaps on account of the still-widespread view of addiction as an illness, this ideal did not collapse quite as fully in the drug context as it did elsewhere; the emergence of "drug courts" in the 1990s supplies some belated evidence of this contextual resilience. *Cf.* Morris B. Hoffman, *The Rehabilitative Ideal and the Drug Court Reality*, 14 FED. SENT. REP. 172, 176 (2002) ("The one exception to the almost universal rejection of the rehabilitative ideal lay in the area of drug laws.").

505. People v. Mosley, 78 Misc. 2d 736 (N.Y. Cty. Ct. 1974), *rev'd sub nom.* People v. McNair, 46 A.D.2d 476 (N.Y. App. Div. 1975).

506. Carmona v. Ward, 436 F. Supp. 1153 (S.D.N.Y. 1977), *rev'd*, 576 F.2d 405 (2d Cir. 1978).

507. *Id.* at 1168, 1172.

508. People v. Broadie, 332 N.E.2d 338, 343–44 (N.Y. 1975).

509. 576 F.2d 405, 410–11 (2d Cir. 1978).

510. *Id.* at 417–32 (Oakes, J., dissenting). Chief Judge Breitel had also included a historical appendix in his *Broadie* opinion. *Broadie*, 332 N.E.2d at 347–54.

511. Carmona v. Ward, 439 U.S. 1091, 1096 (1979) (Marshall, J., dissenting from denial of certiorari). Although the Second Circuit majority had purported to test the Rockefeller laws for gross disproportionality,

Marshall maintained that its antidrug polemics amounted to an "abdication" of this duty. *Id.* at 1102.

512. Coker v. Georgia, 433 U.S. 584 (1977); Gregg v. Georgia, 428 U.S. 153 (1976); Furman v. Georgia, 408 U.S. 238 (1972).

513. Most significantly, the *Coker* plurality advised that "a punishment is 'excessive' and unconstitutional if it (1) makes no measurable contribution to acceptable goals of punishment . . . *or* (2) is grossly out of proportion to the severity of the crime." *Coker*, 433 U.S. at 592 (plurality opinion) (emphasis added).

514. Rummel v. Estelle, 445 U.S. 263, 272 (1980).

515. Hutto v. Davis, 454 U.S. 370, 374–75 (1982) (per curiam) (quoting Rummel v. Estelle, 445 U.S. 263, 272 (1980)); *id.* at 388 (Brennan, J., dissenting). *Hutto*'s procedural history was more complicated than this summary conveys. For the details, see *id.* at 371–72 (per curiam).

516. 463 U.S. 277 (1983).

517. Harmelin v. Michigan, 501 U.S. 957, 966–94 (1991) (opinion of Scalia, J.). According to a news report, Justice Scalia was assigned the majority opinion in *Harmelin* but lost the votes of Justices Kennedy, O'Connor, and Souter when he sought to jettison the proportionality principle rather than narrow it. Paul M. Barrett, *The Loner: Despite Expectations, Scalia Fails to Unify Conservatives on Court*, WALL ST. J., Apr. 28, 1992, at A1.

518. *Harmelin*, 501 U.S. at 996–97, 1002–05 (Kennedy, J., concurring in part and concurring in the judgment); *see also id.* at 1002 ("Petitioner's suggestion that his crime was nonviolent and victimless . . . is false to the point of absurdity. To the contrary, petitioner's crime threatened to cause grave harm to society.").

519. Richard A. Posner, *Pragmatic Adjudication*, 18 CARDOZO L. REV. 1, 12 (1996). Subsequent cases reaffirming *Harmelin*'s narrow approach to proportionality include *Lockyer v. Andrade*, 538 U.S. 63 (2003), and *Ewing v. California*, 538 U.S. 11 (2003).

520. People v. Bullock, 485 N.W.2d 866 (Mich. 1992). In finding this penalty to be unduly excessive, the Michigan Supreme Court stressed that the state constitution forbids "cruel *or* unusual" punishments, not just "cruel *and* unusual" punishments, and employed the *"Lorenzen-Solem"* approach to proportionality analysis that the *Harmelin* majority had effectively discarded. *Id.* at 872–77.

521. State v. Lane, 826 S.E.2d 657 (W. Va. 2019); Wilson v. State, 830 So. 2d 765 (Ala. Crim. App. 2001).

522. *See, e.g.*, State v. Lee, 305 So. 3d 1048 (La. App. 2020); State v. Wallace, 92 So. 3d 592 (La. App. 2012); State v. Allen, 849 So. 2d 82 (La. App. 2003).

523. William W. Berry III, *Cruel and Unusual Non-capital Punishments*, 58 Am. Crim. L. Rev. 1627, 1636–37 (2021).

524. For critical overviews of civil forfeiture's role in the war on drugs and the dearth of procedural safeguards, see Blumenson & Nilsen, *supra* note 24; Annemarie Bridy, *Carpe Omnia: Civil Forfeiture in the War on Drugs and the War on Piracy*, 46 Ariz. St. L.J. 683 (2014); Eric L. Jensen & Jurg Gerber, *The Civil Forfeiture of Assets and the War on Drugs: Expanding Criminal Sanctions While Reducing Due Process Protections*, 42 Crime & Delinquency 421 (1996); Marc B. Stahl, *Asset Forfeiture, Burdens of Proof, and the War on Drugs*, 83 J. Crim. L. & Criminology 274 (1992).

525. *See* Jensen & Gerber, *supra* note 524, at 424; *see also* Lisa Knepper et al., Inst. for Just., Policing for Profit: The Abuse of Civil Asset Forfeiture (3d ed. 2020), https://ij.org/wp-content/uploads/2020/12/policing-for-profit-3-web.pdf [https://perma.cc/XNK8-Y94U] (detailing revenue data from the 2000s).

526. Austin v. United States, 509 U.S. 602 (1993).

527. United States v. Bajakajian, 524 U.S. 321 (1998). On the confusion generated by *Bajakajian*, see Kevin Arlyck, *The Founders' Forfeiture*, 119 Colum. L. Rev. 1449, 1460–64 (2019). *But cf.* Stefan D. Cassella, *Bulk Cash Smuggling and the Globalization of Crime: Overcoming Constitutional Challenges to Forfeiture Under 31 U.S.C. § 5332*, 22 Berkeley J. Int'l L. 98, 104 n.29 (2004) (contending that, notwithstanding the Court's mixed signals, lower courts have routinely "held that the *Bajakajian* gross disproportionality test applies equally in civil and criminal cases").

528. 139 S. Ct. 682 (2019).

529. State v. Timbs, 169 N.E.3d 361 (Ind. 2021); *see also, e.g.*, Deborah F. Bruckman, *When Does Forfeiture of Real Property Violate Excessive Fines Clause of Eighth Amendment—Post-Austin Cases*, 168 A.L.R. Fed. 375, § 6[b] (2001) (collecting cases as of 2001 holding that civil forfeitures under the federal drug laws violate the Excessive Fines Clause).

530. Transcript of Oral Argument at 14, Timbs v. Indiana, 139 S. Ct. 682 (2019) (No. 17-1091), https://www.supremecourt.gov/oral_ar

guments/argument_transcripts/2018/17-1091_1bn2.pdf   [https://perma.cc/
Q9TD-NCPE] (punctuation added).

531. Rachel E. Barkow, *The Court of Life and Death: The Two Tracks of Constitutional Sentencing Law and the Case for Uniformity*, 107 Mich. L. Rev. 1145 (2009). For the 99.999 percent figure, see John F. Stinneford, *Rethinking Proportionality Under the Cruel and Unusual Punishments Clause*, 97 Va. L. Rev. 899, 902–03, 925 (2011).

532. *See generally* Frase, *supra* note 478 (describing this discrepancy).

533. Stuntz, *supra* note 432, at 72–73.

534. Hutto v. Davis, 454 U.S. 370, 374 (1982) (per curiam).

535. Rummel v. Estelle, 445 U.S. 263, 281 (1980).

536. Wilson v. State, 830 So. 2d 765, 786 (Ala. Crim. App. 2001) (Baschab, J., dissenting); *id.* at 791 (Shaw, J., dissenting).

537. People v. Malloy, 41 Cal. App. 3d 944, 958 (1974) (Gardner, J., concurring and dissenting).

CHAPTER 5

538. Davis v. Beason, 133 U.S. 333, 342–43 (1890).

539. Reynolds v. United States, 98 U.S. 145, 167 (1879).

540. State v. Big Sheep, 243 P. 1067, 1068, 1073 (Mont. 1926); *see also id.* at 1073 ("Ruling Case Law says that, while laws cannot interfere with mere religious belief and opinions, they may inhibit acts or practices which tend toward the subversion of the civil government, or which are made criminal by the law of the land."). The Montana justices found much more difficult the question whether the defendant, a Crow Indian whose alleged acts had taken place within the Crow Reservation, could be subject to the state court's jurisdiction.

541. *See, e.g.*, West Va. State Bd. of Educ. v. Barnette, 319 U.S. 624 (1943); Murdock v. Pennsylvania, 319 U.S. 105 (1943); Cantwell v. Connecticut, 310 U.S. 296 (1940).

542. 374 U.S. 398, 403, 406–07 (1963) (holding that South Carolina violated a Seventh-Day Adventist's free exercise rights by denying her unemployment benefits after she was fired for refusing to work on Saturday, her Sabbath). The other leading case in this line was *Wisconsin v. Yoder*, 406

U.S. 205 (1972), which held that a state could not require Amish children to attend school through age fifteen.

543. United States v. Seeger, 380 U.S. 163, 180–83 (1965).

544. Note, *Toward a Constitutional Definition of Religion*, 91 HARV. L. REV. 1056, 1068 (1978).

545. *See* CHRISTOPHER PARTRIDGE, HIGH CULTURE: DRUGS, MYSTICISM, AND THE PURSUIT OF TRANSCENDENCE IN THE MODERN WORLD 225–87 (2018); Note, *supra* note 544, at 1069–71; John R. Phillips, Comment, *Free Exercise: Religion Goes to "Pot,"* 56 CALIF. L. REV. 100, 114–15 (1968); Comment, *The Drug Religions and the Free Exercise Clause*, 1 U. TOL. L. REV. 202, 202–03 (1969); *see also* Joel Jay Finer, *Psychedelics and Religious Freedom*, 19 HASTINGS L.J. 667, 693 (1968) ("In recent years, many recognized authorities in the field of religion have discovered that psychedelic drugs, of which marihuana is the mildest, can produce profound religious experiences.").

546. Donald A. Giannella, *Religious Liberty, Nonestablishment, and Doctrinal Development—Part I. The Religious Liberty Guarantee*, 80 HARV. L. REV. 1381, 1426 (1967). Giannella accurately predicted in 1967 that the "recent establishment of the League for Spiritual Development by Dr. Timothy Leary portends sustained efforts by those who advocate the use of drugs for more expansive self-realization to draw about them the protective mantle of the free exercise clause." *Id.* at 1426 n.141.

547. Arizona v. Attakai, Crim. No. 4098 (Ariz. Super. Ct. 1960) (unreported decision). *Attakai* was reprinted in the December 1961 issue of the American Anthropological Association's flagship journal. *Court Decision Regarding Peyote and the Native American Church*, 63 AM. ANTHROPOLOGIST 1335 (1961).

548. People v. Woody, 394 P.2d 813, 816–17 (Cal. 1964); *see also id.* at 817 ("Although peyote serves as a sacramental symbol similar to bread and wine in certain Christian churches, it is more than a sacrament. Peyote constitutes in itself an object of worship; prayers are directed to it much as prayers are devoted to the Holy Ghost. On the other hand, to use peyote for nonreligious purposes is sacrilegious.").

549. *Id.* at 818 (quoting the California attorney general).

550. *Id.* at 818–21.

551. *In re* Grady, 394 P.2d 728, 729 (Cal. 1964). Following remand, it appears that the peyote preacher was released without a trial. *See* Robert S.

Michaelsen, *"We Have a Religion": The Free Exercise of Religion Among Native Americans*, 7 AM. INDIAN Q. 111, 125 (1983).

552. State v. Whittingham, 504 P.2d 950, 954 (Ariz. App. 1973); Whitehorn v. State, 561 P.2d 539 (Okla. Crim. App. 1977). In contrast, a three-judge panel of the Oregon Court of Appeals declined to follow *Woody*, over a dissent that accused the majority of contravening *Sherbert* and "effectively nullif[ying] the religious freedom guarantees of the federal and Oregon constitutions." State v. Soto, 537 P.2d 142, 147 (Or. App. 1975) (Fort, J., dissenting).

553. *See* Emp. Div. v. Smith, 494 U.S. 872, 912 n.5 (1990) (Blackmun, J., dissenting) (indicating that, as of 1990, twenty-three states had "statutory or judicially crafted exemptions in their drug laws for religious use of peyote"). Two of these statutory exemptions, in Montana and New Mexico, predated *Attakai* and *Woody*.

554. For an overview of these federal exemptions, see Peyote Exemption for Native American Church, 5 Op. O.L.C. 403, 404–09 (1981) [hereinafter OLC Peyote Opinion].

555. ALEXANDER S. DAWSON, THE PEYOTE EFFECT: FROM THE INQUISITION TO THE WAR ON DRUGS 108–11 (2018).

556. Robert N. Clinton, *Peyote and Judicial Activism*, 38 FED. B. NEWS & J. 92, 95 (1991).

557. Bonnie & Whitebread, *supra* note 10, at 1143. *See generally* C.T. Foster, *Free Exercise of Religion as Defense to Prosecution for Narcotic or Psychedelic Drug Offense*, 35 A.L.R.3d 939 (1971) (compiling cases).

558. *See, e.g.*, Gaskin v. State, 490 S.W.2d 521, 523–24 (Tenn. 1973); State v. Bullard, 148 S.E.2d 565, 568–69 (N.C. 1967); State v. Soto, 537 P.2d 142, 144 (Or. App. 1975); Lewellyn v. State, 489 P.2d 511, 515–16 (Okla. Crim. App. 1971). These courts either simply ignored *Sherbert* or asserted that it was inapplicable in the context of a drug prosecution. Some also sermonized against illicit drugs. *See, e.g., Lewellyn*, 489 P.2d at 516 ("We are of the opinion that the danger is too great, especially to the youth of this state at a time when the psychedelic [*sic*] experience is the 'in thing' to so many, for this Court to yield to the arguments that the use of marihuana, for so-called religious purposes, should be permitted under the free exercise clause.").

559. *See, e.g.*, United States v. Kuch, 288 F. Supp. 439, 444–45 (D.D.C. 1968); *see also* OLC Peyote Opinion, *supra* note 554, at 409 & nn.15–16

(discussing two separate unreported decisions from the early 1980s in which the federal district court for the Southern District of New York ruled that drug law challengers were not part of a bona fide religious organization).

560. People v. Mitchell, 244 Cal. App. 2d 176, 182 (1966); *see also, e.g.,* State v. Brashear, 593 P.2d 63, 67–68 (N.M. App. 1979); State v. Randall, 540 S.W.2d 156, 160 (Mo. App. 1976).

561. State v. Blake, 695 P.2d 336, 340 (Haw. App. 1985); People v. Torres, 133 Cal. App. 3d 265, 277 (1982); People v. Mullins, 50 Cal. App. 3d 61, 72 (1975); People v. Collins, 273 Cal. App. 2d 486, 488 (1969); People v. Crawford, 328 N.Y.S.2d 747, 755 (1972); *cf.* NAT'L COMM'N ON MARIHUANA & DRUG ABUSE, *supra* note 21, app. at 1131 (discussing the "judicial test of essentiality" for a drug to receive free exercise protection).

562. Hernandez v. Comm'r, 490 U.S. 680, 699 (1989); *see* D. Bowie Duncan, Note, *Inviting an Impermissible Inquiry? RFRA's Substantial-Burden Requirement and "Centrality,"* 2021 PEPP. L. REV. 1, 7–10 (tracing the history of this doctrinal precept).

563. *See, e.g.,* United States v. Rush, 738 F.2d 497, 512–13 (1st Cir. 1984); United States v. Middleton, 690 F.2d 820, 825–26 (11th Cir. 1982); Leary v. United States, 383 F.2d 851, 859–62 (5th Cir. 1967), *rev'd on other grounds,* 395 U.S. 6 (1969); United States v. Warner, 595 F. Supp. 595, 597–99 (D.N.D. 1984); Randall v. Wyrick, 441 F. Supp. 312, 315–16 (W.D. Mo. 1977); Native American Church v. United States, 468 F. Supp. 1247, 1249–50 (S.D.N.Y. 1979); State v. Rocheleau, 451 A.2d 1144, 1148–49 (Vt. 1982); Town v. State ex rel. Reno, 377 So. 2d 648, 650–51 (Fla. 1979). Among the judicial decisions declining to follow *Woody,* the Fifth Circuit's decision in *Leary* was widely considered the leading case. For an extended criticism of this decision by Leary's lawyer, see Finer, *supra* note 545.

564. *See, e.g.,* Olsen v. DEA, 878 F.2d 1458, 1463 (D.C. Cir. 1989) (citing the final DEA order denying petitioner's exemption request); McBride v. Shawnee Cnty., 71 F. Supp. 2d 1098, 1102–03 (D. Kan. 1999); State v. Hardesty, 214 P.3d 1004, 1010 (Az. 2009) (en banc); State v. McBride, 955 P.2d 133, 140 (Kan. App. 1998). According to then-Judge Ruth Bader Ginsburg, this difference in demand fully "explained why a tightly-cabined exemption for peyote use in a religious rite need not mean that religious use of marijuana (or any other widely used controlled substance) must be accommodated." *Olsen,* 878 F.2d at 1463; *see also* United States v. Christie, 825 F.3d 1048, 1059 (9th Cir. 2016) ("As courts have repeatedly emphasized,

cannabis differs critically from peyote and hoasca precisely because there is a thriving market for diverted cannabis . . . ."); Mark R. Brown, *Marijuana and Religious Freedom in the United States, in* PROHIBITION, RELIGIOUS FREEDOM, AND HUMAN RIGHTS, *supra* note 47, at 45, 61 ("Exempting marijuana . . . in contrast, could swallow the criminal prohibition completely. Everyone, the government argues, would convert to religions that follow the god of marijuana!").

565. In the oddest of these rulings, the U.S. Court of Appeals for the Ninth Circuit found that the federal regulation limiting the peyote exemption to the NAC creates an impermissibly "arbitrary classification," only to preserve the regulation because the Church of the Awakening's proposed remedy—extending the exemption to itself and no additional churches—would be equally arbitrary. Kennedy v. Bureau of Narcotics & Drugs, 459 F.2d 417 (9th Cir. 1972); *cf.* Peyote Way Church of God, Inc. v. Smith, 556 F. Supp. 632, 637 (N.D. Tex. 1983) (stating that the plaintiff in *Kennedy* "won the battle but lost the war"). The Justice Department has taken the position that granting a peyote exemption to the NAC while denying it to comparable religious groups *would* violate the Establishment Clause, except that no comparable groups exist. OLC Peyote Opinion, *supra* note 554, at 409, 420–21. In the courts, the argument that exempting the NAC violates the Establishment Clause has been accepted only in dissent. *See* Peyote Way Church of God, Inc. v. Thornburgh, 922 F.2d 1210, 1220–21 (5th Cir. 1991) (Clark, C.J., dissenting); *Olsen*, 878 F.2d at 1468–72 (Buckley, J., dissenting). One district judge has suggested that any attempt to limit the NAC's exemption to Native American members of the church would be inconsistent with the Establishment Clause. United States v. Boyll, 774 F. Supp. 1333, 1339–40 (D.N.M. 1991).

566. *Drug Abuse Control Amendments of 1970: Hearings on H.R. 1170 and H.R. 13743 Before the Subcomm. on Pub. Health & Welfare of the H. Comm. on Interstate & Foreign Commerce*, 91st Cong. 118 (1970) (statement of Michael Sonnenreich, deputy chief counsel, Bureau of Narcotics and Dangerous Drugs).

567. DAWSON, *supra* note 555, at 112–13; *cf.* Kevin Feeney, *Peyote, Race, and Equal Protection in the United States, in* PROHIBITION, RELIGIOUS FREEDOM, AND HUMAN RIGHTS, *supra* note 47, at 65, 85 (arguing that the peyote exemption "runs into the danger of eliminating rather than

preserving peyotism," insofar as it leads to "racial and political restrictions" on NAC membership or exemption eligibility).

568. Smith v. Emp. Div., 763 P.2d 146 (Or. 1988) (per curiam); Black v. Emp. Div., 721 P.2d 451 (Or. 1986); Smith v. Emp. Div., 721 P.2d 445 (Or. 1986).

569. Emp. Div. v. Smith, 494 U.S. 872, 881–82 (1990).

570. *Id.* at 908 (Blackmun, J., dissenting). Although she agreed with the dissent on these general points, Justice O'Connor concurred in the result on the ground that Oregon's anti-peyote laws satisfied strict scrutiny. *Id.* at 891–907 (O'Connor, J., concurring in the judgment).

571. *See* Michael W. McConnell, *Religious Freedom at a Crossroads*, 59 U. CHI. L. REV. 115, 127–28 (1992); Adam Winkler, *Fatal in Theory and Strict in Fact: An Empirical Analysis of Strict Scrutiny in the Federal Courts*, 59 VAND. L. REV. 793, 858–59 (2006). "[S]o consistently has the Court held for the government in rejecting free exercise exemption claims under supposedly strict scrutiny," one distinguished constitutional scholar wrote in 1992, "that *Employment Division v. Smith* might well be viewed as a mercy killing." Sullivan, *supra* note 191, at 300.

572. State v. Flesher, 585 N.E.2d 901, 903 (Ohio App. 1990); *see also,* *e.g.*, Peyote Way Church of God, Inc. v. Thornburgh, 922 F.2d 1210, 1213 (5th Cir. 1991) (declining to review the district court's analysis of a peyote ban because *Smith* "eviscerates judicial scrutiny of generally applicable criminal statutes in response to free exercise challenges"); People v. Trippet, 56 Cal. App. 4th 1532, 1541 (1997) (stating that *Smith* provides the "short and simple answer" to any free exercise claim involving marijuana).

573. 1991 Or. Laws 329, § 1.

574. Pub. L. No. 103-141, § 2(b)(1), 107 Stat. 1488, 1488 (1993).

575. Louis Fisher, *Indian Religious Freedom: To Litigate or Legislate*, 26 AM. INDIAN L. REV. 1, 32 (2001) (quoting CAROLYN N. LONG, RELIGIOUS FREEDOM AND INDIAN RIGHTS 213 (2000)); *see also* Ira C. Lupu, *Hobby Lobby and the Dubious Enterprise of Religious Exemptions*, 38 HARV. J.L. & GENDER 35, 55 (2015) ("Almost everyone in the enacting Congress was a fan of religious freedom; not a single one stood up and said that members of the Native American Church had a constitutional right to use peyote in their sacraments.").

576. American Indian Religious Freedom Act Amendments of 1994, Pub. L. No. 103-344, § 2, 108 Stat. 3125, 3125. Limiting the impact of

this amendment, the Supreme Court has held that the American Indian Religious Freedom Act does not create a cause of action or judicially enforceable rights. Lyng v. Nw. Indian Cemetery Protective Ass'n, 485 U.S. 439, 455 (1998).

577. Justice Blackmun made a brief reference to this exemption in his *Smith* dissent. Emp. Div. v. Smith, 494 U.S. 872, 913 n.6 (1990) (Blackmun, J., dissenting). For a thorough analysis of the exemption's origins, scope, and effects, see Michael deHaven Newsom, *Some Kind of Religious Freedom: National Prohibition and the Volstead Act's Exemption for the Religious Use of Wine*, 70 BROOK. L. REV. 739 (2005).

578. 521 U.S. 507, 532 (1997).

579. For an overview of state RFRAs as of 2010, see Christopher Lund, *Religious Liberty after Gonzales: A Look at State RFRAs*, 55 S.D. L. REV. 466 (2010).

580. *See, e.g.*, United States v. Meyers, 95 F.3d 1475, 1482–84 (10th Cir. 1996); United States v. DeWitt, 95 F.3d 1374, 1376 (8th Cir. 1996).

581. *See, e.g.*, United States v. Forchion, 2005 WL 2989604, at *5–*6 (E.D. Pa. 2005); State v. Pedersen, 679 N.W.2d 368, 376–77 (Minn. App. 2004); People v. Peck, 52 Cal. App. 4th 351, 359–60 (1996).

582. *See, e.g.*, United States v. Israel, 317 F.3d 768, 772 (7th Cir. 2003); Nesbeth v. United States, 870 A.2d 1193, 1197–98 (D.C. 2005); State v. Balzer, 954 P.2d 931, 937–42 (Wash. App. 1998).

583. *See Nesbeth*, 870 A.2d at 1198 (noting that "courts, before and after the RFRA was enacted, have explicitly rejected the claim that a religious exemption is a viable less-restrictive means of enforcing the marijuana prohibition").

584. *See generally* Ronald J. Krotoszynski, Jr., *If Judges Were Angels: Religious Equality, Free Exercise, and the (Underappreciated) Merits of Smith*, 102 Nw. U. L. REV. 1189, 1219–49 (2008) (reviewing quantitative and qualitative evidence of bias against minority religionists in RFRA and free exercise case law).

585. 546 U.S. 418, 434 (2006).

586. *Id.* at 436.

587. *Id.* at 438.

588. Church of the Holy Light of the Queen v. Mukasey, 615 F. Supp. 2d 1210 (D. Or. 2009).

589. For an overview of this petition process and a suggestion that the DEA is starting to take psychedelic religions more seriously, see Victoria Litman, *Psychedelic Policy, Religious Freedom, and Public Safety: An Overview*, OHIO ST. J. CRIM. L. (forthcoming). For representative criticisms of the DEA process, see Martha Hartney & Brad Bartlett, *DEA and the Religious Exemption: A Fox Guarding the Henhouse*, CHACRUNA (Oct. 13, 2020), https://chacruna.net/dea-prohibition-religious-freedom-ayahuasca-ceremonies/ [https://perma.cc/J46A-YKY6]; Griffen Thorne, *How DEA Denies Religious Exemption Petitions*, PSYCHEDELICS L. BLOG (Nov. 7, 2022), https://harrisbricken.com/psychlawblog/how-dea-denies-religious-exemption-petitions/ [https://perma.cc/F5XG-XJS8].

590. Lupu, *supra* note 575, at 64 (citing Matthew Nicholson, Note, *Is O Centro a Sign of Hope for RFRA Claimants?*, 95 VA. L. REV. 1281 (2009)). Within the psychedelic community, *O Centro* continues to be celebrated. *See, e.g.*, Matt Zorn, *Don't Count on RFRA to Protect Psychedelic Churches*, LUCID NEWS (June 2, 2022), https://www.lucid.news/dont-count-on-rfra-to-protect-psychedelic-churches/ [https://perma.cc/ZBD7-ALB6] ("This case is often seen as a talisman for endorsing entheogenic churches.").

591. Emp. Div. v. Smith, 494 U.S. 872, 888 (1990).

592. *See* Jeremy K. Kessler, The Puzzling Disappearance of Sincerity Testing 2 (2023) (unpublished manuscript) (explaining that "judicial and administrative interrogation of the sincerity of religious objections to federal regulation [has] become disfavored, almost anticanonical," since abolition of the draft).

593. *See, e.g.*, Luke W. Goodrich & Rachel N. Busick, *Sex, Drugs, and Eagle Feathers: An Empirical Study of Federal Religious Freedom Cases*, 48 SETON HALL L. REV. 353, 379–81, 388–90 (2018) (finding, in a study of Tenth Circuit decisions from the mid-2010s, that successful RFRA and free exercise claims are "rare"); Robert R. Martin, *Compelling Interests and Substantial Burdens: The Adjudication of Religious Free Exercise Claims in U.S. State Appellate Courts*, 9 SAGE OPEN 1 (2019) (finding, in a study of state appellate decisions from the late 1990s and 2000s, that state RFRA claims typically lose, albeit substantially less often than claims adjudicated under a rational basis test); *see also* Ira C. Lupu, *The Failure of RFRA*, 20 U. ARK. LITTLE ROCK L. REV. 575, 585 (1998) (arguing, five years into RFRA's existence, that the legislation "did not prove to be the guarantor of religious liberty its proponents promised").

594. *See* MELISSA BONE, HUMAN RIGHTS AND DRUG CONTROL: A NEW PERSPECTIVE 136–68 (2019) (reviewing case law from the United Kingdom, South Africa, and the U.N. Human Rights Committee). To date, the Italian judiciary has been an outlier in its receptiveness to Rastafarians' religious liberty claims regarding marijuana. *See id.* at 154. Before being reversed by a Ninth Circuit panel, the Supreme Court of Guam held in 2000 that the prosecution of a Rastafarian for importing marijuana violated the Free Exercise Clause of the Organic Act of Guam. *See* Guam v. Guerrero, 290 F.3d 1210 (9th Cir. 2002).

595. DAWSON, *supra* note 555, at 104; *cf.* BONE, *supra* note 594, at 155 (contending that the U.S. judiciary's "cultural favouritism or bias" toward the NAC can be seen as an instance of a general tendency to valorize "'the noble but doomed ways of exotic others'" (quoting Mark Hulsether, *Religion and Culture, in* THE ROUTLEDGE COMPANION TO THE STUDY OF RELIGION 489, 493 (John R. Hinnells ed., 2005))); Brown, *supra* note 564, at 61–62 (suggesting that *Woody*'s acceptability to "mainstream America" is bound up with white guilt over historic injustices committed against Native peoples).

596. *Smith*, 494 U.S. at 881; *see also id.* at 882 ("The present case does not present such a hybrid situation, but a free exercise claim unconnected with any communicative activity . . . .").

597. Whitney v. California, 274 U.S. 357, 375 (1927) (Brandeis, J., dissenting).

598. United States v. Schwimmer, 279 U.S. 644, 654–55 (1929) (Holmes, J., dissenting) (punctuation added).

599. Palko v. Connecticut, 302 U.S. 319, 326–27 (1937).

600. *See, e.g.*, Griswold v. Connecticut, 381 U.S. 479, 482 (1965) (stating that the "right of freedom of speech and press includes . . . freedom of inquiry, freedom of thought, and freedom to teach"); Wieman v. Updegraff, 344 U.S. 183, 195 (1952) (Frankfurter, J., concurring) (suggesting that the free speech right "protects" against "inhibition of freedom of thought").

601. *See, e.g.*, Wooley v. Maynard, 430 U.S. 705, 714 (1977) ("We begin with the proposition that the right of freedom of thought protected by the First Amendment . . . includes both the right to speak freely and the right to refrain from speaking at all."); West Va. State Bd. of Educ. v. Barnette, 319 U.S. 624, 645 (1943) (Murphy, J., concurring) ("The right of freedom of

thought and of religion as guaranteed by the Constitution . . . includes both the right to speak freely and the right to refrain from speaking at all . . . .").

602. *Griswold*, 381 U.S. at 482.

603. Marc Jonathan Blitz, *Freedom of Thought for the Extended Mind: Cognitive Enhancement and the Constitution*, 2010 WIS. L. REV. 1049, 1099.

604. Stanley v. Georgia, 394 U.S. 557, 564–65 (1969); *see also* United States v. Reidel, 402 U.S. 351, 359 (1971) (Harlan, J., concurring) (discussing "the First Amendment right of the individual to be free from governmental programs of thought control, however such programs might be justified in terms of permissible state objectives").

605. Spence v. Washington, 418 U.S. 405 (1974) (per curiam) (peace symbol on flag); Tinker v. Des Moines Indep. Sch. Dist., 393 U.S. 503 (1969) (black armbands in school); *see also* Cohen v. California, 403 U.S. 15 (1971) (First Amendment protects wearing jacket with words "Fuck the Draft" in courtroom). *But cf.* United States v. O'Brien, 391 U.S. 367, 376 (1968) (upholding the conviction of an activist who burned his draft card, although indicating that "when 'speech' and 'nonspeech' elements are combined in the same course of conduct, a sufficiently important governmental interest in regulating the nonspeech element" may be required).

606. *Marihuana-Hashish Epidemic and Its Impact on United States Security: Hearings Before the Subcomm. to Investigate the Admin. of the Internal Sec. Act and Other Internal Sec. Laws of the S. Comm. on the Judiciary*, 93d Cong. at V (1974) (Introduction of Sen. James O. Eastland).

607. Bruce Brashear, *Marijuana Prohibition and the Constitutional Right of Privacy: An Examination of* Ravin v. State, 11 TULSA L.J. 563, 580 n.82 (1976). For other early references to the symbolic speech argument in the academic literature, see Jonathan A. Weiss & Stephen B. Wizner, *Pot, Prayer, Politics and Privacy: The Right to Cut Your Own Throat in Your Own Way*, 54 IOWA L. REV. 709, 718–23 (1969); Note, *Symbolic Conduct*, 68 COLUM. L. REV. 1091, 1121–22 & n.164 (1968); Town, *supra* note 107, at 767–69; Peter Kay Westen, Introduction, *Symposium: Drugs and the Law*, 56 CALIF. L. REV. 1, 7 n.52 (1968).

608. THE BEATLES, *Revolution 1, on* THE BEATLES (Apple Records 1968); FUNKADELIC, FREE YOUR MIND . . . AND YOUR ASS WILL FOLLOW (Westbound Records 1970); ALDOUS HUXLEY, THE DOORS OF PERCEPTION (1954).

609. Michael A. Town, *Privacy and the Marijuana Laws, in* THE NEW SOCIAL DRUG: CULTURAL, MEDICAL, AND LEGAL PERSPECTIVES ON MARIJUANA 118, 131 (David E. Smith ed., 1970).

610. Stanley K. Laughlin, Jr., *LSD-25 and the Other Hallucinogens: A Pre-Reform Proposal*, 36 GEO. WASH. L. REV. 23, 41–43 (1967). Without necessarily stating a clear First Amendment conclusion, similar sentiments were voiced in Boyko & Rotberg, *supra* note 107, at 793–94; Brashear, *supra* note 607, at 580 n.82; Weiss & Wizner, *supra* note 607, at 735; Dichter, *supra* note 415, at 862; Note, *supra* note 107, at 254–57.

611. TRIBE, *supra* note 106, at 908, 910.

612. Leary v. United States, 383 F.2d 851, 858 (5th Cir. 1967) (describing testimony of Dr. Ralph Metzner).

613. State v. Renfro, 542 P.2d 366, 369 (Haw. 1975) (quoting an expert witness at trial).

614. *Id.* The Hawaii justices explicitly flagged the possibility of a "symbolic speech" claim even though the defendants' lawyers had not raised it. *Id.* at 369 & n.5.

615. Borras v. State, 229 So. 2d 244, 246 (Fla. 1969); *see also* Marcoux v. Att'y Gen., 375 N.E.2d 688, 690 (Mass. 1978); United States v. Maiden, 355 F. Supp. 743, 746 (D. Conn. 1973); *cf.* Commonwealth v. Leis, Nos. 28841-2, 28844-5, 28864-5 (Mass. Super. Ct. 1968) (unreported decision), *excerpted in* 3 SUFFOLK L. REV. 23, 39 (1968) ("[Marijuana] use is not so much a symbol of dissent in order to effectuate changes in our social system, but rather a manifestation of a selfish withdrawal from society.").

616. Stanley v. Georgia, 394 U.S. 557, 568 n.11 (1969); *see, e.g.*, United States v. Drotar, 416 F.2d 914, 917 (5th Cir. 1969); State v. Murphy, 570 P.2d 1070, 1073–74 (Ariz. 1977) (en banc); Laird v. State, 342 So. 2d 962, 964–65 (Fla. 1977).

617. On the origins of and contemporary debate over the term "entheogens," see Katie Givens Kime, *Entheogens, in* ENCYCLOPEDIA OF PSYCHOLOGY AND RELIGION 792 (David A. Leeming ed., 3d ed. 2020); Joanna Steinhardt, *Entheogen: What Does This Word Actually Mean?*, DOUBLE BLIND (Sept. 15, 2022), https://doubleblindmag.com/what-does-entheogen-actually-mean/ [https://perma.cc/Z32E-FX3M].

618. Note, *Hallucinogens*, 68 COLUM. L. REV. 521, 548 (1968).

619. *See* Genevieve Lakier, *The First Amendment's Real Lochner Problem*, 87 U. CHI. L. REV. 1241, 1311–22 (2020) (documenting how,

beginning in the early 1970s, "there was a marked shift in the Court's First Amendment jurisprudence" away from "equality-promoting, context-sensitive" approaches that sometimes yielded positive entitlements to information or other expressive resources).

620. State v. Kantner, 493 P.2d 306, 312 (Haw. 1972) (Abe, J., concurring).

621. Stanley v. Georgia, 394 U.S. 557, 564 (1969).

622. Seana Valentine Shiffrin, *A Thinker-Based Approach to Freedom of Speech*, 27 CONST. COMMENT. 283, 287 (2011).

623. Blitz, *supra* note 603, at 1054.

624. *See, e.g.*, Lojuk v. Ouandt, 706 F.2d 1456, 1465 (7th Cir. 1983) (explaining that since the 1960s, "several courts have found that compulsory treatment with mind-altering drugs may invade a patient's First Amendment interests in being able to think and communicate freely"); *see also* Blitz, *supra* note 603, at 1094–98 (reviewing case law); *id.* at 1105–11 (exploring the potential relevance of these decisions for challenges to prohibitory drug laws).

625. *See, e.g.*, Jan-Christoph Bublitz, *My Mind Is Mine!? Cognitive Liberty as a Legal Concept, in* COGNITIVE ENHANCEMENT: AN INTERDISCIPLINARY PERSPECTIVE 233 (Elisabeth Hildt & Andreas G. Franke eds., 2013); Mason Marks, *Cognitive Content Moderation: Freedom of Thought and the First Amendment Right to Receive Subconscious Information*, 76 FLA. L. REV. (forthcoming 2024); Dustin Marlan, *Beyond Cannabis: Psychedelic Decriminalization and Social Justice*, 23 LEWIS & CLARK L. REV. 851, 880–84 (2019); Thomas B. Roberts, *You Have a Constitutional Right to Psychedelics: Academic Freedom, Personal Conscience, and Psychotechnologies, in* THE PSYCHEDELIC POLICY QUAGMIRE: HEALTH, LAW, FREEDOM, AND SOCIETY 3 (Harold J. Ellens & Thomas B. Roberts eds., 2015); Osiris Sinuhé González Romero, *Decolonizing the Philosophy of Psychedelics, in* PHILOSOPHY AND PSYCHEDELICS: FRAMEWORKS FOR EXCEPTIONAL EXPERIENCE 77 (Christine Hauskeller & Peter Sjöstedt-Hughes eds., 2022); Charlotte Walsh, *Psychedelics and Cognitive Liberty: Reimagining Drug Policy Through the Prism of Human Rights*, 29 INT'L J. DRUG POL'Y 80 (2016); *Entheogen & Drug Pol'y Project*, CTR. FOR COGNITIVE LIBERTY & ETHICS (undated), https://www.cognitiveliberty.org/ccle1/drug_policy/stmnt.htm [https://perma.cc/Y4GV-A3MS]; *see also* NITA A. FARAHANY, THE BATTLE FOR YOUR BRAIN: DEFENDING THE RIGHT TO THINK FREELY IN THE AGE OF

NEUROTECHNOLOGY 111–29 (2023) (suggesting a cognitive-liberty-based right to use "brain-enhancing" drugs); ROAR MIKALSEN, CONSTITUTIONAL CHALLENGES TO THE DRUG LAW: A CASE STUDY 55 (2017) (describing the war on drugs as "an authoritarian attempt to control consciousness").

626. *See generally* Jeremy K. Kessler & David E. Pozen, *The Search for an Egalitarian First Amendment*, 118 COLUM. L. REV. 1953 (2018) (reviewing such criticisms and progressives' proposed reforms).

627. TRIBE, *supra* note 106, at 908, 910.

628. On Pollan's contributions to the contemporary "psychedelic renaissance," see Sam Woolfe, *How Michael Pollan Made Us Re-Think Psychedelics as Therapy*, HEALING MAPS (Feb. 28, 2022), https://healingm aps.com/michael-pollan-rethink-psychedelics-therapy/ [https://perma.cc/ CS8N-LPPL].

629. Pleasant Grove City v. Summum, 555 U.S. 460, 469 (2009); *see also* Matal v. Tam, 582 U.S. 218, 234 (2017) ("[O]ur cases recognize that the Free Speech Clause . . . does not regulate government speech." (internal quotation marks and brackets omitted)). Although the government speech doctrine wasn't articulated as such until the 1990s, First Amendment scholars typically trace it to the 1977 case *Wooley v. Maynard*, 430 U.S. 705 (1977), which blocked New Hampshire from requiring drivers to display the state motto on their license plates in part because this was *not* government speech. *See* Carl G. DeNigris, Comment, *When Leviathan Speaks: Reining In the Government-Speech Doctrine Through a New and Restrictive Approach*, 60 AM. U. L. REV. 133, 139–50 (2010) (reviewing the evolution of the doctrine).

630. Walker v. Tex. Div., Sons of Confederate Veterans, Inc., 576 U.S. 200, 207 (2015).

631. *See* Steven J. André, *Government Election Advocacy: Implications of Recent Supreme Court Analysis*, 64 ADMIN. L. REV. 835, 899 (2012) ("There is no salient difference as far as the government speech doctrine goes from 'drugs can kill you,' 'cigarettes are unhealthy,' 'racism is nasty,' or all sorts of wartime propaganda attacking the national enemy on an ideological level."). Congress has imposed statutory restrictions on particular forms of executive branch propaganda, *see generally* KEVIN R. KOSAR, CONG. RSCH. SERV., RL32750, PUBLIC RELATIONS AND PROPAGANDA: RESTRICTIONS ON EXECUTIVE AGENCY ACTIVITIES (2005), but none of these restrictions applies directly to drug policy or implements what is understood to be a constitutional command.

632. Caroline Mala Corbin, *The Unconstitutionality of Government Propaganda*, 81 OHIO ST. L.J. 815 (2020).

633. Nelson Tebbe, *Government Nonendorsement*, 98 MINN. L. REV. 648 (2013).

634. André, *supra* note 631.

635. Helen Norton, *The Government's Lies and the Constitution*, 91 IND. L.J. 73 (2015). *See generally* Kessler & Pozen, *supra* note 626, at 2000–06 (reviewing "systemic" theories of the First Amendment that ask which rules "would best serve the expressive environment as a whole").

636. *See generally* DAN BAUM, SMOKE AND MIRRORS: THE WAR ON DRUGS AND THE POLITICS OF FAILURE (1997); WILLIAM N. ELWOOD, RHETORIC IN THE WAR ON DRUGS: THE TRIUMPHS AND TRAGEDIES OF PUBLIC RELATIONS (1994); MATTHEW B. ROBINSON & RENEE G. SCHERLEN, LIES, DAMNED LIES, AND DRUG WAR STATISTICS: A CRITICAL ANALYSIS OF CLAIMS MADE BY THE OFFICE OF NATIONAL DRUG CONTROL POLICY (2014). In the succinct summary of one legal scholar, government prohibitionists "routinely lie or willfully mislead the public about nearly every aspect of both drugs and the policy of prohibition." Randy E. Barnett, *Bad Trip: Drug Prohibition and the Weakness of Public Policy*, 103 YALE L.J. 2593, 2603 (1994).

637. *See* D.M. Gorman, *The Irrelevance of Evidence in the Development of School-Based Drug Prevention Policy, 1986–1996*, 22 EVALUATION REV. 118 (1998); German Lopez, *How the Internet Freed America from Ridiculous Anti-Drug Propaganda*, Vox (Dec. 22, 2015), https://www.vox.com/2015/12/22/10621810/internet-marijuana-legalization-drugs [https://perma.cc/X3L2-QXFQ]; Tom McKay, *The Five Big Lies That D.A.R.E. Told You About Drugs*, MIC (July 3, 2014), https://www.mic.com/articles/92675/the-5-big-lies-that-d-a-r-e-told-you-about-drugs [https://perma.cc/RZ33-KAU3]. *See generally Articles About the D.A.R.E Program: Another Look at Police in Our Schools*, DRUG LIBRARY, https://www.druglibrary.org/think/~jnr/dare.htm [https://perma.cc/4J6W-7MNX] (collecting critical sources on DARE).

638. Brandenburg v. Ohio, 395 U.S. 444, 449 (1969).

639. Conant v. Walters, 309 F.3d 629 (9th Cir. 2002). For more on the impact of this decision, which the DEA did not challenge, see Robert A. Mikos, *The Evolving Federal Response to State Marijuana Reforms*, 26 WIDENER L. REV. 1, 7–10 (2020).

640. *See* Morse v. Frederick, 551 U.S. 393 (2007).

641. Federal law, for example, makes it a felony "to sell or offer for sale drug paraphernalia." 21 U.S.C. § 863(a)(1).

642. Flipside, Hoffman Estates, Inc. v. Village of Hoffman Estates, 639 F.2d 373, 384 (7th Cir. 1981), rev'd, 455 U.S. 489 (1982). For detailed overviews of this line of cases, see U.S. Dep't of Just., Drug Paraphernalia: Federal Prosecution Manual 1–26 (1991), https://www.ojp.gov/pdffiles1/Digitization/134764NCJRS.pdf [https://perma.cc/U8HW-XL5T]; Michael D. Guinan, Note, Constitutionality of Anti-Drug Paraphernalia Laws—The Smoke Clears, 58 Notre Dame L. Rev. 833 (1983).

643. 425 U.S. 748, 764 (1976).

644. Cent. Hudson Gas & Elec. Corp. v. Pub. Serv. Comm'n, 447 U.S. 557, 564–65 (1980).

645. See Kathleen M. Sullivan, Cheap Spirits, Cigarettes, and Free Speech: The Implications of 44 Liquormart, 1996 Sup. Ct. Rev. 123, 130. In Virginia Pharmacy itself, Justice Blackmun contended that "[t]hose whom the suppression of prescription drug price information hits the hardest are the poor, the sick, and particularly the aged." 425 U.S. at 763.

646. Robert Post & Amanda Shanor, Adam Smith's First Amendment, 128 Harv. L. Rev. F. 165, 168 (2015); see also Ronald K.L. Collins & David M. Skover, The Landmark Free-Speech Case That Wasn't: The Nike v. Kasky Story, 54 Case W. Rsrv. L. Rev. 965, 980 (2004) (discussing commercial speech doctrine's evolution from "a liberal cause" into "a libertarian one").

647. Virginia Pharmacy, 425 U.S. at 781 (Rehnquist, J., dissenting).

648. Herzberg, supra note 325, at 271; see also Courtwright, supra note 53, at 242 (reviewing evidence that "commercial promotion matter[s] just as much as, or even more than, legal availability" in determining consumption rates for dangerous products); Kathleen Frydl, The Pharma Cartel, in The War on Drugs, supra note 46, at 303, 311 (suggesting that the opioid crisis reflects an effective delegation of "medical decision-making to Madison Avenue advertising budgets"); Art Van Zee, The Promoting and Marketing of OxyContin: Commercial Triumph, Public Health Tragedy, 99 Am. J. Pub. Health 221, 225 (2009) (describing the "unprecedented" "amount of money spent in promoting" OxyContin in the late 1990s and early 2000s). Although "some commentators have suggested imposing a blanket prohibition on the advertising of opioids . . . any such move would surely run afoul of the First Amendment" under Virginia Pharmacy. Lars Noah, Federal

Regulatory Responses to the Prescription Opioid Crisis: Too Little, Too Late?, 2019 UTAH L. REV. 757, 768.

649. *See* CAULKINS ET AL., *supra* note 54, at 135.

650. *See, e.g.*, Yingxi Chen et al., *Premature Mortality from Drug Overdoses: A Comparative Analysis of 13 Organisation of Economic Co-operation and Development Member Countries with High-Quality Death Certificate Data, 2001 to 2015*, 170 ANN. INTERNAL MED. 352 (2019) (finding that the United States has had premature drug overdose mortality rates more than twice those of any other OECD country).

651. *See generally* Charlotte Garden, *The Deregulatory First Amendment at Work*, 51 HARV. C.R.-C.L. L. REV. 323 (2016); Kessler & Pozen, *supra* note 626; Elizabeth Sepper, *Free Exercise Lochnerism*, 115 COLUM. L. REV. 1453 (2015); Amanda Shanor, *The New* Lochner, 2016 WIS. L. REV. 133; Tim Wu, *The Right to Evade Regulation: How Corporations Hijacked the First Amendment*, NEW REPUBLIC (June 3, 2013), https://newrepublic.com/article/113294/how-corporations-hijacked-first-amendment-evade-regulation [https://perma.cc/F7TN-BEN8]. For more on the *Lochner* case and its legacy, see chapter 1.

CHAPTER 6

652. On the concept of a "constitutional order," see MARK TUSHNET, THE NEW CONSTITUTIONAL ORDER 1 (2003) (defining a constitutional order as "a reasonably stable set of institutions through which a nation's fundamental decisions are made over a sustained period, and the principles that guide those decisions").

653. HERODOTUS, THE HISTORIES 61 (Robin Waterfield trans., 1998) (c. 440 BCE).

654. Put another way, I focus in this chapter on extradoctrinal features of American constitutional practice that (1) seem to have limited the frequency, diversity, and efficacy of constitutional objections to the war on drugs and that (2) could feasibly be changed without a formal amendment to the Constitution.

655. PHILIP BOBBITT, CONSTITUTIONAL INTERPRETATION 9 (1991).

656. PHILIP BOBBITT, CONSTITUTIONAL FATE: THEORY OF THE CONSTITUTION 6 (1982).

657. *See* Jamal Greene, *Pathetic Argument in Constitutional Law*, 113 COLUM. L. REV. 1389, 1467 (2013) ("Although disputed on the margins, mainstream legal and constitutional scholars tend to agree that reasoning outside of Bobbitt's modalities or its equivalent is not recognizable as constitutional law . . . .").

658. David E. Pozen & Adam M. Samaha, *Anti-Modalities*, 119 MICH. L. REV. 729 (2021).

659. "Prudential arguments" are accepted in contemporary constitutional practice, but unlike "policy arguments" they "typically abstract away from first-order welfare effects and emphasize second-order considerations of judicial administrability, manageability, or the like." *Id.* at 732–33. In addition to the examples given in the main text, our list of anti-modalities includes "popularity arguments" that look to the preferences of the general public and "logrolling arguments" that propose an exchange of favors, or a splitting of differences, between competing parties or positions in the interest of compromise. *Id.* at 746–68.

660. *See supra* notes 1–6, 48–49 and accompanying text; *see also, e.g.*, KOFI ANNAN ET AL., WAR ON DRUGS: REPORT OF THE GLOBAL COMMISSION ON DRUG POLICY 2 (2011), https://www.globalcommissionondrugs.org/wp-content/themes/gcdp_v1/pdf/Global_Commission_Report_English.pdf [https://perma.cc/6GTY-P2G8] ("The global war on drugs has failed, with devastating consequences for individuals and societies around the world."); LISA MCGIRR, THE WAR ON ALCOHOL: PROHIBITION AND THE RISE OF THE AMERICAN STATE 250 (2016) (discussing the "wide consensus that Prohibition of the liquor traffic was a fundamentally flawed crusade with devastating consequences"); Cole, *supra* note 319, at 252 ("By all accounts, the war on drugs has been a failure."); cummings & Ramirez, *supra* note 316, at 457–59 & nn.19–30 (collecting sources depicting the contemporary war on drugs as an "epic failure"); Erik Luna, *Drug War and Peace*, 50 U.C. DAVIS L. REV. 815, 854 (2016) (noting that even during the drug war's most intensive phases, "high-ranking government officials . . . acknowledged that they were unaware of any study showing that the costs of prohibition were outweighed by its benefits").

661. Barnett, *supra* note 636, at 2619.

662. *See supra* notes 66–69, 231–254 and accompanying text.

663. The distinguished philosopher of drug rights Douglas Husak observed more than two decades ago that "no very good argument for drug prohibition has ever been given" in the academic literature. Douglas Husak, *Four Points About Drug Decriminalization*, 22 CRIM. JUST. ETHICS, Winter/Spring 2003, at 21, 23. As far as I can tell, this "utterly astounding" observation remains true to this day, at least with regard to the version of prohibition used in the United States. *Id.* For a succinct sketch of the weightiest pro-criminalization arguments, in the abstract, see George Sher, *On the Decriminalization of Drugs*, 22 CRIM. JUST. ETHICS, Winter/Spring 2003, at 30.

664. BOBBITT, *supra* note 655, at 12.

665. *See* Jamal Greene, *The Supreme Court, 2017 Term—Foreword: Rights as Trumps?*, 132 HARV. L. REV. 28, 60–65 (2018).

666. The amendment procedures set forth in Article V of the U.S. Constitution are widely seen as among the most demanding of any modern constitution, and the U.S. rate of formal amendment is among the lowest in the world. *See* Richard Albert, *The World's Most Difficult Constitution to Amend?*, 110 CALIF. L. REV. 2005 (2023). Albert describes the U.S. Constitution as "constructively unamendable." *Id.* at 2013–16.

667. Pozen & Samaha, *supra* note 658, at 784; *see also id.* at 794 ("The anti-modalities . . . wall off constitutional decisionmaking from the better parts of policy analysis, comprehensive normative theory, emotional empathy in context, and complex arrangements for multiparty compromise."). For discussion of the various indirect and truncated ways in which the anti-modalities figure in constitutional decisionmaking, see *id.* at 772–79. For discussion of the advantages and disadvantages of the prevailing constitutional grammar, see *id.* at 768–72, 779–87.

668. Michael Coenen, *Combining Constitutional Clauses*, 164 U. PA. L. REV. 1067, 1070 (2016).

669. *See generally* Kerry Abrams & Brandon L. Garrett, *Cumulative Constitutional Rights*, 97 B.U. L. REV. 1309 (2017); Coenen, *supra* note 668, at 1077–101. As the previous chapter noted, Justice Scalia controversially adverted to the possibility of "hybrid" constitutional rights in his opinion for the Court in *Employment Division v. Smith*. 494 U.S. 872, 881–82 (1990).

670. For a valuable treatment of this issue with respect to marijuana prohibition specifically, see Scott W. Howe, *Constitutional Clause Aggregation and the Marijuana Crimes*, 75 WASH. & LEE L. REV. 779 (2018).

671. *Cf.* Francisca Pou Giménez & Catalina Pérez Correa, *Prohibitionist Drug Policy in Mexico: A Systemic Constitutional Underminer*, 31 WASH. INT'L L.J. 58, 116 (2021) (describing drug prohibition as a " 'systemic constitutional underminer,' since it generates many interconnected normative problems that penetrate all social domains").

672. The Sixth Amendment instructs that "[i]n all criminal prosecutions, the accused shall enjoy the right to a speedy and public trial, by an impartial jury of the State and district wherein the crime shall have been committed," while Article II gives the president the "Power to grant Reprieves and Pardons for Offenses against the United States, except in Cases of Impeachment." Every state constitution gives the governor or another executive body a comparable pardon power. *See* Kathleen Ridolfi & Seth Gordon, *Gubernatorial Clemency Powers: Justice or Mercy?*, 24 A.B.A. CRIM. JUST. 26, 31 (2009).

673. *See* Lafler v. Cooper, 566 U.S. 156, 170 (2012) ("[C]riminal justice today is for the most part a system of pleas, not a system of trials. Ninety-seven percent of federal convictions and ninety-four percent of state convictions are the result of guilty pleas."); HUM. RTS. WATCH, AN OFFER YOU CAN'T REFUSE: HOW US FEDERAL PROSECUTORS FORCE DRUG DEFENDANTS TO PLEAD GUILTY 31 (2013), https://www.hrw.org/sites/default/files/reports/us1213_ForUpload_0_0_0.pdf [https://perma.cc/3BTG-WXZD] ("[F]rom 1980 to 2010, the percentage of federal drug cases resolved by a plea increased from 68.9 to 96.9 percent . . . .").

674. Santobello v. New York, 404 U.S. 257, 261 (1971); *see also id.* at 260 ("Properly administered, [plea bargaining] is to be encouraged. If every criminal charge were subjected to a full-scale trial, the States and the Federal Government would need to multiply by many times the number of judges and court facilities."); RACHEL ELISE BARKOW, PRISONERS OF POLITICS: BREAKING THE CYCLE OF MASS INCARCERATION 129 (2019) (describing *Santobello* as giving plea bargaining "the official stamp of approval").

675. BARKOW, *supra* note 674, at 130–32. If enough defendants went on a "plea strike" and insisted on taking their cases to trial, they could crash the system. But at least to date, the collective action problems in organizing any such strike have proven insurmountable. *See* Andrew Manuel Crespo, *No Justice, No Pleas: Subverting Mass Incarceration Through Defendant Collective Action*, 90 FORDHAM L. REV. 1999 (2022).

676. The leading case remains *Sparf v. United States*, 156 U.S. 51 (1895).

677. *See* Kenneth Duvall, *The Contradictory Stance on Jury Nullification*, 88 N.D. L. Rev. 409, 414 (2012) (discussing "the official judicial consensus against jury nullification," pursuant to which all federal district judges and almost all state trial judges decline to tell jurors about their power to nullify); Nancy J. King, *Silencing Nullification Advocacy Inside the Jury Room and Outside the Courtroom*, 65 U. Chi. L. Rev. 433 (1998) (documenting the spread of judicial and prosecutorial mechanisms to restrict nullification advocacy and exclude potential nullifiers from juries); Jordan Paul, *How Courts Robbed Juries of a Powerful Tool for Doing Justice*, Balls & Strikes (Oct. 7, 2021), https://ballsandstrikes.org/legal-culture/how-courts-robbed-juries-of-a-powerful-tool-for-doing-justice/ [https://perma.cc/VY73-XW2D] (summarizing and criticizing judicial practices that "effectively gutted" jury nullification).

678. Brief for the United States at 29, Smith v. United States, 2023 WL 2265706 (No. 21-1576) (internal quotation marks omitted).

679. Paul Butler, *The Evils of American Criminal Justice: A Reply*, 44 UCLA L. Rev. 143, 148 (1996); *see also* United States v. Dougherty, 473 F.2d 1113, 1143 (D.C. Cir. 1972) (Bazelon, C.J., concurring in part and dissenting in part) ("The reluctance of juries to hold defendants responsible for unmistakable violations of the prohibition laws told us much about the morality of those laws and about the 'criminality' of the conduct they proscribed."); Alan Scheflin & Jon Van Dyke, *Jury Nullification: The Contours of a Controversy*, Law & Contemp. Probs., Autumn 1980, at 51, 71 ("The repeal of [Prohibition] laws is traceable to the refusal of juries to convict those accused of alcohol traffic.").

680. Paul Butler, *Racially Based Jury Nullification: Black Power in the Criminal Justice System*, 105 Yale L.J. 677 (1995).

681. Separate from Butler's proposal, fear of nullification may have deterred some prosecutors from bringing certain sorts of drug cases to court. *See, e.g.*, Anna Offit, The Imagined Juror: How Hypothetical Juries Influence Federal Prosecutors 44 (2022) (discussing federal prosecutors' concerns that "reverse sting" tactics used in narcotics investigations "would be perceived by jurors as unfair").

682. Schick v. Reed, 419 U.S. 256, 262 (1974) ("unfettered"); *Ex parte Garland*, 71 U.S. (4 Wall.) 333, 380 (1866) ("unlimited"). I describe the pardon power as "virtually" unlimited because many constitutional scholars believe the president could not, for instance, issue a self-pardon or attach

NOTES TO PAGES 144–145

certain conditions to a pardon. *See, e.g.*, Albert W. Alschuler, *Limiting the Pardon Power*, 63 ARIZ. L. REV. 545 (2021); Note, *The President's Conditional Pardon Power*, 134 HARV. L. REV. 2833 (2021).

683. *See generally* Clifford Dorne & Kenneth Gewerth, *Mercy in a Climate of Retributive Justice: Interpretations from a National Survey of Executive Clemency Procedures*, 25 NEW ENG. J. ON CRIM. & CIV. CONFINEMENT 413 (1999); Margaret Colgate Love, *Reinvigorating the Federal Pardon Process: What the President Can Learn from the States*, 9 U. ST. THOMAS L.J. 730 (2012).

684. *See Clemency Statistics*, U.S. DEP'T OF JUST. (Feb. 10, 2023), https://www.justice.gov/pardon/clemency-statistics [https://perma.cc/ W2BM-9369]. This trend followed, and took further, another sharp drop-off in pardon rates that occurred in the early 1900s. *See* JAMES Q. WHITMAN, HARSH JUSTICE: CRIMINAL PUNISHMENT AND THE WIDENING DIVIDE BETWEEN AMERICA AND EUROPE 183 (2005).

685. *See* MARGARET COLGATE LOVE, RELIEF FROM THE COLLATERAL CONSEQUENCES OF A CRIMINAL CONVICTION: A STATE-BY-STATE RESOURCE GUIDE 18–38 (2006).

686. Margaret Colgate Love, *The Twilight of the Pardon Power*, 100 J. CRIM. L. & CRIMINOLOGY 1169, 1173 n.17 (2010).

687. President Obama commuted hundreds of sentences for nonviolent drug crimes during his second term. *See A Nation of Second Chances: President Obama's Record on Clemency*, WHITE HOUSE (Jan. 17, 2017), https://obam awhitehouse.archives.gov/issues/clemency [https://perma.cc/6SJ5-2XPM]. President Biden followed up in 2022 with a mass pardon of federal convictions for simple possession of marijuana. *See supra* note 4. A number of governors and mayors have also recently issued mass pardons for low-level marijuana convictions. *See Marijuana Pardons and Expungements: By the Numbers*, NORML (2023), https://norml.org/marijuana/fact-sheets/mariju ana-pardons-and-expungements-by-the-numbers/ [https://perma.cc/ F3UC-YGE6].

688. For an incisive elaboration and critique of this dynamic, see Rachel E. Barkow, *The Ascent of the Administrative State and the Demise of Mercy*, 121 HARV. L. REV. 1332 (2008); *see also* Austin Sarat & Nasser Hussain, *On Lawful Lawlessness: George Ryan, Executive Clemency, and the Rhetoric of Sparing Life*, 56 STAN. L. REV. 1307 (2004) (analyzing executive clemency as a form of "lawful lawlessness" or "legally sanctioned alegality" in a

modern constitutional democracy). For discussion of other possible factors behind the late twentieth-century decline in executive clemency, see Paul J. Larkin, Jr., *Revitalizing the Clemency Process*, 39 HARV. J.L. & PUB. POL'Y 833, 856–82 (2016); Paul Rosenzweig, *Reflections on the Atrophying Pardon Power*, 102 J. CRIM. L. & CRIMINOLOGY 593, 603–08 (2012).

689. *See* Mark Tushnet, *The Rise of Weak-Form Judicial Review*, in COMPARATIVE CONSTITUTIONAL LAW 321 (Tom Ginsburg & Rosalind Dixon eds., 2011); Mark Tushnet & Rosalind Dixon, *Weak-Form Review and Its Constitutional Relatives: An Asian Perspective*, in COMPARATIVE CONSTITUTIONAL LAW IN ASIA 103 (Rosalind Dixon & Tom Ginsburg eds., 2014).

690. *See* David E. Pozen, *Judicial Elections as Popular Constitutionalism*, 110 COLUM. L. REV. 2047, 2056 (2010). *See generally* William Baude, *The Judgment Power*, 96 GEO. L.J. 1807 (2008).

691. These arguments are the subject of a vast and growing literature. Leading U.S. works from the turn of the century include LARRY D. KRAMER, THE PEOPLE THEMSELVES: POPULAR CONSTITUTIONALISM AND JUDICIAL REVIEW (2004); MARK TUSHNET, TAKING THE CONSTITUTION AWAY FROM THE COURTS (1999); Robert C. Post & Reva B. Siegel, *Legislative Constitutionalism and Section Five Power: Policentric Interpretation of the Family and Medical Leave Act*, 112 YALE L.J. 1943 (2003); Saikrishna Prakash & John Yoo, *Against Interpretive Supremacy*, 103 MICH. L. REV. 1539 (2005).

692. Lawrence Gene Sager, *Fair Measure: The Legal Status of Underenforced Constitutional Norms*, 91 HARV. L. REV. 1212 (1978).

693. *See supra* notes 281–92 and accompanying text. The Michigan Court of Appeals, for instance, "urge[d] the Legislature," as the branch of government "better equipped to make the findings and decisions in this area," "to reevaluate the entire marijuana 'problem.'" People v. Schmidt, 272 N.W.2d 732, 736 (Mich. App. 1978).

694. Telephone Interview with R. Keith Stroup (Dec. 16, 2022).

695. William J. Brennan, Jr., *State Constitutions and the Protection of Individual Rights*, 90 HARV. L. REV. 489, 503 (1977).

696. Robert F. Williams, *State Courts Adopting Federal Constitutional Doctrine: Case-by-Case Adoptionism or Prospective Lockstepping?*, 46 WM. & MARY L. REV. 1499, 1502 (2005); *see also* Jessica Bulman-Pozen & Miriam Seifter, *State Constitutional Rights and Democratic Proportionality*, 123 COLUM. L. REV. 1855, 1881 (2023) ("Despite the distinctive state constitutional rights

tradition, state courts liberally import practices, doctrinal frameworks, and rhetoric from the pages of the U.S. Reports when deciding state constitutional rights claims."); Robert A. Schapiro, *Contingency and Universalism in State Separation of Powers Discourse*, 4 ROGER WILLIAMS U. L. REV. 79, 79 (1998) ("[S]tudies confirm that in construing their states' constitutions, state courts frequently defer to federal case law and seldom deviate from federal analysis.").

697. Obergefell v. Hodges, 576 U.S. 644 (2015); McDonald v. City of Chicago, 561 U.S. 742 (2010); District of Columbia v. Heller, 554 U.S. 570 (2008); Lawrence v. Texas, 539 U.S. 558 (2003). *McDonald* incorporated the Second Amendment right recognized in *Heller* against the states.

698. *See* Michael Boucai, *Glorious Precedents: When Gay Marriage Was Radical*, 27 YALE J.L. & HUMAN. 1, 4 (2015) ("To claim a right to marry a same-sex partner in the early 1970s was necessarily to seek something other than a favorable judgment in court . . . ."); Reva B. Siegel, *Dead or Alive: Originalism as Popular Constitutionalism in* Heller, 122 HARV. L. REV. 191, 224 (2008) ("At the end of the 1980s, the bench and bar still did not see the Second Amendment as authorizing judicial intervention [to enforce individual rights claims].").

699. *The MacNeil/Lehrer NewsHour* (PBS television broadcast Dec. 16, 1991); *see also* JOSEPH BLOCHER & DARRELL A.H. MILLER, THE POSITIVE SECOND AMENDMENT: RIGHTS, REGULATION, AND THE FUTURE OF *HELLER* 60 (2018) ("The militia-oriented view [of the Second Amendment] dominated not only doctrine, but most commentary and scholarly writing, for most of American history. It was endorsed by leading voices left, right, and center.").

700. U.S. DEP'T OF HEALTH & HUMAN SERVS., SUBSTANCE ABUSE & MENTAL HEALTH SERVS. ADMIN., RESULTS FROM THE 2007 NATIONAL SURVEY ON DRUG USE AND HEALTH: NATIONAL FINDINGS 250, 252 (2008), https://www.dpft.org/resources/NSDUHresults2007.pdf [https://perma.cc/U85M-2JVC].

701. *See* Gary J. Gates, *How Many People Are Lesbian, Gay, Bisexual, and Transgender?*, WILLIAMS INST. (Apr. 2011), https://williamsinstitute.law.ucla.edu/publications/how-many-people-lgbt/ [https://perma.cc/748H-N9WT]; Lydia Saad, *What Percentage of Americans Own Guns?*, GALLUP (Nov. 13, 2020), https://news.gallup.com/poll/264932/percentage-americans-own-guns.aspx [https://perma.cc/W27J-MCVZ].

702. Derrick A. Bell, Jr., Brown v. Board of Education *and the Interest-Convergence Dilemma*, 93 HARV. L. REV. 518 (1980).

703. Jack M. Balkin, *How Social Movements Change (or Fail to Change) the Constitution: The Case of the New Departure*, 39 SUFFOLK L. REV. 27 (2005). Balkin's article is rare in the literature for considering a social movement that *failed* to change constitutional law; most such studies focus on successful movements and therefore risk selecting on the dependent variable. For other important works on social movements and constitutional change, see Scott L. Cummings, *Law and Social Movements: Reimagining the Progressive Canon*, 2018 WIS. L. REV. 441, 443 n.7 (collecting sources). For evidence and theory on the Supreme Court justices' embeddedness in, and responsiveness to, elite networks, see NEAL DEVINS & LAWRENCE BAUM, THE COMPANY THEY KEEP: HOW PARTISAN DIVISIONS CAME TO THE SUPREME COURT (2019).

704. DAVID COLE, ENGINES OF LIBERTY: HOW CITIZEN MOVEMENTS SUCCEED (rev. ed. 2017); David Cole, *Where Liberty Lies: Civil Society and Individual Rights After 9/11*, 57 WAYNE L. REV. 1203 (2011).

705. William N. Eskridge, Jr., *Channeling: Identity-Based Social Movements and Public Law*, 150 U. PA. L. REV. 419 (2001); William N. Eskridge, Jr., *Some Effects of Identity-Based Social Movements on Constitutional Law in the Twentieth Century*, 100 MICH. L. REV. 2062 (2002) [hereinafter Eskridge, *Some Effects*].

706. Reva B. Siegel, *Constitutional Culture, Social Movement Conflict and Constitutional Change: The Case of the De Facto ERA*, 94 CALIF. L. REV. 1323, 1356–57 (2006).

707. *See supra* notes 326, 368, 391–92 and accompanying text; *see also, e.g.*, Donna Murch, *Crack in Los Angeles: Crisis, Militarization, and Black Response to the Late Twentieth-Century War on Drugs*, 102 J. AM. HIST. 162, 170 (2015) (explaining that "the crack crisis proved deeply divisive" in cities like Los Angeles "and helped fracture African American and Latino communities internally along lines of age, class, and faith"). "At the heart of this story," Michael Javen Fortner reflects toward the end of his pathbreaking study of Black civic leaders' support for the Rockefeller drug laws, "is the breakdown of racial solidarity . . . ." FORTNER, *supra* note 326, at 279.

708. *See* Bonnie, *supra* note 468, at 584–85.

709. Lassiter, *supra* note 24, at 133.

710. *See supra* notes 27, 109, 419, 467, 499 and accompanying text; *see also* Bonnie, *supra* note 468, at 578 (explaining that marijuana decriminalization was endorsed in the mid-1970s by "[m]any professional organizations" as well as editorial pages "across the country"). None of these groups continued to push for decriminalization in the 1990s, as far as I can tell. The most dramatic about-face came from the ABA. At the urging of its law student division, the ABA announced in 1990 that it "deplores the use of marijuana and other harmful drugs" and "rescinds" its prior support for decriminalization. *See* Linda P. Campbell, *ABA Gets Tougher on Marijuana*, Chic. Trib. (Feb. 13, 1990), https://www.chicagotribune.com/news/ct-xpm-1990-02-13-9001130036-story.html [https://perma.cc/B7WD-R4B7].

711. For an explicit judicial statement to this effect from the early 1970s, referenced in the book's introduction, see People v. Sinclair, 194 N.W.2d 878, 891 (Mich. 1972) (Williams, J., concurring) ("The name in the [case caption] is happenstance as the defendant could have been any mother's son or daughter.").

712. *See* Bruce Western & Becky Pettit, *Incarceration and Social Inequality*, Daedalus, Summer 2010, at 8, 10.

713. Loïc Wacquant, Punishing the Poor: The Neoliberal Government of Social Insecurity 43, 312 (2009); *see also* Bernard E. Harcourt, The Illusion of Free Markets: Punishment and the Myth of Natural Order 40–44, 202–08 (2011) (describing the post-1970s rise of a logic of "neoliberal penality" that facilitates the expansion of the penal sphere at the same time that it delegitimates other sorts of government intervention); Loïc Wacquant, *Deadly Symbiosis: When Ghetto and Prison Meet and Mesh*, 3 Punishment & Soc'y 95, 96 (2001) (asserting that "rising 'racial disproportionality'" in U.S. imprisonment rates "can be traced directly to a single federal policy, namely, the War on Drugs").

714. *See, e.g.*, Eskridge, *Some Effects, supra* note 705, at 2064 ("My thesis is that most twentieth century changes in the constitutional protection of individual rights were driven by or in response to the great identity-based social movements . . . ."). The phrase "discrete and insular minorities" comes from a canonical footnote in which Justice Harlan Fiske Stone began to articulate, in 1938, which sorts of laws would continue to receive rigorous review in the post-*Lochner* era. *See* United States v. Carolene Prods. Co., 304 U.S. 144, 152 n.4 (1938) ("[P]rejudice against discrete and insular minorities

may be a special condition, which . . . may call for a correspondingly more searching judicial inquiry.").

715. The italicized phrase in the main text is a reference to Bruce Ackerman's argument that discrete and insular minorities may be especially *well* positioned to accomplish their policy goals in a pluralist system, given their reduced collective action problems, and that courts should therefore protect "anonymous and diffuse" groups instead. Bruce A. Ackerman, *Beyond* Carolene Products, 98 Harv. L. Rev. 713 (1985). For the idea of a late twentieth-century "cannabis closet" analogous to the previous generation's gay closet, see The Cannabis Closet: First Hand Accounts of the Marijuana Mainstream (Chris Bodenner ed., 2010).

716. *See generally* Hart, *supra* note 57 (documenting the dearth of affirmative arguments for responsible adult drug use and arguing that it has warped drug research and policymaking). As explained in chapter 2, litigants challenging marijuana laws in the 1970s downplayed the affirmative dimensions of marijuana use in favor of arguments about the harms of prohibition. Religious liberty cases brought under the Free Exercise Clause were the only ones in which litigants routinely advanced anything that might be considered a "pro-drug" position.

717. *See supra* note 186 and accompanying text.

718. *Cf.* Lester Hunt, *A Moral Defense of Recreational Drug Use*, Notre Dame Phil. Revs. (Apr. 4, 2016), https://ndpr.nd.edu/reviews/a-moral-defense-of-recreational-drug-use/ [https://perma.cc/R2CJ-U9VN] ("If your opponent says that the conduct in question clashes with the best life for human beings, it is in a way beside the point to prove, in response, that it is morally permissible to do individual actions that clash with the best life for human beings. Such a response concedes too much territory to your opponent. The only hope of building an effective defense rests on the possibility of an attractive alternative vision of the best life for human beings.").

719. Emily M. Bernstein, *Ginsburg Says He Used Drugs*, Harv. Crimson (Nov. 6, 1987), https://www.thecrimson.com/article/1987/11/6/ginsburg-says-he-used-drugs-psupreme/ [https://perma.cc/8DYB-6HTT] (quoting NPR's Nina Totenberg).

720. Douglas H. Ginsburg, *Delegation Running Riot*, Regulation, Winter 1995, at 83, 84 (describing various seldom-enforced doctrines meant to limit government power as part of "the Constitution-in-exile").

721. Ronald Reagan, *Informal Exchange with Reporters on the Supreme Court Nomination of Douglas H. Ginsburg*, AM. PRESIDENCY PROJECT (Nov. 6, 1987), https://www.presidency.ucsb.edu/documents/informal-excha nge-with-reporters-the-supreme-court-nomination-douglas-h-ginsburg [https://perma.cc/9ZD4-YY2U]; Ronald Reagan, *Remarks to Ethnic and Minority Administration Supporters on the Supreme Court Nomination of Douglas H. Ginsburg*, AM. PRESIDENCY PROJECT (Nov. 6, 1987), https://www. presidency.ucsb.edu/documents/remarks-ethnic-and-minority-administrat ion-supporters-the-supreme-court-nomination-douglas [https://perma.cc/ W8SD-ZH7T].

722. *See Americans Do Not Want Marijuana Legalized, but a Poll . . .* , UPI (Nov. 8, 1987), https://www.upi.com/Archives/1987/11/08/ Americans-do-not-want-marijuana-legalized-but-a-poll/9463563346000/ [https://perma.cc/2YA2-SPZV] (discussing the *Newsweek* poll); *see also* Richard J. Meislin, *Past Marijuana Use Held Insufficient Reason to Rule Out Candidate*, N.Y. TIMES (Nov. 10, 1987), https://www.nytimes.com/1987/11/10/ us/past-marijuana-use-held-insufficient-reason-to-rule-out-candidate. html [https://perma.cc/A34N-5PSQ] (reporting similar results from a poll conducted two days later).

723. 133 CONG. REC. 31,197 (Nov. 6, 1987) (remarks of Sen. Byrd). Joining many members of Congress who made similar statements after the NPR story broke, President Reagan's secretary of education William Bennett, who would go on to serve as the next administration's hardline drug czar, told reporters that "youthful indiscretions" with drugs should not be disqualifying for future office. *Bennett Says Youthful Lapses Shouldn't Bar Office Seekers*, N.Y. TIMES (Nov. 10, 1987), https://www.nytimes. com/1987/11/10/us/bennett-says-youthful-lapses-shouldn-t-bar-office-seek ers.html [https://perma.cc/Y2G3-P7HL].

724. *See* ERIC SCHLOSSER, REEFER MADNESS: SEX, DRUGS, AND CHEAP LABOR IN THE AMERICAN BLACK MARKET 49 (2003) (describing Ginsburg's withdrawal as setting an "unfortunate precedent" that "transmuted" McCarthy-era questions about membership in the Communist Party into "a new litmus test" for politicians, this time focused on pot smoking); Morris J. Blachman & Kenneth E. Sharpe, *The War on Drugs: American Democracy Under Assault*, 7 WORLD POL'Y J. 135, 147–48 (1989) (describing the Ginsburg episode as part of a growing pattern of "drug-related character assassination").

CHAPTER 7

725. *See* Erik Luna, *Drug Exceptionalism*, 47 Vill. L. Rev. 753, 755–56 & nn.13–17 (2002) (noting that "numerous jurists and scholars" have "identified a 'drug exception' to the Bill of Rights created through judicial acquiescence to the activities of narcotics agents," and collecting citations).

726. Mathieu Hikaru Desan, *Realist and Historicist Modes of Critique in Critical Sociology*, 49 Critical Socio. 589, 590, 604 (2023). On "doctrinal realism" as a methodological middle ground between strongly externalist and strongly internalist approaches to studying the development of doctrine, attentive to "background patterns" and to "insights of social science" while also insisting that "the law, if rightly understood, typically makes sense in its own terms," see Richard H. Fallon, Jr., *How to Make Sense of Supreme Court Standing Cases—A Plea for the Right Kind of Realism*, 23 Wm. & Mary Bill Rts. J. 105, 106–07 (2014).

727. *See, e.g.*, Richard A. Posner, Overcoming Law 245 (1995); Barry Friedman & Daniel T. Deacon, *A Course Unbroken: The Constitutional Legitimacy of the Dormant Commerce Clause*, 97 Va. L. Rev. 1877, 1881 (2011); Brian A. Lichter & David P. Baltmanis, *Foreword: Original Ideas on Originalism*, 103 Nw. U. L. Rev. 491, 491 (2009); Yaniv Roznai, *Original Constitutionalist: Reconstructing Richard S. Kay's Scholarship*, 52 Conn. L. Rev. 1299, 1304 (2021). Histories of contemporary originalist theory include Johnathan O'Neill, Originalism in American Law and Politics: A Constitutional History (2005); Lawrence B. Solum, *What Is Originalism? The Evolution of Contemporary Originalist Theory*, in The Challenge of Originalism: Theories of Constitutional Interpretation 12 (Grant Huscroft & Bradley W. Miller eds., 2011).

728. *See supra* note 678 and accompanying text; *see also* Jack Chin, *SG to the Court: Originalism Requires Jury Lawfinding*, Prawfsblawg (Mar. 26, 2023), https://prawfsblawg.blogs.com/prawfsblawg/2023/03/sg-to-the-court-originalism-requires-jury-lawfinding.html [https://perma.cc/52LP-C8NZ] (summarizing scholarship on this point by Rachel Barkow, Darryl Brown, Joan Larsen, and Jenia Iontcheva Turner).

729. Stanton D. Krauss, *An Inquiry into the Right of Criminal Juries to Determine the Law in Colonial America*, 89 J. Crim. L. & Criminology 111, 116, 122, 213–14 (1998).

730. John Stinneford, *Original Meaning and the Death Penalty*, 13 U. St. Thomas J.L. & Pub. Pol'y 44, 57 (2018); *see also, e.g.*, John F. Stinneford, *Experimental Punishments*, 95 Notre Dame L. Rev. 39 (2019); John F. Stinneford, *The Original Meaning of "Cruel,"* 105 Geo. L.J. 441 (2017); Stinneford, *supra* note 531.

731. *See* Lawrence B. Solum, *Surprising Originalism*, 9 ConLawNOW 235, 258 (2018) ("Judged against the relevant baseline—punishment practices that were long in use and approved by the common law in 1791—there is a powerful argument that modern multiyear sentences are both 'cruel' and 'unusual.'").

732. Stuntz, *supra* note 432, at 72–73. For a forceful nonoriginalist argument that the Eighth Amendment should be read to preclude "sentences harsher than those justified under retributivism even if they can be justified under a different rationale, such as deterrence or incapacitation," see Youngjae Lee, *The Constitutional Right Against Excessive Punishment*, 91 Va. L. Rev. 677, 684 (2005).

733. 545 U.S. 1, 58 (2005) (Thomas, J., dissenting).

734. *See, e.g.*, William Baude, *The Contingent Federal Power to Regulate Marijuana*, in Marijuana Federalism, *supra* note 230, at 171, 172 (arguing that "[i]f a state legalizes and regulates a drug in a way that minimizes the risk of spillovers into the interstate black market, the federal drug laws should be forbidden to apply within that state" as a constitutional matter); Friedman & Lakier, *supra* note 221, at 256 n.7 (advancing an earlier version of this argument and citing complementary works by Randy Barnett, Richard Epstein, and Donald Regan).

735. *See* Grodin, *supra* note 63, at 19 (stating that "those courts which have addressed [the happiness clauses in their state constitutions] so far have failed to develop around it any coherent body of jurisprudence"); Lawrence B. Solum, *Themes from Fallon on Constitutional Theory*, 18 Geo. J. L. & Pub. Pol'y 287, 349 (2020) ("The meaning of the Privileges and Immunities Clause . . . is debated by originalists and no clear consensus has emerged."). In two cases from the 1870s that have been excoriated by originalists but have not been overturned, the Supreme Court drained the Privileges or Immunities Clause of much of its potential meaning. United States v. Cruikshank, 92 U.S. 542 (1876); Slaughter-House Cases, 83 U.S. (16 Wall.) 36 (1873).

736. HOWARD MUMFORD JONES, THE PURSUIT OF HAPPINESS 1 (1953). For the view that the Privileges or Immunities Clause was originally understood to protect enumerated federal constitutional rights against state infringement, see Kurt T. Lash, *The Enumerated-Rights Reading of the Privileges or Immunities Clause: A Response to Barnett and Bernick*, 95 NOTRE DAME L. REV. 591 (2019).

737. *See* HART, *supra* note 57, at 1 ("I take drugs as part of my pursuit of happiness, and they work. I am a happier and better person because of them."). Hart is the Mamie Phipps Clark Professor of Psychology at Columbia University.

738. *See, e.g.*, William Baude, Jud Campbell & Stephen E. Sachs, *General Law and the Fourteenth Amendment*, 76 STAN. L. REV. (forthcoming 2024) (noting that the Privileges or Immunities Clause is "often read" by originalists "to have guaranteed a vast swath of substantive rights").

739. RANDY E. BARNETT, RESTORING THE LOST CONSTITUTION: THE PRESUMPTION OF LIBERTY 271 (2014 ed.). For quasi-originalist arguments that recreational drug taking may be protected under the Ninth Amendment, see ROBERT M. HARDAWAY, NO PRICE TOO HIGH: VICTIMLESS CRIMES AND THE NINTH AMENDMENT 87–123 (2003); Robert W. Sweet & Edward A. Harris, *Just and Unjust Wars: The War on the War on Drugs—Some Moral and Constitutional Dimensions of the War on Drugs*, 87 Nw. U. L. REV. 1302, 1346–73 (1993); Kevin S. Toll, Comment, *The Ninth Amendment and America's Unconstitutional War on Drugs*, 84 U. DET. MERCY L. REV. 417 (2007).

740. *See* Randy E. Barnett, *The Presumption of Liberty and the Public Interest: Medical Marijuana and Fundamental Rights*, 22 WASH. U. J. L. & POL'Y 29, 43 (2006) (discussing this approach with reference to *Raich*).

741. *See, e.g.*, Thomas B. Colby, *The Sacrifice of the New Originalism*, 99 GEO. L.J. 713 (2011); Jeremy K. Kessler & David E. Pozen, *Working Themselves Impure: A Life Cycle Theory of Legal Theories*, 83 U. CHI. L. REV. 1819, 1844–48 (2016); Robert Post & Reva Siegel, *Originalism as a Political Practice: The Right's Living Constitution*, 75 FORDHAM L. REV. 545 (2006); *see also* Calvin TerBeek, *"Clocks Must Always Be Turned Back": Brown v. Board of Education and the Racial Origins of Constitutional Originalism*, 115 AM. POL. SCI. REV. 821 (2021) (tracing the origins of originalism to Republican resistance to *Brown v. Board of Education*).

742. *See generally* ERWIN CHEMERINSKY, WORSE THAN NOTHING: THE DANGEROUS FALLACY OF ORIGINALISM 139–65 (2022); Richard H. Fallon, Jr.,

Selective Originalism and Judicial Role Morality, 102 Tex. L. Rev. 221 (2023).

743. *See supra* note 29 and accompanying text.

744. Meanwhile, an ascendant countermovement within conservative constitutional theory known as common good constitutionalism, which privileges the promotion of morality and the prevention of social disorder over the promotion of individual autonomy and the prevention of abuses of power, is even less likely to support drug liberalization. *See generally* Adrian Vermeule, Common Good Constitutionalism (2022).

745. Vicki C. Jackson, *Constitutional Law in an Age of Proportionality*, 124 Yale L.J. 3094, 3098 (2015).

746. BVerfGE 54, 143 (1980) (Ger.).

747. *See* R. v. Oakes, [1986] 1 S.C.R. 103, 138–40 (Can.); Aharon Barak, Proportionality: Constitutional Rights and Their Limitations 131–210 (2012).

748. *See* Jackson, *supra* note 745, at 3104–06. *See generally* Stephen Gardbaum, *The Myth and Reality of American Constitutional Exceptionalism*, 107 Mich. L. Rev. 391 (2008).

749. Greene, *supra* note 665, at 58; *see also* Kai Möller, *US Constitutional Law, Proportionality, and the Global Model, in* Proportionality: New Frontiers, New Challenges 130, 141 (Vicki C. Jackson & Mark Tushnet eds., 2017) (contrasting proportionality's *"comprehensive model,* according to which any interest, however trivial, is sufficient to attract the protection of constitutional rights," with the U.S. *"threshold model,"* according to which only interests that reach a certain threshold of importance receive constitutional protection).

750. Corte Suprema de Justicia de la Nación [CSJN], 25/8/2009, "Arriola, Sebastián y otros," Fallos (2009-332-1963) (Arg.); CSJN, 11/12/1990, "Montalvo, Ernesto Alfredo," Fallos (1990-313-1333) (Arg.); CSJN, 29/8/1986, "Bazterrica, Gustavo Mario," Fallos (1986-308-1392) (Arg.).

751. Corte Constitucional [C.C.], mayo 5, 1994, Sentencia C-221/94 (Colom.); *see also* C.C., junio 6, 2019, Sentencia C-235/19 (Colom.) (invalidating a ban on public consumption of cannabis); Manuel José Cepeda Espinosa & David Landau, Colombian Constitutional Law: Leading Cases 52–59 (2017) (discussing the 1994 ruling and its complicated aftermath). The Supreme Court of Brazil is currently considering

an Extraordinary Appeal that raises similar issues. For background on this appeal, which has been pending for nearly a decade, see Felipe Neis Araujo, *Brazil's Supreme Court Shamefully Ducks Key Drug-Decrim Ruling*, FILTER (May 25, 2023), https://filtermag.org/brazil-supreme-court-drug-decriminalization/ [https://perma.cc/FC64-9575].

752. ORG. AM. STATES, ANNUAL REPORT OF THE INTER-AMERICAN JURIDICAL COMMITTEE TO THE GENERAL ASSEMBLY 101 (2014), http://www.oas.org/en/sla/iajc/docs/infoanual.cji.2014.eng.pdf [https://perma.cc/3D9T-3ATW]. Outside the courts, Ecuador became the first country to codify drug decriminalization in a constitutional text when it amended its constitution in 2008. *See* ECUADOR CONST. 2008, art. 364.

753. BVerfGE 90, 145, 147 (1994) (Ger.), *translated in BVerfGE 90, 145—Cannabis*, GERMAN L. ARCHIVE (Michael Jewell trans., 2001), https://germanlawarchive.iuscomp.org/?p=85 [https://perma.cc/2QHP-N52S].

754. Declaratoria General de Inconstitucionalidad 1/2018, Diario Oficial de la Federación [DOF] 15-07-2021 (Mex.); Cass., sez. un., 19 dicembre 2019, n. 12348/20 (It.); Maccabbee v. Comm'r of Police, No. SKBHCV2017/0234 (2019) (E. Caribbean); Minister of Just. & Const. Dev. v. Prince, [2018] ZACC 30 (CC) (S. Afr.); Tsikarishvili v. Parliament, N1/4/592 (2015) (Geo.). The Constitutional Court of Georgia and the Supreme Court of Mexico have been particularly active in this area. For broader context and summaries of their key rulings as of 2018 and 2022, respectively, see HUMAN RTS. WATCH, HARSH PUNISHMENT: THE HUMAN TOLL OF GEORGIA'S ABUSIVE DRUG POLICIES 56–58 (2018), https://www.hrw.org/sites/default/files/report_pdf/georgia0818_web.pdf [https://perma.cc/B3H8-CD9Q]; Giménez & Correa, *supra* note 671, at 68–76, 93–94. Applying proportionality principles to the interpretation of drug statutes, the Supreme Court of Spain ruled in the early 1970s that the country's criminal drug ban does not apply to possession for personal use, while the Supreme Court of Chile ruled in 2015 that an exemption for personal use of cannabis covers certain groups of people, not just individuals. Corte Suprema de Justicia [C.S.J.], 4 junio 2015, "Ministerio Público con Paulina González Céspedes," Rol de la causa: 4949-2015 (Chile); S. Herrero Álvarez, *El Cannabis y Sus Derivados en el Derecho Penal Español*, 12 ADICCIONES 315, 319–20 (2000) (discussing Spanish cases).

755. For an overview, see Matthew DeCloedt, *Human Rights Litigation and the Medicalization of Cannabis in Canada, ca. 2000–Present*, 61 HIST. PHARMACY & PHARMACEUTICALS 59 (2019).

756. R. v. Taylor [2001] EWCA Crim 2263 [33]; *see also, e.g.*, R. v. Smith, 34 C.C.C. (3d) 97 (1987) (Can.) (invalidating a seven-year mandatory minimum sentence for importing narcotics); Bakhutashvili v. Parliament, N1/8/696 (2017) (Geo.) (invalidating a five- to eight-year sentence for purchase and possession of a small amount of desomorphine); J.Y. Interpretation No. 790 (2020) (Taiwan) (invalidating a five-year mandatory minimum sentence for growing cannabis for personal use).

757. *Cf.* Amber Marks, *Defining 'Personal Consumption' in Drug Legislation and Spanish Cannabis Clubs*, 68 INT'L & COMPAR. L. Q. 193, 218–19 (2019) ("In comparative constitutional case law, the freedom to consume cannabis without State interference has been consistently situated within the right to privacy and associated personality rights, the objective of which is the protection of personal autonomy.").

758. *See generally* Bulman-Pozen & Seifter, *supra* note 696.

759. Ravin v. State, 537 P.2d 494, 498 (Alaska 1975).

760. State v. Russell, 477 N.W.2d 886, 889 (Minn. 1991).

761. People v. McCabe, 275 N.E.2d 407, 409 (Ill. 1971) (per curiam) (punctuation added).

762. People v. Lorentzen, 194 N.W.2d 827, 831 (Mich. 1972).

763. People v. Woody, 394 P.2d 813, 821 (Cal. 1964).

764. People v. Shepard, 409 N.E.2d 840, 847 (N.Y. 1980) (Fuchsberg, J., dissenting); *see also, e.g.*, Seeley v. State, 940 P.2d 604, 630–32 (Wash. 1997) (Sanders, J., dissenting).

765. *See* Tor-Inge Harbo, *The Function of the Proportionality Principle in EU Law*, 16 EUR. L.J. 158, 172 (2010) ("[I]n the literature on the proportionality principle it is common to suggest that the principle is interpreted differently according to what areas it is utilised in, for example, whether it is utilised in relation to public health . . . ."); Valentina Vadi, *The Migration of Constitutional Ideas to Regional and International Economic Law: The Case of Proportionality*, 35 NW. J. INT'L L. & BUS. 557, 575 (2015) (noting the view that proportionality review tends to involve greater deference "in the adjudication of public health related disputes").

766. *See generally* Greene, *supra* note 665.

767. ROBERT ALEXY, A THEORY OF CONSTITUTIONAL RIGHTS 57 (Julian Rivers trans., 2002). More specifically, Alexy describes principles as "optimization requirements," or "norms which require that something be realized to the greatest extent possible given the legal and factual possibilities." *Id.* at 47 (emphasis omitted).

768. *See supra* notes 145–52 and accompanying text (discussing *Ravin* and follow-on cases); ALEXY, *supra* note 767, at 414–15 (observing that the German Constitutional Court did "not establish the truth of the legislature's empirical premises [regarding the dangers of cannabis], but their uncertainty," thus warranting "empirical epistemic discretion"); *see also* MATTHIAS KLATT & MORITZ MEISTER, THE CONSTITUTIONAL STRUCTURE OF PROPORTIONALITY 114–15 (2012) (offering a formal analysis of this point).

769. *Cf.* Álvaro Santos, *Drug Policy Reform in the Americas: A Welcome Challenge to International Law*, 114 AJIL UNBOUND 301, 303 (2020) (explaining that "despite these rulings and a narrative in Latin America that increasingly recognizes the right to personal use of marijuana, [marijuana] remains largely criminalized through the crime of possession" above minimum quantity thresholds).

770. Within drug policy circles, harm reduction refers to "a set of practical strategies and ideas aimed at reducing negative consequences associated with drug use." *Principles of Harm Reduction*, NAT'L HARM REDUCTION COAL. (2023), https://harmreduction.org/about-us/principles-of-harm-reduction/ [https://perma.cc/Z94P-8CSU]. The term may also refer to "a movement for social justice built on a belief in, and respect for, the rights of people who use drugs." *Id.* On the history of harm reduction and its growing popularity in the United States, see MAIA SZALAVITZ, UNDOING DRUGS: THE UNTOLD STORY OF HARM REDUCTION AND THE FUTURE OF ADDICTION (2021); German Lopez, *America's New Drug Policy*, N.Y. TIMES (May 4, 2023), https://www.nytimes.com/2023/05/04/briefing/us-drug-policy-reducing-harm.html [https://perma.cc/F2M8-F955].

771. Lee, *supra* note 732, at 681 (citation and punctuation omitted).

772. *See generally* Möller, *supra* note 749.

773. Greene, *supra* note 665, at 115–16.

774. *Id.* at 63. Mattias Kumm calls this the *"turn from legal interpretation to public reason oriented justification"*: "Instead of attempting to make sense of authoritative legal materials[,] the focus of courts engaged in proportionality analysis is the assessment whether a public action can

be demonstratively justified by reasons that are appropriate in a liberal democracy." Mattias Kumm, *The Idea of Socratic Contestation and the Right to Justification: The Point of Rights-Based Proportionality Review*, 4 LAW & ETHICS HUM. RTS. 141, 142 (2010).

775. *See Controlled Substances—Alphabetical Order*, U.S. DRUG ENF'T ADMIN. (June 6, 2023), https://www.deadiversion.usdoj.gov/schedules/ora ngebook/c_cs_alpha.pdf [https://perma.cc/9JAJ-UTPK]; *see also* Linda J. Ehrlich, *Freedom of Choice: Personal Autonomy and the Right to Privacy*, 14 IDAHO L. REV. 447, 468 (1978) ("The drug situation is particularly difficult because of the immense variety of drugs available; the courts [if they were to embrace the *Ravin* approach] would be burdened with hearing extensive testimony pertaining to the potential harmfulness of each one.").

776. Ross Coomber & Nigel South, *Fear and Loathing in Drugs Policy: Risk, Rights and Approaches to Drug Policy and Practice, in* PROHIBITION, RELIGIOUS FREEDOM, AND HUMAN RIGHTS, *supra* note 47, at 235, 240; *see also* Koppelman, *supra* note 66, at 292 ("Drugs are beneficial for the majority of users, who achieve the effects they seek without adverse consequences. They are harmful, sometimes terribly harmful, for a few."). This contingency applies even to the most feared drugs. As Coomber and South explain, adults "can inject heroin for 20 or 30 years with . . . few harms accruing" if they have a steady supply of unadulterated heroin, the financial means to afford it, and clean injecting equipment, "or they can be subject to serious health harms and/or death if circumstances conspire to make riskier behavior more likely, as can be compounded by prohibition." Coomber & South, *supra*, at 239.

777. *See supra* note 68 and accompanying text.

778. *See, e.g.*, POLLAN, *supra* note 125, at 41–42, 69–70, 420 (discussing the noetic quality of psychedelic drug experiences for some users, who "emerge with the enduring conviction that important truths have been revealed to them").

779. Recall from chapter 2 that when the DEA administrator overruled an administrative law judge's recommendation to reschedule marijuana, he refused to give any weight to the "numerous testimonials and opinions of lay persons" who found the drug to be a source of healing or meaning in their lives, on the ground that these opinions have "no scientific merit." Marijuana Scheduling Petition; Denial of Petition, 54 Fed. Reg. 53,767, 53,769–71 (Dec. 29, 1989).

780. Jeremy Waldron, Law and Disagreement 290 (1999).

781. *See, e.g.*, Kate Andrias, *Building Labor's Constitution*, 94 Tex. L. Rev. 1591, 1592 (2016) (explaining that "contemporary worker movements make almost no appeal to the Constitution"); Brando Simeo Starkey, *Why the Black Lives Matter Movement Should Claim the 14th Amendment*, Andscape (July 30, 2020), https://andscape.com/features/why-the-black-lives-mat ter-movement-should-claim-the-14th-amendment/ [https://perma.cc/ SJP6-DE6T] (noting that "the webpage that outlines the [Black Lives Matter] movement's philosophical underpinnings mentions nothing about the Constitution"). *See generally* Amna A. Akbar, *Demands for a Democratic Political Economy*, 134 Harv. L. Rev. F. 90 (2020) (discussing "abolitionist, antiracist, and anticapitalist" movements of the past decade and their dis- avowal of legal liberal strategies).

782. Oteri & Silverglate, *supra* note 255, at 65; *see also Challenging the Cocaine Laws*, *supra* note 269 (describing Oteri as "the first lawyer in the U.S. to challenge the government's right to legislate against private mari- juana use").

783. Classic works in this vein include Gerald N. Rosenberg, The Hollow Hope: Can Courts Bring About Social Change? (1991); Stuart A. Scheingold, The Politics of Rights: Lawyers, Public Policy, and Political Change (1974); Marc Galanter, *Why the "Haves" Come Out Ahead: Speculations on the Limits of Legal Change*, 9 Law & Soc'y Rev. 95 (1974). *See also* Scott L. Cummings & Ingrid V. Eagly, *A Critical Reflection on Law and Organizing*, 48 UCLA L. Rev. 443, 450–60 & 454 n.38 (2001) (collecting works "specifically on the inability of litigation to produce mean- ingful reform" and contextualizing these works within the larger body of skeptical writing on law and lawyers as vehicles for social change).

784. *See generally, e.g.*, Martin Loughlin, Against Constitutionalism (2022); Louis Michael Seidman, On Constitutional Disobedience (2013); Ryan D. Doerfler & Samuel Moyn, *The Constitution Is Broken and Should Not Be Reclaimed*, N.Y. Times (Aug. 19, 2022), https://www.nyti mes.com/2022/08/19/opinion/liberals-constitution.html [https://perma.cc/ QH2M-FXGA].

785. Pozen & Samaha, *supra* note 658, at 787–96.

786. Bonnie & Whitebread, *supra* note 10, at 1177.

787. *See, e.g.*, Giménez & Correa, *supra* note 671, at 94 (explaining that the Constitutional Court of Colombia, after holding that personal drug use

may not be criminalized, "approved a new legal framework [that] made drug addiction a matter of public health and obliged state authorities to guarantee treatment for those who voluntarily seek it" (citing C.C., junio 28, 2011, Sentencia C-491/12 (Colom.))).

788. JOSEPH FISHKIN & WILLIAM E. FORBATH, THE ANTI-OLIGARCHY CONSTITUTION: RECONSTRUCTING THE ECONOMIC FOUNDATIONS OF AMERICAN DEMOCRACY (2022).

789. *See id.* at 456–61.

790. *See* Jonathan S. Gould, *Puzzles of Progressive Constitutionalism,* 135 HARV. L. REV. 2053, 2087–91 (2022); David Pozen, *Inside or Outside the Modalities?,* BALKINIZATION (Apr. 21, 2022), https://balkin.blogs pot.com/2022/04/inside-or-outside-modalities.html [https://perma. cc/94W7-GC5U].

791. *Drug Related Crime Statistics,* NAT'L CTR. FOR DRUG ABUSE STATS. (2023), https://drugabusestatistics.org/drug-related-crime-statistics/ [https:// perma.cc/9RBG-SKF4]. The number of drug arrests dropped to 1.16 million in 2020. *Id.; see also* Jennifer D. Oliva & Taleed El-Sabawi, *The "New" Drug War,* 110 VA. L. REV. (forthcoming 2024) (arguing that the drug war remains largely intact, notwithstanding the rise of public health-oriented policy rhetoric).

792. ABA STANDARDS FOR CRIMINAL JUSTICE: DEFENSE FUNCTION 4-1.2(b) (4th ed. 2017).

793. Dorothy E. Roberts, *The Supreme Court, 2018 Term— Foreword: Abolition Constitutionalism,* 133 HARV. L. REV. 1, 108–10 (2019).

794. *See, e.g.,* CAULKINS ET AL., *supra* note 54, at 247–49 (discussing the growing global rift over marijuana policy specifically and drug liberalization more generally); David Bewley-Taylor, *Politics and Finite Flexibilities: The UN Drug Conventions and Their Future Development,* 114 AJIL UNBOUND 285, 288–89 (2020) (describing Russian, Chinese, and Japanese opposition to Canada's legalization of marijuana).

795. *See* Boister, *supra* note 151, at 67–68.

Index

. . .

For the benefit of digital users, indexed terms that span two pages (e.g., 52–53) may, on occasion, appear on only one of those pages.

INDEX

Mann, Coramae Richey, 69
marijuana
  arguments regarding fundamental
    right to, 37
  arrests per year for, 14, 29
  cannabis equity programs and, 86–88, 89
  classification as a narcotic or with narcotics
    of, 2, 33–34, 49, 52–66, 77–78, 174
  Commerce Clause and, 48, 162–63
  consciousness-expanding properties of, 129
  Cruel and Unusual Punishment Clause
    and, 103–4
  decriminalization of, 4, 10, 29–30, 70–71,
    153–54, 164, 166–67, 177–78, 187n.11
  disproportionate prison sentences as
    basis for constitutional challenges and,
    103–5, 109–10
  Equal Protection Clause and, 32–34, 56,
    61–65, 140–41
  euphoriant classification of, 130
  fears of social dislocation regarding, 63–65
  freedom of religion claims and, 120–
    21, 123
  increased use during 1960s and 1970s
    of, 29, 50
  legalization for medical uses of, 2, 48, 49,
    50, 70–71, 86–87, 166–67
  legalization for recreational uses of, 2, 49,
    50, 172–73, 175–76
  liberal professional-managerial class
    and, 153–54
  liberty rights and, 28–29, 30–31, 32–
    34, 116
  mandatory minimum sentences for, 103–6
  Marihuana Tax Act of 1937 and, 31, 46–47
  medical uses of, 57–58, 65
  physically nonaddictive nature of, 14,
    50–52, 171
  privacy rights and, 28–29, 30–36,
    37–38, 77
  property rights and, 33–34
  proportionality model of rights review
    and, 103–4, 166–68, 169
  psychoactive effects of, 65–66, 70
  pursuit of happiness and, 40–41, 65–66
  racial equality and, 64–65, 70, 77–78
  religious dogmatism and prohibitions
    against, 64–65
  short-term effects of, 52
  state bans on, 23, 31–35, 57–58
  substantive due process jurisprudence
    and, 28–29, 41

symbolic speech arguments
  regarding, 128
U.S. rates of using, 151–52
war on drugs and, 9, 14
"whitening" of image of, 70–71, 78,
  226–27n.356
Marks v. United States, 97–98
Marshall, John, 44–45
Marshall, Thurgood, 96–99, 100–2, 108
Maryland, 87
Massachusetts, 56–57, 77
McCabe decision (People v. McCabe), 55–58,
  150, 167–68
McDonald v. City of Chicago, 150–51
McLaughlin v. Florida, 61
McReynolds, James Clark, 45–46
MDMA. See Ecstasy
mescaline, 52–53, 116, 118–19, 128–30
Mexican Americans, 70. See also Latinos
Meyer v. Nebraska, 36
Michigan, 33–34, 104–5
Micronesia, 57–58
Mill, John Stuart, 33–34, 43, 139–40
Minnesota, 82–83
Mississippi, 4
Mitchell, John, 98
modalities of constitutional interpretation
  detachment from political-moral
    judgments and, 141, 173–74
  doctrinal arguments and, 138–39
  fundamentalist arguments and, 139
  norm against combining clauses
    and, 141–42
  originalist arguments and, 138–39
  positive rights and, 175
  textual arguments and, 138–39
Model Drug Paraphernalia Act of
  1979, 134–35
morphine, 23
Morrison decision (United States v.
  Morrison), 47–48
Musto, David, 69

Narcotics Control Act of 1956, 12, 145
National Commission on Marihuana and
  Drug Abuse (Shafer Commission), 28,
  37–38, 50, 52–53, 63–64, 99–100
National Organization for the Reform of
  Marijuana Laws (NORML)
  founding (1970) of, 4, 29
  marijuana's classification opposed by,
    58, 77, 78

[288]